THE NEW POLITICS OF
SURVIVAL:
GRASSROOTS MOVEMENTS IN CENTRAL AMERICA

THE NEW POLITICS OF
SURVIVAL:

GRASSROOTS MOVEMENTS IN CENTRAL AMERICA

EDITED BY
MINOR SINCLAIR

FOREWORD BY
JUNE NASH

Monthly Review Press
New York

An *EPICA* Book

The Ecumenical Program on Central America and the Caribbean (EPICA)
Washington, D.C.

An EPICA/Monthly Review Press Book
All Rights Reserved

Library of Congress Catalog Card Number: 94-062066
ISBN Number: 0-85345-951-7

Graphic credits: Roberto Aguirre (166), Ayuda Archives (49), Steve Cagan (182, 208, 238), Corinne Dufka (170, Back Cover), EPICA Archives (46, 108, 152), Jim Harney (24), Latin America Bureau (107), Jonathan Moller (97), Nicaragua Network Educational Fund Archives (Title Page), NISGUA Archives (66, 74), Ron Selden (Cover), Rod Sinclair (119, 252, 264), and Kimberly White (35, 40).

Monthly Review Press
122 West 27th Street
New York, NY 10001

Manufactured in the United States of America

10 9 8 7 6 5 4 3 2 1

for Jesus,
who as a seven year-old child
survived the massacre in Rió Negro, Guatemala,
who witnessed the brutal slaying of his sister
--her head beaten against a rock--
who lived as a virtual slave in the household
of his sister's assassin, and
who, now, twelve years later,
has organized the Committee of Widows and Orphans
to press for legal justice against those responsible
for the masssacre.

for Rosa, Neto, Gloria, Rafa and Edit,
five remarkable children who have done much
in their short lives to defend human rights,
and who lost their father,
Herbert Ernesto Anaya,
the President of the Salvadoran Human Rights Commssion,
who was gunned down
while taking his children to school.

CONTENTS

Acknowledgements
Foreword

Introduction   1

GUATEMALA

Uncovering the Truth: Political Violence
    and Indigenous Organizations   25
      Rolando Alecio

Weaving Our Future: Campesino Struggles for Land   47
    Rigoberta Menchú and the Committee of Campesino Unity

Faith, Community and Resistance in the Guatemalan Highlands   75
    Minor Sinclair

EL SALVADOR

Repopulated Communities in El Salvador   109
    Martha Thompson

Building an Alternative: The Formation of a Popular Project   153
    Mario Lungo Uclés

NICARAGUA

New Autonomy, New Struggle: Labor Unions in Nicaragua   183
    Trish O'Kane

The Nicaraguan Women's Movement: Feminist
   Reflections From Within   209
     Ana Criquillon

Farmers' Organizations and Agrarian Transformation
   in Nicaragua   239
     Eduardo Baumeister

Unbinding the Ties That Bind:
   The FSLN and the Popular Organizations   265
     Midge Quandt

Notes on Contributors
Index

EDITOR'S ACKNOWLEDGEMENTS

That this collection covers more than just one country I am indebted to the wisdom of Mirna Perla de Anaya, a Salvadoran human rights activist, who persuaded me that the importance of popular movements stretched throughout the Americas.

That this book has reached completion I am indebted to my colleagues at the Ecumenical Program on Central America and the Caribbean who with great patience convinced me that this study must be limited to the realm of the possible.

Hundreds of Central Americans shared with me their time and insights, including exiles, such as Guatemala's Rigoberta Menchú and Frank LaRue, who have now returned to their homes ; activists who became members of the National Assembly of their country, such as El Salvador's Hector DaSilva and Ana Guadalupe Martínez; too many others including El Salvador's Febe Velasquez and Segundo Montes who have been killed for their unwillingness to be silent; and many, many popular movement believers who continue to fight the good fight, year after year.

I cannot hope to thank the many people who assisted in this book, most of whom directly helped the authors of the articles and whom I never had the pleasure of knowing. I would like to give special recognition to the eight authors represented here, Rolando Alecio, Rigoberta Menchú and the CUC team, Martha Thompson, Mario Lungo, Trish O'Kane, Ana Criquillon, Eduardo Baumeister and Midge Quandt, many of whom sacrificied their work building the popular movement in order to offer here their reflections on the popular movement. Students of social change movements will be enormously grateful for their willingness to recount their rich experiences.

I would like to thank particularly Margaret Low and also Scott Wright, my colleagues at EPICA, who made extremely valuable contributions in translation and editing. In addition, many others offered their skills in translating, editing and offering valuable advice. I would like to thank, in particular, Molly Graver, Gretta Tovar Siebentritt, Rebecca Wentling, Rick Jones, Jennifer Casolo, Richard Shaull, Curt Wands, Andrew Kaufmann, and Gene Palumbo. Susan Lowes, editor of Monthly Review Press, deserves special credit as well for her support of this project. Others who played an important role in the development of the project are Margaret Popkin, Judy Butler, David Blanchard, O'Carm., Karen Brandow, Alan Cibils, Miguel Ventura, Beatriz Manz, Solange Muller, Edgar Palacios, Joe Mulligan, S.J., Indiana Acevedo, Angélica Fauné, and Orlando Nuñez.

A special thanks is due as well to the Carmelite Justice and Peace Commission for providing initial support for this project and to the Ecumenical Program on Central America and the Caribbean for allowing me to integrate this project into my work at EPICA.

M.S.

FOREWORD

This publication provides a timely manual for the arts of survival gained in almost two decades of warfare in the Central American states and a prospectus for those who want to understand the reasons for the tragic debacle and how to avoid future disasters. In contrast to past heroic accounts of battles that used to constitute history, we learn of wars with no winners and all are losers. But we also gain comprehension about democratic movements generated in the course of struggle that provide alternative paths of development and progress.

The authors of each of the country studies have been intimately connected with one or more of the grassroots movements described. Their accounts awaken our consciousness of the human dimensions of a warfare that seemed without end or even purpose. They go beyond that to show the recuperative power of people once they gain an awareness of their potential to act politically. Whether they speak of Nicaraguan women, burdened with centuries of denial of their identity as mature political, social and economic actors, who found distinctive voices to articulate an agenda separate from that of the Sandinistas, or of Mayan campesinos marginalized from the political process of Guatemala and mercilessly exploited in the labor markets of export-oriented enterprises, the contributors show the linkages between consciousness of self and how the denial of that selfhood is linked to structures of domination and repression.

Because the authors have been involved in the struggles as participants, they can provide a step by step analysis of the process of transformation that allows the reader to capture the ambiguities, the paths not taken, and the compromises related to survival. This ethnograpic approach allows one to go beyond theoretically predetermined course of human action characteristic of those who are removed from the conflicts. At the same time, the authors provide a reflexive view that situates their entry into the conflict and makes it part of the data. They express moral commitments and value priorities. Why they have chosen commitments and what motivates their actions are as much a part of the data as the commitments and motivations of grassroots leaders and followers they describe.

This is especially clear in the section on Guatemala by Rolando Alecio, Minor Sinclair, and Rigoberta Menchú in which the discourse is imbued with morality and spiritual courage. For those trained to separate "truth" from "evidence," the language may be disconcerting unless one relates it to the violence and obscenities perpetrated in the name of market priorities and political sovereignty. In countries where, as Minor Sinclair points out, "the mere survival of the people continues to be an act of resistance to the Army" struggle is lodged in an identity that remains distinct from the oppressor. Those who lacked this sense of self linked with a collective group even joined the enemy, a common phenomenon in the fascist period in Europe as well. Overcoming fear and the devastation of loss requires recourse to psychic energies denied in the objective discourse of science.

Chapters on repopulation and revitalization of the countryside in El Salvador by Martha Thompson and Mario Lungo Uclés also demonstrate that collective action to rebuild communities could only be accomplished with spiritual appeals. It is clear that these authors understand what that means and they have convincingly conveyed to the readers the significance of spiritual energies. In order to recreate the idea of community in a new mold based on justice and participation rather than opportunism and dominance, the authors show us that a changed conception of self is essential, and this must be linked to others in a strong sense of community.

Trade unions are one among many of the grassroots movements analyzed, neither taken to be the preeminent domain nor rejected as superseded by what some call the "new social movements." Indeed, the strategies incorporated by unions confronting global enterprises and neoliberal policies as described by Trish O'Kane in Nicaragua may be instructive for syndicalists in what were the core industrial countries. Her discussion of "solidarism," associations of workers identified with *patrons* found in Guatemala and Costa Rica indicates the neoliberal attack against labor world-wide. The broad spectrum of rights that these Central American workers include in their agenda advances the basis for mobilization including the specific reproductive issues that concern women. At a time when union membership is declining and unions have been suspended in many U.S. firms, trade unionists throughout the hemisphere should welcome strategies that in Central America, as in

Canada where unions still incorporate 37 percent of the labor force, have expanded the arena for organization.

U.S. military and economic intervention in Central America helped set the agenda for the 1970s and 1980s of a narrow band of large landowners and army officers. *The New Politics of Survival: Grassroots Movements in Central America* addresses the issues raised by the export of arms, military advisors, and capital but goes beyond an indictment of military solutions and unjust economic distribution to consider alternative ways of organizing society. Despite the economic backwardness of the region, Central American countries are forging new democratic processes that could be a model for the hemisphere.

June Nash, Distinguished Professor
The City College of the City University of New York

Introduction: The New Politics of Survival

Minor Sinclair

66 I didn't have the five *colones* which the hospital wanted to charge me," she said. Isabel, in her early 20s and wearing a white cotton dress, spoke in a measured tone much like many other Salvadoran campesinos or campesinas.

Alone and pregnant, Isabel had come from her village to San Salvador to look for a hospital. She had been worried about giving birth in the village--apparently she did not have family support or money--but she had no idea that the state-run hospital would turn her away. "So I gave birth in the street," Isabel said, and added, "No one should have to suffer what I did."

This conversation took place in 1989 and Isabel then was a promoter working with women in marginalized communities on the outskirts of San Salvador. She worked with the National Coordination of Women of El Salvador (CONAMUS). Her job was to encourage women to meet together to talk about their problems and to support each other. Isabel knew that there were too few hours in each day for poor women to carry water and firewood, wash and cook and tend the children. Time for organizing or forming self-help groups did not exist. Yet if there was potable water in their community, they might have more time and could learn to read and to write. And if they could read and write...

Isabel's story is not atypical for those who joined popular movements throughout Central America. Despite desperate conditions of poverty, little or no formal education, exploitation and, in countries such as El Salvador, the guns turned on them, participants in popular movements created options for themselves. Their stories are incredible, in part, because they survived to tell their stories; many others died the early deaths caused by hunger, numbing oppression and political persecution. The experience of giving birth in the street helped Isabel become *consciente* (roughly translated, politically aware) but gaining awareness is not the only factor in breaking the cycle of exploitation and in creating a movement. For a movement to have even limited success, its participants need strong organizing capabilities, political vision and an opportune political moment.

CONAMUS, a women's organization, is just one of more than two hundred popular organizations which have given El Salvador one of the strongest movements in Latin America. CONAMUS promotes social change by encouraging women to resist and to organize, often in small and incremental ways–by asking their husbands to help carry water or by petitioning the local authorities to install water spigots. And often in big and challenging ways: for a time, CONAMUS ran one of the few women's clinics in El Salvador and it was the only medical facility, outside of the military hospital, which was diagnostically capable of proving rape occurred. In El Salvador rape was used by the soldiers as a counterinsurgency tactic to instill terror among the civilian population. Mobilizing women against rape and for their rights against an Army that systematically violated human rights led the government to treat CONAMUS as a guerrilla "front group" and many CONAMUS members were repressed.[1]

The incidents of daily resistance (both armed and unarmed) may well be "short-lived, localized, ephemeral and easily repressed,"[2] as one analyst has described popular organizations. But taken collectively they have made for a social change movement that has altered the political terrain of Central America in a fundamental way. The account of the popular movement in Central America is a story of conscientization of the poor and of the practice of "a politics of the possible" –local actions and demands set in a specific circumstance, but with a vision of fundamental change.

Much has been written about Central America in the past ten years; many authors have rightly focussed on U.S. policy of support for military regimes engaged in counterinsurgency efforts against guerrilla movements. Other authors have described the guerrilla movements themselves and still others have looked at the economic and political roots of the armed conflict. All but overlooked has been the unarmed aspect of the struggle, the role of popular organizations engaged in awareness-raising, community organization and largely unarmed actions of resistance.

Conscientization is a complex process and by no means uniform within each country or within each sector, but in many cases individual conscientization does turn into collective action. Local actions and issues can become, the sum being greater than the parts, a groundswell for change. Daily actions of resistance are not isolated but part of a collective demand for broadsweeping societal transformation. Diverse demands and a multiplicity of organizations become part of a popular movement, or movements, for social change.

In this anthology the first task of the authors has been to narrate the stories of the popular movement in Guatemala, El Salvador and Nicaragua. The articles describe as well as analyze specific popular movements because little first-hand material about these events has found its way into the English language. In broad terms, three themes course through the articles in this collection, chosen because they enhance, not impede, the telling of the story. First of all, the authors show why people participate in popular movements, that is, what motivates people and why and how people become conscienticized in a process. Subjective concerns as well as objective factors are important. Secondly, the authors trace the development of the movements over a historical period. "Development" hardly describes the eruptions and dormancy, crisis and calm, radical and reformist swings, periods of revolution and accommodation which most movements experience. And lastly, many of the authors look at how a particular movement plays a pivotal role in building a political alternative to the dominant power structure.

Charting the popular movement in Central America is an impossible task for even a team of adept investigators. The territory is vast, the terrain impenetrable and the climate turbulent. Frequent visitors to Central America gain the distinct impression that most of the political activity occurs at a subterranean level and given the legitimate need for semi-clandestinity because of repression, the movement's spokespeople rarely reveal the internal processes of popular organizations. This anthology has looked to writers with an insider's perspective, those who know their subject intimately and who, though sympathetic to the cause about which they wrote, are willing to critique the movement as well. To contribute we invited non-Central Americans as well as Central Americans, social scientists as well as leaders in the popular movement. Some articles have been translated from Spanish; others were written originally in English. The result is not an academically uniform collection, but rather an anthology that brings the richness as well as the diversity of different perspectives, styles and backgrounds.

The challenge of covering Guatemala, El Salvador and Nicaragua in one volume, each country with widely varying demographics, political and cultural histories, resistance movements, and modes of dominance, is a demanding one. Yet, there are some remarkably similar social experiences among the countries. One experience has to do with the revolutionary struggle. In Guatemala, the guerrilla struggle has persisted for more than thirty years. In El Salvador, the FMLN proved itself as Latin America's strongest revolutionary movement through the 1980s. In

Nicaragua, the Sandinista government ambitiously undertook a revolutionary program in its eleven years of state power.

The dynamic between the popular movement and the armed revolutionary movement in all three countries (in Nicaragua's case, an armed revolutionary government) is complex and fascinating, yet little studied. Through the 1980s in Guatemala and El Salvador, this relationship could not be openly discussed as their militaries and governments considered popular organizations *fachadas* or fronts for the guerrillas. Given the political climate in Central America, to reveal the interior of the popular movement and their contacts with the insurgent groups would have been to needlessly endanger many lives. This book appears at an opportune moment as perhaps only now can those relationships be further probed.

Another element unifying these essays is that Guatemala, El Salvador and Nicaragua have been fertile grounds for the birth of a wide spectrum of grassroots movements, both traditional ones as well as so-called "new" social movements. Traditional movements in Latin America date back at least twenty-five years or more and include labor unions, revolutionary student groups, mass organizations and peasant unions which have a rich experience in political change. More recently other movements have arisen: land reform cooperatives, women's organizations, squatter movements, environmental groups, grassroots human rights groups, refugee and internally displaced people's organizations and many others.

While attempting to characterize anything as nebulous as social movements is problematic, it can be said that participants in the more traditional movements tend to rely more on class-based analysis and anti-imperialist ideology and have prioritized organizing in the workplace. Within traditional movements organizational models tend towards a vanguard group which gives direction to the mass organizations. Achieving state power is seen as a principal goal.

Participants in many of the newer movements tend to define themselves more and organize more around issues of identity (race/ethnic groupings, gender issues) and community (home, neighborhood, quality of life) as well as the traditional issues of class, anti-imperialism and workers' rights. The Committee of Campesino Unity (CUC) in Guatemala which unites *ladino* and indigenous campesinos around land issues is one example of the blend of ethnic, class-based and religious roots of the struggle of a newer organization(see Chapter 3). There is a smaller number of the new movements, such as some indigenous groups in Guatemala and the Atlantic Coast of Nicaragua, which have explicitly rejected the class element of their struggle and put forward political autonomy as their goal.

Some of the most creative initiatives are the popular organizations' direct responses to state-sponsored repression. Literally rising out of the ashes of massacres, scorched-earth tactics and state-run death squads, these groups have grown from a handful of courageous individuals to a mass movement of thousands during the 1980s. They are made up of the victims–refugees and displaced persons, mothers (and other family members) of the disappeared, political prisoners, widows, war-handicapped, and survivors of violence by the civil defense patrols. While some observers have classified these movements as "ethical or moral movements," because of their human rights focus, they are as threatening to the dominant classes as well-organized labor unions or revolutionary student groups.

Other movements–squatter community organizations, women's groups, environmental organizations, youth movements and others–rise in response to a specific context of marginalization and discrimination. Some are national in scope, others local. Some are spontaneous, others the result of long years of tedious organizing. Some press for greater inclusion in the system, others for fundamental change of the system. All are protest movements; some can be absorbed by the system while others represent too great a threat to the system.

The distinction between the "traditional" and the "new" movements may be a blurred one, at best; what has been more important has been the mushroom growth of popular organizations over the past twenty-five years and the increasing diversity of their identities and demands. It has been, as one writer suggests, "a diaspora of collective action" (which means fragmentation as well as strength). Perhaps it is misleading to speak of *the* popular movement when in reality, in any given country, there are multiple popular movements.

The diversity of popular organizations defies a rigorous definition of what, exactly, is a popular organization. Rather than attempting a comprehensive definition, it would be more helpful to describe certain elements which are generally common to popular movements.

First of all, the movements are *popular,* that is, they have what is generally considered to have a lower or working class connotation. This means that in such highly polarized societies with enormous inequalities of wealth and power *popular* also refers to the vast majority of people. Central Americans also use *popular* to describe people (intellectuals, politicians, church figures and others) who though not poor themselves identify with poor peoples' struggles. *Popular* also signifies a democratic process or a situation where the power is rooted in the *pueblo,* the people.

Secondly, popular organizations are action-oriented and depend on participation and mobilization for their power, rather than institutional structures, state or party power, or financial wealth. Popular movements may develop institutional structures--such as non-governmental organizations (NGOs), political party apparatus, think tanks, lobby groups–but the power of the movement rests in its ability to mobilize people rather than in the power of the institutions.

A third characteristic is that popular organizations seek societal transformation. They are inherently anti-systemic and radical in their goals (although their strategy may be considered moderate). This differentiates popular movements from reform-oriented groups which seek moderate change that only further reinforces the dominant system. The *solidarista* labor organizations are one example of a reformist-oriented group. Popular organizations, it should be noted, may ally themselves with reformist groups for tactical reasons.

Fourthly, popular organizations appeal to the original values expressed in the French Revolution ("liberty, equality and fraternity") and much more recently in the Universal Declaration of Human Rights. Most popular organizations support full guarantees of individual liberties such as freedom of speech, freedom to associate, freedom of religion, and right to life. More so, they are deeply concerned that individual liberties are guaranteed for all and not just the few. The social and economic rights guaranteed in the Universal Declaration should protect, in particular, the most vulnerable population--the poor, women, children and the oppressed. The pledges of self-determination for nations should guarantee a participatory democracy within nations. The deepening of the popular movement in recent years has brought new values into currency: solidarity between and among disenfranchised groups, community in an increasingly alienating world, and assertion of identity among diverse populations.

The Historical Context for Social Change Movements

At the close of the World War II period in Europe, for the first time since its independence, Central America experienced a time of hope. The world economy was in expansion and the attention of the world's only real imperial power, the United States, was focused elsewhere, namely on the task of rebuilding Europe. The Central American region was seen neither as a threat nor a place of promise by the U.S. In 1944, without the fear of U.S. intervention, an alliance of progressive forces and conservative business elites in El Salvador overthrew the dreaded Maximiliano Hernández Martínez dictatorship. In Guatemala moderate change came through the ballot box when in 1944 a civilian, Juan José Arévalo, and then in 1950 a reformist military officer, Jacobo Arbenz, won successive presidential elections and implemented reforms such as social security legislation, minimum wage and a moderate land reform. In Costa Rica the 1948 rebellion of José "Pepe" Figueres prompted a series of reforms including the dissolution of the national army, establishment of tax on private capital and greater government services. Only Nicaragua, under the grip of the Anastasio Somoza dictatorship and the U.S.-trained National Guard, defied the reformist trends in the region.

In the 1950s the Cold War logic took hold of Washington and containment of communism (and expansion of U.S. markets) became the operative policy for the U.S. in Central America. Asserting its right of "manifest destiny" to intervene in Latin America, the U.S. reversed a decade of moderate rule in most of Central America. In 1954 the U.S. sponsored a CIA-led coup in Guatemala which dragged the "land of eternal spring" into a tyranny of military rule for the next 30 years. In 1961 in El Salvador, a right-wing coup further entrenched military domination by installing a regime headed by the National Conciliation Party, the official party of the military.

The triumph of the Cuban revolution in 1959 showed Central Americans that change, even against the will of Washington, was possible. Before the revolutionary spirit could take root in the Central American isthmus, the U.S. pre-empted radical change by funneling unparalleled levels of U.S. aid to social programs in Latin America through the Alliance for Progress ($100 million in the 1960s). It was John F. Kennedy who said that "those who make peaceful revolution impossible will make violent revolutions inevitable,"[3] but the U.S. had little intention in allowing revolution, peaceful or violent, to succeed.

In terms of "developing" Central America, the Alliance for Progress did help break the landed oligarchy's stranglehold on the economy and create a small, "modernizing" manufacturing class, but for the poor the cost of "development" was prohibitively high. Overall trade between U.S. corporations and businesses owned by Central American elites doubled and the average GNP grew at a greater than 5% annual clip through the 1960s (Nicaragua at 7.1%, Guatemala at 5.5%, El Salvador at 5.6%, Costa Rica at 6.1% and Honduras at 5.1%). Though per capita income increased, the gap between the wealthy and the masses who produced wealth for others became cavernous.

The idea that the 1960s represented a "decade of development" for Central America was based on two myths, that trickle down economics works and that political democracy follows capitalist development. In terms of the former, with the exception of Costa Rica in Central America, every social indicator showed worsening conditions for the poor relative to the rich. The situation in Guatemala was representative of the rest of the region. According to U.N. data, in 1950 the richest 5% of the population owned 48% of the wealth and within twenty-five years their "good fortune" had increased to 60%. In 1950 the poorest 50% of the people earned 9% of the total income; by 1977 their share had dropped to 7%. Curable diseases, mainly those caused by the lack of caloric intake,

w/ "sand policy"

were responsible for 42% of the deaths in Guatemala. In 1960 there was only one doctor per each 4,644 inhabitants, an abomination by standards in developing countries, but by 1975 that figure had deteriorated to one physician for every 9,000 persons.[4]

In terms of the second myth, it would have been difficult to convince many Central Americans that a functional democracy, even a fragile one, was taking root. In El Salvador and Guatemala, sham elections posed a choice only between candidates from differing military-dominated parties which was more choice than the dictator Somoza offered his "electorate" in Nicaragua. In El Salvador when a political alliance of Christian Democrats, social democrats and communists (running under another name) did challenge the military party in elections in 1972 and 1977, ballot-stuffing was flagrant and the opposition's leaders were forced into exile. The political system left little space for non-violent change. What did change, however, were the expectations that people held. The political discourse of reformism which the U.S. championed created an expectation of progress. When the only change people experienced was for the worse, people increasingly looked to the more radical vision which students and other sectors were espousing.

In the 1960s and 1970s clandestine guerrilla groups first in Guatemala, then Nicaragua and El Salvador made their initial forays and steadily grew. Though the histories, tactics and ideologies of the guerrilla organizations varied greatly, in each country the guerrillas came to be seen as the primary opposition to the governing regime. In July, 1979 the Somoza regime in Nicaragua fell to the Sandinista Front for National Liberation (FSLN). For the next eleven years Nicaragua's course under the revolutionary Sandinista government diverged from the path of its neighbors.

The Sandinista revolution brought impressive gains in land reform and social welfare to ordinary Nicaraguans and the beginning of changes in the formal democratic process and protection of individual liberties. Its sweeping land reform, second only to Cuba's in Latin America, opened access to arable land to hundreds of thousands of landless peasants and the advances in literacy (reducing illiteracy from 52% to 13% in a six month period) and preventive health care (elimination of polio, full participation of children in the immunization campaigns) were astounding. The contra war, directed by the enemies of the revolution (ex-National Guardsman, wealthy landowners who lost their proprieties in the land redistribution, and the United States), torpedoed the social projects of the Sandinistas. The contras, however, did not have the military power nor popular support to overthrow the Sandinistas.

In the late 1970s and early 1980s in El Salvador and Guatemala political protest swelled as a result of the fraudulent elections and the deteriorating social conditions. In San Salvador hundreds of thousands of people, led by the mass organizations, filled the downtown streets in protest. The mass organizations--such as the Revolutionary Coordination of the Masses (CRM) in El Salvador--were neither alternatives to the guerrillas in the mountains nor appendages to them, but rather significant actors who put forward the demands of the poor majority in the struggle against deteriorating wages, growing unemployment, landlessness and political disenfranchisement. They fought the military regimes in the little political space which remained to them: popular organizing, street demonstrations, wall graffiti and underground newspapers. In Guatemala the dynamic was similar with the labor movement and the Committee of Campesino Unity (CUC) leading the way calling for work stoppages in the factories and in the fields and sponsoring national demonstrations.

Facing the rising challenge of both the guerrillas and mass organizations, the Salvadoran and Guatemalan militaries closed all political space for opposition. National armies and security forces fired on demonstrators and opposition figures, and their sympathizers or suspected sympathizers were hunted down, disappeared or killed. In El Salvador anyone wearing blue jeans or tennis shoes was suspect; in Guatemala carrying a student ID was tantamount to being a guerrilla in the view of the military. In 1980, 1981 and 1982 hundreds of brutally tortured bodies appeared *every week* on the streets and highways of Guatemala and El Salvador. In an attempt to eradicate support for the guerrillas in the countryside, the Salvadoran Army and Guatemalan Army launched "scorched earth" campaigns, burning and destroying crops, animals and homes, and exterminating human life.

Popular organizations such as CUC in Guatemala and the Federation of Christian Campesinos in El Salvador (FECCAS-UTC) bravely attempted to resist in clandestinity, but the military-led onslaught was too ferocious and popular organizations passed into oblivion. Many of the survivors joined the guerrillas or fled into exile. The popular organizations were, literally, decapitated, and only the most innocuous forms of opposition were permitted.

In the early 1980s the United States was faced with the choice of cutting support for the repressive militaries which the U.S. had largely created and thereby risking victories by the guerrillas, or staying the course despite the "distastefulness" of the atrocities of its allies. Pulling the plug on the Salvadoran and Guatemalan governments was never seriously considered, and the U.S. continued to provide economic and political support to the repressive regimes though briefly cutting military aid to El Salvador in 1980 after the assassination of the four U.S.

church women and restricting military aid to Guatemala from 1978 to 1986.

In the mid 1980s the United States, under heavy domestic criticism for its militaristic policy towards the region, pressured Central American regimes to allow a political opening through what became known as the Esquipulas II process. Elections, national forums and negotiations with the guerrillas were supposed to be the elements that would bring peace to the region. But the formal electoral processes, particularly when held in countries at war, did not bring democratic participation, and even though civilians formally took the reins of government, the military continued to dominate. The political opening, though falling far short of establishing fledgling democracies, did offer the popular movements in El Salvador and Guatemala new political space in which to organize.

Grassroots human rights organizations such as the Mutual Support Group (GAM) in Guatemala and CoMadres (Committee of the Mothers of the Disappeared) in El Salvador, formed by the victims of government abuses, held public protests and demanded that the authorities return their loved ones who had been disappeared. *"Vivos los llevaron, vivos los queremos"*("Alive, you took them; alive, we want them back!") was their cry during demonstrations which openly confronted the regimes. From 1985 on, the popular movements in both Guatemala and El Salvador took on new life as many organizations came out of clandestinity, and many new ones were formed.

For the Army, inducing terror was a means of social control; the most hideous killing, or forcing neighbor to kill neighbor or family member to kill their own family member, was justified in the interests of national security. International human rights groups, however, were calling attention to the overt atrocities and so the regimes looked for other methods. Another effective form of social control (and which did not attract the attention of international human rights groups) was Army "psych-ops," or psychological operations, such as interrogating children about the suspicious activities of their parents or sending military doctors and clowns to communities in conflictive areas. The battle, as the Army defined it, was over "winning the hearts and minds." A U.S. colonel, assigned to El Salvador as a military advisor, noted, "The most important territory to win is the six inches between a peasant's ears." For the popular movement, instilling courage within the civilian population who faced state terror and Army psych ops became a vital aspect of their struggle.

Though counterinsurgency greatly conditioned the course of the popular movements, perhaps insurgency was an even more important influence. The popular movements in Guatemala and El Salvador, unlike in other countries in Latin America, developed alongside the political/military organizations of the guerrillas, namely the URNG in Guatemala and the FMLN in El Salvador. Complete autonomy from larger political forces was not an option, and popular organizations tended to form ties with revolutionary groups; the space for independence did not exist. Neither completely autonomous from nor completely dependent on the guerrilla organizations, the popular organizations nonetheless asserted a different political space than the guerrilla organizations; their "front" was a *barrio*, a workplace, a university campus and the plaza in front of the National Palace. Their "weapons" were *popular*-mobilizations, strikes and street graffiti. Though their struggle was not an armed one, it was neither more nor less revolutionary or crucial for social change than the struggle of the guerrilla forces.

For every guerrilla in the field fighting to overthrow an anti-popular regime, there have been dozens of people involved in strikes, demonstrations, and other forms of unarmed protest and dozens more involved in intelligence or logistical support for the guerrillas. For every guerrilla killed in fighting, there were dozens of unarmed civilians whose daily acts of resistance cost them their lives. Guerrilla and popular movement leaders have described the struggle as 90% non-violent and 10% armed struggle. This is not to say, however, that the popular movement in El Salvador, Guatemala and Nicaragua has defined itself as "non-violent." Members of popular organizations positioned themselves on the front lines of the unarmed struggle, but also many made up the "rear guard" of the armed struggle aiding in supply, information and even part-time militia networks. What has been often overlooked, largely because of the constant accusations by the Guatemalan and Salvadoran militaries that popular organizations are *fachadas* (fronts) for the guerrillas, is that the relationship between popular organizations and guerrilla structures has been one of mutual influence.[5] Most of the FMLN members, in fact, were recruited from the ranks of the popular movement when the repression forced the popular organizations underground in 1980.

In Nicaragua the Sandinistas took power through a popular insurrection, which means they counted on both a guerrilla force and a high degree of popular participation. In the early years of Sandinista rule, mass organizations such as ATC (campesino organization), UNAG (cooperatives and farmers' organization) and CDS (*barrio* committees) played a critical rule in forming and implementing state policy in areas such as literacy programs, land reform and neighborhood security. The popular organizations operated more as extensions of the government and the Sandinista party than as independent movements. During the contra war, popular organizations were on the front lines of the war--cooperatives were a primary target of contra attacks--as well as in the rear guard recruiting troops and consoling the family members of fallen *just as human resources are postponed until "economic goals" are ( ) achieved*

Sandinistas. The relationship between popular organizations and the revolutionary state in Nicaragua was hardly harmonious, however. The demands of the popular organizations were often postponed until later for the "good of the revolution" and then never addressed. The U.S. economic blockade and the U.S.-backed contra war forced the Sandinistas to divert its human and economic resources to national defense rather to programs of social transformation. Sandinista verticalism, the dangers of co-optation, lack of participation in decision-making, little space for criticism and the need for autonomy by popular organizations also contributed to the tensions and have become major issues for the Nicaraguan popular movement in the 1990s.

Not only in Nicaragua but in El Salvador, and to a lesser extent in Guatemala, the popular movement has created experiences of popular power. In the northern mountainous regions of El Salvador and to a lesser extent in parts of the highlands and low-lying areas of northern Guatemala, guerrilla forces had successfully cordoned off areas and were able to establish "liberated zones." In these communities, known as the Local Popular Powers in El Salvador[6] and the Communities of Population in Resistance in Guatemala,[7] popular organizations had the chance in a limited way to put into practice their demands for democracy and popular participation. They set up alternative health care and education, democratically-elected councils which responded to the will of the people, and community-shared forms of production and income distribution. The experiment was limited by the isolation and extreme economic deprivation of the communities, by the constant attack or threat of attack by Army troops, and by the limits to democracy which the military needs and the vertical structures of the guerrillas imposed. Notwithstanding the constraints, popular organizations developed a communitarian economic and political model and learned from its successes as well as its shortcomings.

Present International Context

Ideas about political power--by those who wield it and by those who seek it--have changed in the past two decades in Central America. Twenty-five years ago young guerrilla leaders strategizing in the mountains assumed that if the opposition could overthrow the repressive regimes and take the reins of state power, they would be able to successfully defend national sovereignty and chart a socialist course. Often popular movement leaders would share that goal.

By the late 1980s, however, revolutionaries had begun to question whether achieving state power, even if attainable, would be worth the cost. The eight year assault by the Reagan Administration and the U.S.-backed contras on the Sandinista experiment in Nicaragua--at a cost of 30,000 lives (including combatants and civilians) and $14 billion in economic losses[8]--have forced contemporary revolutionaries to rethink the assumption that state power can guarantee national sovereignty. For Salvadoran or Guatemalan revolutionaries, control of state power-- either by seizing power or by winning an election--would mean fending off the constant attacks of U.S.-backed Salvadoran or Guatemalan contras or elites intent on sabotaging the economy.

Even the goal of achieving state power has come into question. Given the collapse of the Soviet Union and the formerly Communist-controlled Eastern European countries, the socialist ideology has been met with skepticism and even abandonment by some of its former proponents. Attempts to pose an alternative to capitalism in the international sphere are just beginning. For revolutionaries, managing state power seems an increasingly untenable goal and even if attainable, revolutionaries have asked, to what end?

By the mid 1980s neoliberalism had hit the region with "the force of a tropical storm."[9] The structural adjustment programs, intended to stabilize the currency, reduce state intervention in the economy and open the economy to private investment, have had a devastating impact on the poor. After nearly a decade of neoliberal policies, Central American economies are showing only modest growth rates and reduced inflation, and the income levels of the bottom 60% have deteriorated significantly. Countries such as Mexico and Argentina, which have gone further in terms of structural adjustment, are showing even lower growth rates. To gain access to international loans, Central American governments have been forced by international lending agencies to cut government spending; public spending on health, education, other services and social security were the first budgetary victims. Denied access to international loans through the multilateral lending agencies, the Sandinistas as well had little alternative but to cut their budget across the board (including a devastating 40% cut in 1988). A group of Central American analysts wrote,[10]

> In reality, Central America's [governments] have very little space in which to define a national or regional development strategy. The path toward reconstruction has already been drawn by the International Monetary Fund and the World Bank... All the region's countries are applying stabilization and structural adjustment programs designed by these multi-lateral institutions.

The analysts go on to ask,[11]

> Is [the struggle for power] thus reduced to a simple dispute over who can best administer this model designed from the outside? Is the left's only alternative to enter the election race under the banner of progressive administration of this same model?

The mid-1990s present a markedly different context for those seeking change in Central America. Not only· has the revolutionary struggle faded, but also the electoral prospects for the left have dimmed throughout the region. As the situation in Nicaragua and El Salvador has shown, the fomer guerrilla groups (the FSLN in Nicaragua and the FMLN in El Salvador), now political parties, have been unable to maintain their unity and project a consensus vision capable of building an electorate. The left's position in Guatemala is no more hopeful in the short term. For the popular movement, the linkage with a national revolutionary "project" has become less relevant as popular organizations and community groups look to address in a local and immediate way the dire problems which their members face.

In addition, winning state power can no longer be the primary goal of opposition organizing because power no longer resides in the National Palace or the National Assembly. National governments have less power than they ever did in planning the course of their country, as some new and some old outside forces largely shape the internal policies of Latin American countries. If popular movements seek a greater voice in the political, economic and social policy decisions which affect the lives of their members, the popular movements must be part of a process which puts forward viable alternatives and engages those forces who do have power over Central Americans' destinies.

That means, first of all, addressing the International Monetary Fund (IMF), the World Bank, and other multilateral and private lending sources that enforce narrow parameters of policy options for national governments. Currently, if the Central American countries want access to international credit, they must be willing to accept the lenders' harsh terms. To reject credit or to gain credit on the borrowers' terms, as Peru attempted in the early 1980s limiting its payments to 10% of its GNP, is economic suicide.

A second locus of power resides with the U.S. government and US AID which, even though it now offers less than half of the international aid than it did through the 1980s, still has tremendous influence in the region. The U.S. has tremendous influence within the multilateral agencies and sets the terms for trade, aid and financing in bilateral, multilateral and regional terms.

The third force which the popular movements must address is the national military within each country. The creation of national security states in Central America was a strategic decision by the U.S. in the late 1970s. Now the Salvadoran and Guatemalan militaries refuse to relinquish their control over civilian affairs even though the armed opposition which justified their tyranny are no longer present or represent a threat. The militaries retain *de facto* veto power over virtually every civilian decision, and claim constitutional rights to intervene if the "national security" is, in their view, threatened.

The Role of the Popular Movements in Seeking Change

With the heady dreams of revolutionary triumphs distant and the situation of the region's poor increasingly bleak, the popular movement represents the best hope for offering strategies of survival and creating real alternatives to the economic and political crisis which Central America is facing. How? The articles in this collection analyze the following points in greater depth, but it may be helpful to present them briefly here.

a. Alternatives can be proposed and experimented with at a local level. Within the informal economy and within local communities there exists greater space to propose, tinker with and build economic alternatives. Production cooperatives, community savings and loan associations, job training, and literacy programs and many other alternative ideas have greater chance for success in local communities where people know and trust each other. Within local communities the effects of the neoliberal model are felt most harshly and opposition to neoliberalism is most clear and organized. At a local level popular organizations are more able to empower people to create an alternative and most able to build a democratic revolution from below where people can participate in local decisions.

b. The vision of the popular movements is based on people's needs, not on ideology. The collapse of socialism, in political and ideological terms, has not been a major setback to the popular movements in Central America. Even though it cannot be said that a clear alternative to the neoliberal agenda exists, the popular movements represent the best hope for developing that alternative. Their process of conscientization, participation and organization of the grassroots in order to seek solutions for the poor majority is the kind of process that is absolutely critical to the search for an alternative.

c. Neoliberalism is vulnerable to a process of democratization. As Central American countries progress from rigidly controlled, militarily dominated societies to more open ones, necessary for the modernization of the economy, some measure of democratization will also take place. A strengthening of civil society may permit the victims of neoliberal policies to become more politically active, allowing their mobilization, their vote and their pressure for change. The danger is that this process may become stagnated just like the Alliance for Progress-style democracies three decades earlier.

d. People will continue to resist in an organized way because they have little other choice but to resist if they are to survive. Unless another wave of repression is unleashed, the worse the economic situation becomes for the poor, the more explosive the situation becomes. At its core, the neoliberal system is an exclusionary one; an unrestricted economy, internationalization of commerce and capital-intensive production will benefit primarily the elites, and increasingly the poor will find themselves neither as producers nor consumers. The neoliberal model will not be able to satisfy the demands of the majority of the people, and opposition through popular movements will continue to grow.

The challenge facing popular movements in Guatemala, El Salvador, Nicaragua and elsewhere in Latin America is how to form strategic alliances and develop political strategies so that local and issue-specific movements can confront policies which are formulated outside of their reach. Popular organizations form in response to poverty-inducing policies of the World Bank and the IMF; movements protest the hegemony which the United States exercises over national politics; and groups resist when possible the increasing militarization of civil society. Yet popular movements have not found sufficiently adequate ways to influence those with real power.

The greater challenge for protest movements in Central America, and around the world, is to move from protest to proposal, from actions of resistance and protest to well-defined political projects which can assert themselves as alternatives to the dominant structures. This calls for long-range planning and vision, and it is our hope that these nine articles help push the boundaries of the possible and generate new ideas for forming a progressive alternative.

OVERVIEW OF ARTICLES

Guatemala

The period of *la violencia* during the early 1980s in Guatemala is almost always described in terms of its national impact: as many as six hundred indigenous communities eliminated, a million people displaced, upwards of a hundred thousand persons killed and another seven thousand disappeared. But what has been its impact at a community level? How has it affected social organization, particularly among the indigenous? Guatemalan anthropologist Rolando Alecio, who researched for 18 months the effects of political violence in Rabinal in the Department of Baja Verapaz, documents nineteen massacres committed by the Army or civil defense patrols killing more than 4,000 indigenous people in a municipality of 28,000 persons. The vast majority of victims were Mayan Achís. In the process nearly all forms of social organization were annihilated. Twelve years later, the indigenous communities are organizing themselves again–as a response to the violence. Popular organizations such as the National Council for

Displaced Persons (CONDEG) and the National Coordination of Widows in Guatemala (CONAVIGUA) are increasingly active in the region. Even more significant have been independent, community-led initiatives to exhume the clandestine graves and press legal prosecution against the military. Alecio compares the period of violence and the current period and offers his conclusions in "Uncovering the Truth: Political Violence and Indigenous Organization."

The history of one of Guatemala's most innovative and long-standing popular organizations, the Committee of Campesino Unity (*Comité de Unidad Campesina* - CUC), has never been told, for reasons of the personal security of its members. In 1978 CUC shocked the nation by mobilizing tens of thousands of campesinos to support a tin miners' march from Huehuetenango to the capital. Two years later, thirty-nine CUC activists and foreign dignitaries were burned alive in the massacre at the Spanish Embassy, and two years after that the organization was forced into clandestinity. The resurgence of CUC in 1986 demonstrated that the peasants' struggle for land could be repressed but not denied. When CUC leader Rigoberta Menchú was named the 1992 Nobel Peace laureate during the year of the quincentennary, the international community recognized the vitality of what CUC members had been saying for years: "They can cut off our branches, they can burn our trunk, but they cannot destroy our roots." "Weaving Our Future: Campesino Struggles for Land," written by a team of CUC members headed by Rigoberta Menchú, tells the story of the CUC in a powerful narrative.

It has been said that people resist exploitation as actively as they can and as passively as they must. But from where do the victimized, particularly those whose oppression dates back generations, summon the power to take their first actions of resistance? For some people, at least, their faith plays a pivotal role in helping them recognize their oppression and claim their human dignity. In "Faith, Community and Resistance in the Guatemalan Highlands," the editor of this collection traces thirty years of pastoral work in indigenous communities in the Department of El Quiché, from the Catholic Church's program of evangelization known as Catholic Action to the radicalization of pastoral workers and their persecution, to the resurgence of pastoral work in the Communities of Population in Resistance and in the Ixcán jungle. The article reveals the relationship of pastoral work and community organization and, inevitably, the political consequences of a pastoral program that confronts the structures of oppression.

El Salvador

It is ironic that the counterinsurgency policies of the Salvadoran Army gave more impetus to popular organizing than the guerrilla insurgency did. From 1986-1989 more than two hundred popular organizations were founded, many of these by victims of the Army's repression. The largest and perhaps the most well-organized group were the 35,000 Salvadoran refugees in Honduras and the hundreds of thousands internally displaced people. How did the refugees and displaced persons, forced from their homes and denied their livelihood, organize into one of the country's most significant social movements? How did the survivors of Army bombings, massacres and scorched earth policies return, after ten years in exile, to reclaim their land and face the Army? In her essay entitled "Repopulated Communities in El Salvador," Martha Thompson, a development worker who monitored the refugee issue for eight years, describes the repatriation of refugees in Mesa Grande refugee camp during 1987-89 to their homes in Chalatenango, Cabañas and Cuzcatlan and the return of refugees from Colomoncagua to Segundo Montes City in Morazán.

In "Building an Alternative: The Formation of a Popular Project," Salvadoran social scientist Mario Lungo Uclés discusses the role of the popular movement in the building of a political alternative to the policies of conservative and military-dominated governments. Lungo, who won the esteemed Premio de las Americas award from Havana, Cuba for his book *El Salvador en los 1980s: insurgencia y contrainsurgencia*, writes, "Throughout most of the war in El Salvador, the popular project was seen as revolutionary... and the FMLN spent a great deal of time defining what the popular project was. But the working class and poor seldom had a precise idea what that was." In this piece, Lungo explores the origins of the popular movement in El Salvador, its relationship to the FMLN, its strengths and weaknesses and its capacity to respond to the needs of the poor in the midst of repression. In conclusion Lungo lays out the process for building an alternative popular project.

Nicaragua

During the Sandinista years in government (1979-1990) the popular movement enjoyed high levels of official support, including access to government resources and freedom from the terror of state repression faced by popular movements in other Central American countries. Nearly across the board, however, the popular organizations were not able to consistently articulate a critique of Sandinista policies, even when those policies were against their interest. The women's rights movement, for example, habitually found its concerns on specific gender issues relegated to second tier as mobilization to "defend the revolution" took priority.

It is not surprising that Nicaraguan popular organizations, particularly the labor movement, regained their voice in the four years since the Chamorro government took power. During that time, more than 50,000 union members lost their jobs, yet the Sandinista party (now out of power) gave labor unions the cold shoulder. While in power the FSLN had been a strategic ally of labor, but in the past four years the party has shown more interest in maintaining a working alliance with the Chamorro government than backing its class allies. For the first time in twelve years, labor unions had to rely extensively on labor tactics--strikes, demonstrations and collective bargaining--rather than revolutionary sloganeering and insider's influence to hold the line against layoffs and wage concessions. In "New Autonomy, New Struggle: Labor Unions in Post-Sandinista Nicaragua," Trish O'Kane, a U.S. journalist formerly based in Nicaragua, outlines the onslaught of neoliberalism which has so debilitated organized labor. She then goes on to analyze the flighty "marriage of convenience" between organized labor and the FSLN, and the newly found autonomy of the unions.

Often the sharpest criticism of a revolutionary movement comes not from its adversaries but from its supporters, and such is the case with the Sandinista revolution and the Nicaraguan women's movement. As Ana Criquillon argues convincingly in "The Nicaraguan Women's Movement: A Feminist Reflection From Within," the notion of empowerment, liberation and the elimination of elite privilege was not a Sandinista priority, at least in terms of the position of women in a heavily patriarchal society and party. Instead, the Sandinistas tended to use women's organizations as tools to mobilize public support for the Sandinista cause, particularly during the course of the contra war. In doing so, the Sandinista party left its mark of verticalism and broken promises on the women's movement. Recently however, an increasingly independent and diverse women's movement has had success in asserting its own agenda and mobilizing women in behalf of their own demands. These new forms of resistance have helped to revolutionize the revolution from within.

The medium-sized producers in agriculture are key to Nicaragua's economy and key to the success of any government, whether revolutionary or neoliberal. Eduardo Baumeister, a Nicaraguan sociologist, has been a consultant for many years with the National Union of Farmers and Ranchers (UNAG by its Spanish acronym) including the period of crucial negotiations of *concertación* (consensus-building) in the first year of the Chamorro government (1990). In analyzing the role of UNAG as a moderating influence both on the Sandinista government and on the Chamorro government, Baumeister describes the impact of a popular organization, which is also one of the country's leading producers, on national policies in his article "Farmers' Organizations and Agrarian Transformation in Nicaragua." UNAG has played a moderating role. During the Sandinista period, UNAG preserved space for privately owned producers in agriculture; during the Chamorro government UNAG ensured that the government did not eradicate the gains of the revolutions for small and medium-sized farmers.

In our last article in this collection, "Unbinding the Ties: The FSLN and the Popular Organizations in Nicaragua," Midge Quandt argues that the Sandinistas lost power partly through their mishandling of the relationship between the government and the popular organizations. Said one party activist, "The FSLN should let the popular organizations alone. It should stop being the father; let the children wander, leave home and grow up. Then they can reunite later on different terms."[12] The struggle for social change no longer revolves around the strategy for taking state power but around empowering the oppressed in the *barrios*, sweatshops and migrant labor camps. It belongs less to the party professionals and more to the myriad faces of civil society. This is a step away from verticalism, towards greater democratic participation, but it also involves its own risks: dispersion, fragmentation and the lack of a unified vision. These obstacles can be overcome, the author argues, using the experience of the farmworkers' association (ATC) as an example, through a process of seeking common ground and creating popular alliances.

Conclusion

The armed conflicts in Central America have wound to a close. The bloody contra war in Nicaragua ended with neither the contras nor the Sandinistas in power and only sporadic fighting over local demands initiated by armed re-contras or re-compas. In El Salvador peace accords led to the full demobilization of the FMLN and its integration into the political process. In Guatemala the government and the URNG have entered negotiations and agreed to end the 34 year conflict. The peace accords call for democratization and demilitarization of Guatemalan society as well as the demobilization and political integration of the URNG guerrilla forces.

Throughout the region, the struggle has shifted from the military battlefield to the political arena where the forces of civil society compete to assert their interests. Currently within civil society nowhere are the goals of social justice, political participation and economic democracy more clearly articulated than in the popular organizations. Campesinos, widows, Christian base community members, returned refugees and others do not pursue justice or political participation out of an idealistic or ideological commitment. Rather they form their organizations in order to defend themselves and to assert their rights in the face of a desperate struggle for survival.

Their search for survival--banding together to demand potable water from the municipality, building a cooperative to sell their grains at higher prices or to obtain more inexpensive agricultural services–can lead to experimenting with alternatives: alternative production methods, alternative education, alternative forms of self-organization or governance. Not all alternatives are good ideas or work. The unworkable ideas are discarded; the possible alternatives are pursued. When as individuals the poor compete to survive by selling their labor and their body, most often they are super-exploited. But when oppressed individuals form groups to defend themselves they can change their relationship with the economic and political forces which shape their lives.

Isabel, the Salvadoran campesina who helped found a women's organization after being forced to give birth in the street, may have asked herself what the life of her newborn would have been like if not for the organization. Would the infant have survived? Would Isabel herself have surrendered to the harshness of life in a marginalized community? How would her and her baby's lives been different? Clearly CONAMUS has improved Isabel's life and has made a significant impact on oppressed women living in marginalized communities. The alternatives fashioned by Isabel and her *compañeras* who promote the work of CONAMUS will not turn back neoliberal policies nor bring about a more democratic government in El Salvador, but they do create options for women who previously had very few. Alternatives do help break the cycle of exploitation. If alternatives can be generated at a local level, they can also be built at a regional level and a national level.

By themselves popular organizations may not be able to create a political and economic alternative in the 1990s, but they do allow people living on the margin to survive when that is often in doubt. The politics of survival in shantytowns, rural villages, sweatshops and large plantations contain the seeds of alternatives for the future. The popular movement is fertile ground for experimentation of different forms of social organization, production, communication, and education. The popular movement, too, helps keep hope alive when that resource is in short supply.

FOOTNOTES:

[1] One of CONAMUS' early leaders, Maria Cristina Gómez, was a Baptist and a school teacher. She was a leader in CONAMUS' demonstrations and sponsored a women's radio program. For her work, in early 1989 she was kidnapped, tortured with acid and killed by death squad members.

[2] See Gabriel Escobar, *The Making of Social Movements in Latin America* (Boulder, Colorado: Westview, 1992), p. 327.

[3] *Public Papers of the Presidents ... John F. Kennedy ... 1962* Washington, 1963), 223. Cited in Walter LeFeber's *Inevitable Revolution* (New York: W.W. Norton & Company, Inc., 1984) p. 154.

[4] Landau, Saul. *The Guerrilla Wars of Central America* (New York: St. Martin's Press, 1993), p. 176.

[5] In the recently concluded negotiations process in El Salvador, for example, most of the socio-economic demands which the FMLN presented were drawn from demands asserted first by popular organizations. Yet no one accused the FMLN as serving as a "front group" for the popular movement.

[6] See Jenny Pierce, *Promised Land: Peasant Rebellion in Chalatenango, El Salvador* (London: Latin America Bureau, 1986).

[7] See Chapter 2 of this collection.

[8] Estimated by the World Court in The Hague in its landmark ruling against the U.S. for support of the contras.

[9] *Envío,* April 1992, p. 36.

[10] Arturo Grigsby and Napoleon Alvarado, SJ, "Central America's Economic and Political Backdrop," in *Envío,* August 1993. pp.5-6.

[11] *Ibid.*

[12] Quoted in "Unbinding the Ties," by Midge Quandt in this collection.

GUATEMALA

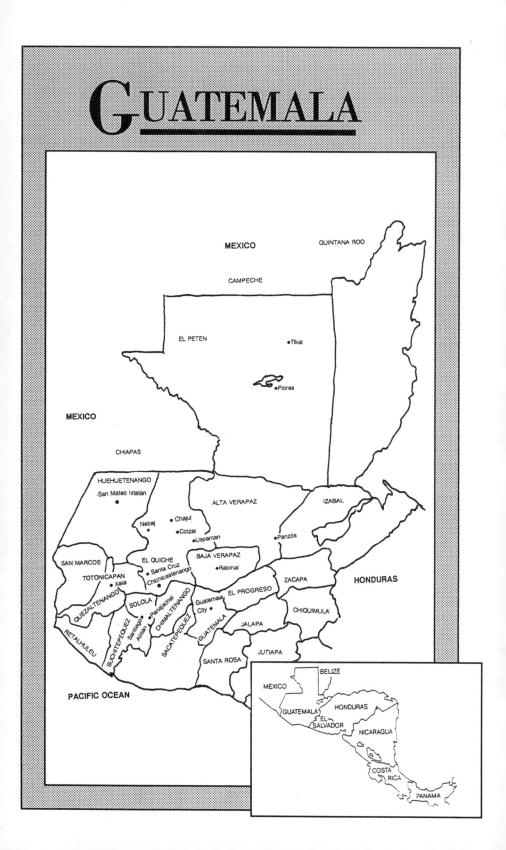

In Mayan communities, for the first time people are beginning to publicly denounce the massacres of the past fifteen years and demand legal justice.

Uncovering the Truth: Political Violence and Indigenous Organizations

Rolando Alecio

In November 1993 the public exhumation of a clandestine mass grave began outside the village of Río Negro, Guatemala. For two weeks members of an international forensic team dug away the covering dirt. As family members of the victims looked on, the forensic team unearthed, one by one, 177 skeletons. The victims were women and children exclusively. The exhumation had uncovered the truth that a horrible massacre against defenseless people had been committed. It was a truth which had long been denied by authorities and ignored by the international community. Now, eleven years after the massacre which had ended political organizing in the municipality, the unearthed skeletal remains have become the spark of a new stage of organizing among the indigenous of Río Negro.

Earlier in the year the surviving members of Río Negro, many of whom had been displaced across the country or resettled into a nearby government camp, organized themselves to petition for the exhumation of their loved ones and for the right to grant the deceased a dignified burial. They had heard of exhumations in other parts of the country and in the nearby community Chichupac. The Río Negro community called on the assistance of popular organizations who had formed *Sectores Surgidos por la Violencia* (Groups Arising Out of the Violence).

Only in the past three years had the survivors showed any signs that as a community Río Negro would survive. Four massacres in 1982 had eliminated over half of the residents of the village. Some of the survivors had hidden themselves among the burgeoning displaced population; others had been forced into the resettlement camp. They had lived paralyzed by fear. Organizing themselves to reclaim their lands, to rebuild their homes and above all to reclaim their history has been a slow, halting process.

Beginning in 1975 the Río Negro community had been the scene of intense campesino organizing. An internationally-funded hydroelectric dam on the River Chixoy threatened to, and eventually did, forcibly displace hundreds of poor, indigenous (mainly Achís) campesino families who lived in the Upper Chixoy Valley. The dam project and the subsequent land confiscations conscienticized hundreds of small farmers from Río Negro and surrounding communities who organized to hold on to their land or to receive fair compensation.

In 1981-1982 as the local opposition to the dam and demand for compensation became more heated, the Guatemalan Army's counterinsurgency war spilled into Río Negro and the municipality of Rabinal, the capital of the department of Baja Verapaz, even though there was little armed presence of the guerrillas. Opposition to the dam was seen as a pro-guerrilla movement and Río Negro and the municipality of Rabinal suffered severe repression at the hands of the Army and the Army-directed civil defense patrols. In the late 1970s leaders of community organizations had been selectively targeted but by early 1982 massacres committed against entire villages ended any further protest against the Chixoy dam project. A pastoral worker who lived in the area commented, "The Chixoy dam was built with the blood of the inhabitants of Río Negro and Rabinal." During this period, virtually all forms of community organization were annihilated.

The Río Negro massacre, committed by the civil defense patrol from a neighboring village, was neither the only nor the largest massacre committed in the Rabinal municipality. All told, at least nineteen massacres took place killing between four thousand and five thousand people. Over a 32 month period, 15% of the entire population of the municipality had been exterminated.

In July 1982, just a few months after the massacres took place, the community of Río Negro itself was flooded and disappeared under the waters backed up by the dam. Since the Chixoy dam went on line, no one–neither the international funders nor the government–has been willing to address the violence that the dam project provoked in Río Negro. The silence has been broken, however, as the victims themselves have begun to organize.

The first part of this article characterizes the social organization in the Rabinal area, both the traditional as well as the organizations formed in the indigenous communities. Given that Rabinal was not a conflict zone and that the guerrilla organizations were not strong in the area, community organizations, not the guerrilla insurgency, were the real targets in Rabinal. This article shows how the impact of such high levels of all types of political violence--harassment, arbitrary arrest, torture, rape, death squad killing and massacre--has been immeasurable. Particularly the widespread use of massacres has been devastating in terms of raw numbers of victims and in terms of the psychological and cultural trauma. Foremost has been an overpowering fear of even the most innocuous form of community organization.

The second part of the article describes the difficult rebuilding of community organizations in an area devastated by political violence. Community organizations, to the extent that they exist at all, are still in nascent forms, but they represent the seeds of stronger structures. The first step for the survivors has been to overcome fear, a process in which outside popular organizations and the Church have been helpful. The second step has been for victims as well as victimizers to recognize the truth of what has occurred. The third step is to restore community, both in the physical sense of rebuilding homes and replanting fields, and in the social sense of rebuilding security, confidence and communication.

Violence as a Response to Social Organization

Rabinal is a municipality in the department of Baja Verapaz, situated to the north of Guatemala City in the geographic center of the country. According to estimates based on the 1981 national census there are currently 36,363 inhabitants, 82% of whom are indigenous and belong to the linguistic group Achí.[1] Approximately one-fourth of the population lives in Rabinal, and the other 76% of the population lives among the 74 small rural communities called *aldeas* or *casarios*.[2]

The basic services in this municipality are scarce. There is only one health clinic. The town of Rabinal and the village Xococ are the only communities which have electricity or potable water in the homes. Local roads are few and often impassable, and transportation between the communities is limited or non-existent. Of the 74 rural communities, only 30 have elementary schools, and the level of illiteracy is 58.30%. There is no telephone service.[3]

The principal economic activity has been the cultivation of corn for family consumption. Most farmers work small plots with an average size of 2.28 hectares,[4] which is not sufficient to cover the minimum nutritional needs of each family. This, in turn, has forced seasonal migrations to the sugar cane, coffee or cotton plantations on the southern coast where working conditions are miserable, and salaries are often a half to a third of the national minimum wage.[5]

Many people in Rabinal also make traditional crafts as a supplementary source of income. Though the cultural benefits of artisan work are significant, the economic benefits are minimal. For example, in the village of Xococ, which is the second largest community following

Rabinal, women who weave straw mats, producing on the average one mat every two days, earn 0.48 *quetzales* (US$0.09) for each day of work.[6]

During the last ten years, because of such low levels of income and the resulting poverty, different strategies of survival have emerged. They include an increase in trade between communities, principally by women, including many widows due to the violence of the 1980s, who gather fruits or beans in their communities and walk anywhere from two to six hours to sell or exchange them for other products in the different villages. What they receive in return is hardly quantifiable, and often consists only in a few tortillas or a little coffee to feed themselves and some of their children.

Another survival strategy has been the non-traditional migrations to Guatemala City and to the United States. This has had a serious effect on the communities involved as particularly the young have left.

A third strategy involves joining the military, an option which is prominent in several rural communities. Enlistment guarantees an income to the family of the soldier, and housing, clothing and food to the soldier for a period of 30 months.[7] It is not uncommon for a man who lost parents, siblings and cousins to Army repression ten years before to be grateful today for the fact that he has four sons in military service who can guarantee economic survival for his family and simultaneously prove their "loyalty" to the Army.

Social Organization among the Indigenous

The traditional form of organization in Rabinal has been based on the family and the land. The family is the nucleus of biological, social and cultural survival; the family's relationship with the land enables survival. Other institutions such as the Catholic Church and its associations such as the *cofradías* and the *hermandades* have lent cohesion and identity to the community life but also have acted as a means of controlling the indigenous population by dominant groups. Before the violence of the 1980s there were 18 important *cofradías* (and still others of lesser importance) in Rabinal.[8]

Military commissioners were also key figures used to control the civilian population. Appointed by the military to be a link between the civilian population and the military, the commissioners frequently abused their power in order to defend the political and economic interests of the local elite. From 1963 until the late 1960s they initiated a wave of terror in the communities in response to the guerrilla insurgency which was based in eastern Guatemala. In the late 1970s and early 1980s under the direction of the Army, the commissioners formed civil defense patrols to be the eyes and ears of the Army. The commissioners and the patrols were key instruments of repression during the period of the massacres.

The 1960s signified profound changes in other forms of social organization in the rural communities of Guatemala. The traditional social organizations of the campesino and indigenous communities of Guatemala were quickly influenced by the ideas of development programs, self-help projects, and cooperatives brought by missionaries and other pastoral agents. This caused serious confrontations between those who defended the traditional order and those who supported creating new organizations which allowed for improving the quality of community life. The reservations of the traditionalists limited the development of new organizing models in several communities; still, by 1970 many communities were already organized in community improvement committees, cooperatives, Catholic base communities and campesino organizations. One of the most important cooperatives, *La Huella del Baron,* was one founded by Catholic pastoral workers. The Center for Family Development, another non-governmental organization, was deeply involved in training and human development.

In 1976 two events led to increased campesino organizing. In February an earthquake devastated much of Guatemala, affecting particularly the poor who lived in poorly made, *barreque-* constructed (made of wooden slats and clay) homes. Tens of thousands were killed, and hundreds of thousands were left homeless. To coordinate relief efforts, the poor had to organize themselves engendering new levels of community trust as well as, in view of the exorbitant governmental corruption of international aid, new levels of cynicism towards authorities.

The other event was the approval of the financing of the Chixoy dam which would become the largest hydroelectric plant in the Central American region. Funded by the Central American Economic Integration Bank ($7.8 million in 1974), the World Bank ($145 million in 1975) and the Inter-American Development Bank ($105 million in 1976), the dam was projected to generate 300,000 kilowatts. The overriding concern of the lending agencies were the cost over-runs (the final cost of the dam more than doubled the original estimate of $400 million), the extensive delays and the technical failures encountered in construction. Of lesser importance seemed to be the situation of the peasants whose land would be flooded and who were being systematically exterminated when they attempted to defend their land.[9]

The conflict between Río Negro and the National Electrification Institute (INDE) erupted in mid-1978 when construction of the dam began. Residents of Río Negro resisted the government plan for resettlement and formed an organization to represent their views and defend their interest in jobs offered in the construction. The residents of Río Negro and neighboring communities sought the support of the Committee of Campesino Unity (CUC was its acronym in Spanish) which for a number of years had been active in the area working with cooperatives and church based social development organizations. CUC had strong contacts nationally and internationally and played an important role by taking up the cause of the poor majority and by denouncing government abuses.

Río Negro: The Beginning of the Violence[10]

The first casualties of the violence over the dam occurred on March 4, 1980 when three soldiers assigned to guard the Chixoy Hydroelectric Project arrived at the community of Río Negro just as people were meeting in the church to discuss the evictions from their lands. The soldiers fired shots on the large group, killing seven persons. The people responded by chasing the soldiers and captured one of them who was killed by the crowd. The other two fled, one of whom drowned when he attempted to swim across the reservoir to escape. The rifle of the drowned soldier was never found and, though probably lost in the reservoir, was the basis of the Army accusation that the Río Negro community were guerrillas because they refused to return the rifle.[11] In fact, the Guerrilla Army of the Poor (EGP), one of the insurgent groups which would later make up the URNG, had begun to operate in the Rabinal area some years previously. Their aim, however, was primarily political formation and recruitment of members and not insurgent activity. Rabinal was not a conflictive zone and there is no evidence that the Río Negro community supported the fledgling guerrilla presence.

The lost weapon in Río Negro became the army's justification for unleashing a wave of repression against most of the communities of the municipality of Rabinal. In the beginning, the objective was to eliminate anyone who was a leader of any kind (heads of *cofradías*, catechists, health promoters, cooperativists, captains of sports teams, heads of families, etc.) because of the role such people played in the social organization. This was true above all in the case of Río Negro but it was also true of other communities in the municipality in which grassroots movements of the Catholic Church, such as *La Huella del Barón* cooperative and the Center for Family Development (CIF), had developed an important community infrastructure.

Later, however, the pattern of killings changed. The slaughter became indiscriminate. Almost all the communities suffered some level of repression (from threats to kidnapping and torture to individual assassinations and massacres). Mass killings occurred in nearby communities such as Canchún, Los Encuentros and in Rabinal itself (where between 300 to 500 people were massacred by Army troops and death squads on September 15, 1981). In February 1982 the Army and civil defense patrol of Xococ massacred 73 persons, Río Negro residents who had come to Xococ to the market. When word of the massacre reached

Río Negro the next morning, the men from the village fled. As one man, who lost his wife, two children and two sisters in the massacre, stated

> We left our village [Río Negro] and sought refuge in the woods. Our wives said that they would never leave their homes and their children because they could not survive in the woods, but they told us to leave and hide because life isn't respected and that we must not go to Xococ or Rabinal.
>
> One morning at 6:00 a.m. the armed patrols came to Río Negro. They went house to house obliging all the women and children to attend a "meeting" under the *conacaste* tree while the Xococ patrollers ransacked our houses taking all things of value.
>
> The patrollers then asked the women, "What do you do when the guerrillas come? You dance with them, no? You have no shame. Show us how you dance with the guerrillas!"
>
> They then claimed that the men of the village had all joined the guerrillas even though all knew that the patrols had killed them the day before. Then the patrollers played *marimba* music on tape recorders and forced the poor women to dance.
>
> Despite the women's claims that they didn't dance with or know the guerrillas, the patrollers took the women and children--at about 1:00 p.m.--to what is now the clandestine cemetery. Two women, each carrying a child on their back and another in their hands, threw themselves down a ravine and escaped. They hid all afternoon then ran to find us.
>
> We did not witness the killing because we were in hiding. When we came to the village, we saw the tragedy. Their bodies mutilated, horribly killed, decapitated, throats cut, tortured, raped... The children had been beaten against big rocks until they died. Others were killed with clubs.
>
> On this day, there was a great silence in our village. In our home I found only coffee brewing on the fire and corn *masa* on the grinding stone. All of the survivors were like chicks without the mother hen, widowers and two widows, some children without mother or father, with hardly the strength or spirit to bury the bodies.

"The Time of Punishment"

Why Río Negro? As with the other massacres in Guatemala, there was a combination of local factors and the national context of counterinsurgency repression. The Army feared the Río Negro community because they were organized with CUC. For the Army, being involved with CUC was tantamount to being a guerrilla even though there was no evidence of insurgent activity in the area. The Río Negro community had already opposed the resettlement program offered by INDE and caused an international incident because of their resistance to being flooded out by the dam. INDE, the Army and the financial backers of the dam did not want the example of resistance by Río Negro to spread to the other communities which were being forcibly resettled.

The Army took advantage of village rivalry and pre-existing land conflicts between Río Negro and the nearby village of Xococ.[12] Río Negro and Xococ were similar in terms of living conditions, socio-cultural characteristics, history and class position. By 1981 most of the inhabitants of Xococ collaborated with the Army, giving information and recruiting conscripts. Xococ was one of the first villages to form a civil defense patrol, at the direction of the Army. The Army accused the residents of Río Negro of aiding the guerrillas and then warned the Xococ villagers that they better organize to defend their lands and homes and that the Xococ villagers should eliminate the threat of the community of Río Negro before Xococ is attacked. Led by an Army officer, the Xococ civil defense patrols committed a series of brutal atrocities against the Río Negro community as well as other communities, apparently without remorse. In the March 13th massacre in Río Negro, after slaying the 177 victims, the civil defense patrollers proceeded to kidnap the sixteen remaining surviving children and took them as virtual slaves. In addition to the Río Negro massacre, the Xococ patrol was also involved in mass killings: Xococ (73 killed), Agua Fria (92 killed) and Plan de Sánchez (268 killed). Still today as one enters the village, a sign reads: "WELCOME TO THE COMBATIVE VILLAGE OF XOCOC."

Between March 1980 and August 1983, a period which residents still refer to as the "time of punishment" or "time of judgement," as many as 5,000 people were killed in the municipality. The following table gives details on nineteen of the massacres that were committed during that period.

TABLE 1: Massacres Committed in the Rabinal Area (1980-1983)

No.	Date	Community	No. of Victims
1.	3/4/1980	Río Negro	7
2.	3/13/1981	Canchún	14
3.	5/2/1981	Los Encuentros	13
4.	9/15/1981	Rabinal	300-500
5.	9/19-20/1981	Multiple villages[13]	200
6.	12/1981	La Ceiba	51
7.	12/4/1981	Panacal	104
8.	1/6/1982	Chichupac	62

9.	2/13/1982	Xococ[14]	73
10.	3/13/1982	Río Negro	177
11.	5/14/1982	Los Encuentros	89
12.	7/18/1982	Plan de Sánchez[15]	268
13.	7/18/1982	El Sauche	15
14.	9/13/1982	Agua Fria[16]	92
15.	1982	Chichupac-Xeabaj	104
16.	1982	Xesiguán	79
17.	1982	Pichec	60
18.	Unknown	Nimacabaj	54
19.	Unknown	Coyajá	46

The Rabinal tragedy was part of a policy of counterinsurgency developed on a national level which included "scorched earth" military operations, the creation of model villages, Civil Defense Patrols (PACs), and development poles. The results are devastating: 440 communities were exterminated; 1,650,000 people displaced from the communities or homes, including 150,000 who sought protection in other countries (especially Mexico, and later Honduras and Belize); and 72,000 dead or disappeared in a period of four years between 1980 and 1984[17].

The Army justified its repression against the Rabinal communities as counterinsurgency. Yet unlike many other highland communities, the armed insurgency did not exist there. The people of Rabinal never took up arms or joined the Guerrilla Army of the Poor (EGP). Although there were some isolated cases of young people in Rabinal who did join the guerrillas, and some guerrillas and groups of guerrillas did appear in the villages, collective participation in the armed struggle never occurred. At most, the EGP considered the zone an area of reserve, a recruiting area for logistical support. What evidence that did exist of armed guerrilla actions was fabricated by the Army to justify the mass killings.[18] Many of the early selective killings of community leaders were also attributed, most likely unfairly so, to the guerrillas.

One of the most insidious aspects of the Army repression in the Rabinal area was its manipulation and use of civilian neighbors as either accusers or executioners. Particularly, civil defense patrols, directed by the Army and military commissioners, or other "spontaneous" groups committed the bulk of the killings.[19] The population was divided into victims and victimizers. Based on our interviews with local functionaries, witnesses, indirect informants and others, it is estimated that in more than three-fourths of the mass executions, members of the same community or a neighboring community participated in the killing. Victims and victimizers lived alongside each other; they were of the same ethnic group and often of the same family. It was not uncommon for a victim to be a victimizer, and a victimizer to be a victim.

One community perpetuates violence against another community generally when they are instigated or threatened to by the Army (or its agents) and when there exists longstanding disputes between the communities involved: The people in community A made accusations against the people in community B because they had long wanted to get control of community A's water source; the people of community C made accusations against the people of community D because of a boundary dispute; the people of community E killed the first people in community F because these people refused to sell them their lands; the people of community G went ahead of the soldiers who entered community H by night because they were jealous of the people of H because they are *ladinos*.

The goal of the repression was not just elimination of community leaders or suspected guerrilla sympathizers. The Army and its agents attempted to make life untenable for the survivors by destroying all things of value. This included not only property and other possessions (houses, clothes, furniture, handmade objects that were used for both every day purposes and ceremonial purposes) but also the essentials needed to sustain life (crops, livestock, tools, seeds, trees, water supply, etc.).

The Effects of the Violence

The effects of the violence can be observed today at all levels in the life of the Rabinal communities. At a personal level, survivors felt extreme traumatization as an immediate effect. Extreme traumatization is the product of "catastrophic experiences that occur in a socio-political context which affects the subject to such a way one's basic structure of personhood is left damaged."[20] The trauma was a result of people's personal loss and also, for many, from their degree of guilt for either directly or indirectly being involved in the repression. For most people, resistance to the repression was not an option. None of the massacres occurred in a context of armed confrontation or physical resistance by the victims. The survivors paid a high personal cost for their survival. Most, consciously or unconsciously, collaborated with the Army by *chillando* (accusing their neighbors of subversion) or in other ways showing their sympathy with the Army. One man who lost family members in the repression relates[21]

> What hurt the most was that our own neighbors were the ones. When they came at night, maybe they thought that we wouldn't recognize them, but you know your own people. A lot of acquaintances from other villages stole from us, accused us ... massacred us. This can't be pardoned. One expects this from soldiers or ladinos but from your own people is a sin.

In other ways, the victims internalized the repression, sometimes by claiming that they deserved the repression (calling that period "time of punishment" or "time of judgement") or by identifying with their oppressor. The Rabinal and Xococ cemeteries, where hundreds of innocent people died at the hands of the Army and civil defense patrols, are virtual monuments to the military. Gravestones, including those marking victims of the Army, have been painted in camouflage and decorated with military symbols–guns, crossed swords and five-sided stars. Others are decorated with a replica of The Combatant's Plaque given to foot soldiers who have killed an enemy in combat. Throughout the Rabinal area, military style is in fashion: combat t-shirts, pants, boots and berets and also camouflage-painted buckets, lanterns, towels, batteries, combs, pencils, handkerchiefs, toys and lotions.

Nearly all forms of independent community organizations disappeared after the repression partly out of the continuing threats against organizations and partly out of people's inability to function in any "normal" way. Social change groups such as Christian base communities,

Twelve years after the masscre, the Rió Negro community is finally allowed to bury their dead. Here Rigoberta Menchú, Guatemala's Nobel Peace laureate, joins the funeral procession in the burial of 177 remains which were exhumed in November 1993.

cooperatives, and self-help groups were disbanded, and traditional organizations such as the *cofradías* and *hermandades* also became inactive. The only groups left untouched by the violence have been the civil defense patrols and the military commissioners. The repression left its mark on social organization in other ways as well.

1. The high number of deaths in a short period of time (approximately 15% of the total population was killed in 32 months), principally heads of families, caused the disintegration of the nuclear family. This contributed to the disintegration of social organization, since organizations frequently were based on systems of family relationships.

2. Repression and fear also caused the displacement of large numbers of people who fled for their lives to the mountains or to urban areas, especially Guatemala City. This resulted in the total disintegration of the community's forms of social organization, including those related to organization for production.

3. The death of one or more members of a family, especially of men of productive age, led to the abandonment of cultivable land. Moreover, people were often too scared to venture to their outlying plots to farm. The inability of the community to farm destroyed the local economy and damaged the community's sense of identity and cohesion.

4. The death and displacement of important groups of the population caused profound changes in the socio-demographic patterns of the municipality to the degree that there exist today communities populated almost entirely by women and children. The scarcity of men of productive and reproductive age has resulted in serious morale problems, which in turn constitute another factor contributing to the social disintegration of the community. The group most affected by this has been the widows, who are characterized as "prostitutes" by the rest of the community and as "subversives" by the military authorities.

5. The fear has prevented the population from organizing in any way; as a result of this, the majority of the communities face greater obstacles in overcoming their poverty. Almost all the programs for development and community assistance undertaken between 1984 and the present have failed because of the lack of community organization. The degree of the military's control over the population and the level of fear is such that Rabinal is one of the few communities in which CONAVIGUA, the organization of widows whose husbands were killed in the violence, has not been able to organize until recently.

6. In order to avoid becoming targets for repression, family members of the victims have enlisted in the Army or have become enthusiastic members of local civil defense units. The department of Baja Verapaz has a volunteer enlistment rate three times higher than the national average. The guilt and even self-hatred of those who joined the ranks of their repressors has had a devastating impact at a psychological level.

7. The military has dominated the civilian authorities in large as well as small affairs. The imposition of new leaders, military commissioners and *jefes* of the civil defense patrols has destroyed Rabinal's traditional hierarchies of authority. The new authorities are appointed by the Army and rule with counterinsurgency objectives. Land and resources are stolen from families seen as sympathizing with the opposition and given to military sympathizers. Small groups of affluent campesinos have thus emerged as new beneficiaries of the local leadership structure controlled by the military.

8. Land tenancy has been altered for counterinsurgency objectives. Instead of the traditional pattern of clusters of people dispersed over the area which was the basis for the community's social organization, people are forced to live in more concentrated settlements. This has changed fundamentally people's sense of connection to the land, of space and of relationships (interpersonal, intercommunity, etc.) since these are based on the pattern of settlement.

In conclusion, the former structures of social organization of Rabinal have completely ceased to exist and, up until recently, restoring them has proven difficult owing to the strong social control exercised by the military and paramilitary organizations. Other institutions involved in social services and in development (including governmental institutions) as well as popular organizations have tried to involve the people in their programs with discouraging results. Up until 1990 the situation could be summarized by a comment offered by a staffperson with a development institution which has programs in a number of communities in the municipality:[22]

> It is very difficult to work here because the people refuse to participate. It's not because they don't want to, but because they're afraid. If the women are asked to get together to talk about participating in a project, they won't do so; they say, "They're going to kill us; they're going to think that we're trying to get ourselves killed."

A foreign anthropologist who has been close to the residents of Rabinal concurs. He said in a June 1994 interview,

> There has been a brutal deterioration of the social fabric, a psychosis and trauma at both a personal and collective level. The massacres left the communities without leadership. These are sad people, people full of fear. The violence has been internalized and the sadness has led to an enormous amount of drinking and other forms of escapism, including suicide.

Violence as a Form of Social Control

As we have seen, in the Rabinal area the Guatemalan state resorted to the use of extreme violence in an effort to eliminate all organizations attempting social change. Institutionalized violence was used as a form of social control. The indigenous communities were victims of a counterinsurgency policy based on terror, one of whose principle objectives has been to destroy the traditional forms of social organization of the indigenous cultures--which are fundamental in the making of a peoples' identity--in order then to impose models of social organization consistent with "national security."

According to Arturo Arias, a Guatemalan anthropologist who wrote *Guatemala: Polos de Desarrollo,*[23] one of the objectives of the efforts to destroy the traditional social organization of the indigenous ethnic groups was to promote these groups' integration into a model of a nation which does not recognize cultural diversity but, rather, demands cultural and ideological homogeneity. As a result of this homogeneity, there will be new kinds of social organization created. Collective participation by the community, for example, in independent projects for the benefit of the entire community is too threatening.

While not completely foregoing the use of violence, the military has developed other ways of controlling the indigenous population through development projects. These new ways of trying to influence the indigenous population are designed to "reach the hearts and minds" of the campesinos. Simultaneous with the large military offensives, the army has carried out "civic campaigns" involving literacy, vaccination, construction of latrines, and agricultural training.

However, the military's plans for supplanting the former community structures with new Army-dominated civic structures have not been entirely successful. As the next section shows, as the military threat diminishes, independent community organizations tend to emerge. In Rabinal many communities suffered extreme loss of life and near total, if not total, destruction of community organization. Yet their basic values, which are the elements most important in maintaining the unity of the communities, have survived and been passed on to the next generation. New forms of organization have adapted to the conditions which the dominant sectors have imposed on them. Not surprisingly, these organizations have tried to respond to the violence, utilizing the spaces available to them.

Social Organization as a Response to Political Violence

What happens so that the culture of fear and escapism--in a community still dominated by the Army--begins to lose its death grip on a people? How is passivity converted into action, submission turned into acts of opposition? Whatever change has taken place in Rabinal since 1990 has been gradual as people are testing the limits of control.

The first signs of the emergence of community life from the shadow of Army control were the declining enlistments in the Army and the dropping participation in the civil defense patrols. Then slowly people began to re-establish informal community associations based on their need for economic survival. Only most recently has there been the most significant third development: an ethical demand arising from the family members of the victims. Their cry began with the right to exhume and then give a dignified burial to those who died in such an undignified way, then deepened to the right to assert the truth about the Army-inspired violence, and has become bolder still. The family members of the victims are demanding justice and are pressing ahead with attempts at legal prosecution of the Army officers and civil patrol leaders who ordered and carried out the mass killings.

In regards to the first point, there has been a passive resistance towards militarization in Rabinal. Without openly confronting the military or the civil patrol leaders, seventy communities have succeeded in eliminating the patrols. People feel less incumbent to prove their loyalty to the military and hence feel less obligated to join the patrols. Participation in the patrols has also been difficult to enforce due to the seasonal migration of nearly all community laborers who go to the coastal plantations for the harvests. The disbandment of the patrols should not be seen entirely as community opposition to the patrols or to the military. In many instances, their disbandment reflects the success of the counterinsurgency--it is widely recognized that the patrols are unnecessary because there is no guerrilla presence--and that the social control has been so internalized by the population, that there is less need for overt mechanisms of control. Patrols continue in only two communities, Xococ and Vegas de Santo Domingo,[24] where patrol leaders use their authority to put down any attempts to accuse them of human rights violations.

The Guatemalan Army, too, has become a less appealing option for Rabinal's young, precisely because the threat from the Army has lessened. Since the state-led repression has declined, the indigenous do not have to join the Army in order to prove their loyalty to the Army or the government. So enlistment has declined. Neither tendency, the disappearance of the patrols nor the declined enlistment in the military, however, should be interpreted as any kind of active resistance to the patrols and the military. There have been no protests, anti-military education campaigns or organizing against the patrols or military. Popular organizations which have organized opposition to the patrols in other parts of the country have not been, until very recently, present in Rabinal.

A nascent form of community organization in the Rabinal area has been the informal grouping of people who organize themselves in order to survive economically. Increasingly, campesinos are forming work groups to collectively farm the land furthest from the village which the Army historically has prevented them from farming. Though collective farming is a traditional work practice in Rabinal, the military had seen it as a threat. Since the early 1980s, some people lived in hiding and others were afraid to work or show any sign of collective organizxation. Most people were even afraid to identify themselves as from a village which the Army considered subversive (Río Negro, Plan de Sánchez or any other site of a massacre).

The seeds of these informal work groups were their experiences living as displaced people in the mountains as small "communities in resistance." They survived by moving constantly to avoid being

In Guatemala City, children protest the forced disappearance of their parents.

captured by the Army and by eating roots, berries and the gleanings from their abandoned fields. When after as many as 36 months of extreme hardship the displaced people decided to return to the Army-controlled towns, they sent delegations to appeal to military and judicial authorities to allow their "legal" return. The experience of organization--which allowed their survival in the mountains and guided them through negotiations with the authorities to permit their returns--gave people the basis for future organization.

Beginning in 1992 the displaced from Río Negro and other communities affected by the violence began to return to their lands to live and to replant. Since 1982 there had been a *de facto* military prohibition against even visits to their abandoned homes and farms. Later people were allowed to plant their fields but not live in their former communities (even though their fields lay a full day's walk from Rabinal). Now twenty families have returned to the area of Río Negro (even though the original site remains under water) and are rebuilding their community. The Catholic Church has provided some financial assistance for the community to build a water supply and the community has rebuilt the school and sought government teachers. The next step, according to one community member who lost 40 relatives in the political violence, is to create income generation projects for the widows and orphans (organized as the *Comité de Vuidas y Huérfanos)* and possibly re-found *La Huella del Baron* cooperative.

The return to Río Negro and other communities has been possible only through a strong sense of organization among the returnees; individual families would be too fearful and the obstacles too over-whelming for any one family to attempt a return on their own. Those who have been affected by the violence have been clear that their work groups and other economic associations are directed towards their own economic survival and should not be seen as challenges to the military or the two remaining civil defense patrols in Xococ and Vegas de Santo Domingo. The strategy of non-confrontation with the military is becoming difficult to maintain, however, as the public exhumations and the search for the truth is once again leading to a clash of victims and their victimizers.

For the thousands of Achí families in Rabinal who lost close relatives during the political violence, what began as a deeply held conviction that their loved ones deserved a dignified burial has turned into a strong political challenge to the legitimacy of the military. In the words of one resident, "The bones have started to talk, and they are telling the truth about the massacres." The search for the truth inevitably will lead to legal charges against those accused of being responsible for the widespread repression as people continue to speak out against Army threats and beatings and refuse to be intimidated.

The struggle for the truth began in 1989 when former Río Negro residents had returned to their lands and saw in a ravine three skulls which the rain had left exposed. Stunned, they returned to Rabinal and asked a local priest to return to the area and perform a spiritual cleansing of evil from the site of the mass killing. One pastoral worker who was present told what happened.[25]

> It was an incredible pilgrimage that lasted a week. We did a mass at the burned chapels in each of the six villages of Río Negro which had been massacred. People cried to see their land, to see the trees, to see the bones of those who had been killed.

Before people rarely had talked about the violence. Even during mass, when people prayed for the dead they would not reveal exactly how their loved ones had died, namely that they were killed by the Army. Now people are beginning to express themselves, tell their feelings, to give air to their infected wounds.

The first public exhumation in the Rabinal area took place in May 1993. The exhumation was initiated at the urging of an Achí woman who had lost her entire family in the massacre at Chichupac (on January 6, 1982 sixty-two people were killed) and was presently living in Guatemala City. She approached CONAVIGUA (National Commission for the Widows in Guatemala) to ask for their help to exhume the remains of her family. CONAVIGUA had helped form the *Sectores Surgidos por la Violencia* (Groups Arising from the Violence) which worked with an international forensic team in a number of previous exhumations. With an order from the local judge, the forensic team uncovered dozens of bodies. Even though the exhumation was initiated from the outside and military commissioners threatened people against attending the exhumation, dozens of family members of the victims came to identify the remains. CONAVIGUA played a critical role in meeting with the widows in Chichupac "to help give us the courage to speak out" as one widow explained.

In October 1993 the exhumation of one of the four massacres against the Río Negro community brought out an even more open expression of sentiment against the Army. With daily arrivals of national and international press, human rights groups and representatives of popular organizations, survivors of the Río Negro community openly told their stories and expressed their feelings–sadness, anger and for some, revenge. The unearthing of 177 skeletal remains of women and children was a powerful experience. For the first time since the killing, family members of the victims could openly visit the site of the massacre, place a candle where their bodies had been uncovered and publicly pray. People openly described the history of persecution against them and named the killers. For the first time in twelve years the exhumation had allowed for public acknowledgement of the massacre and gave the space for human response among the victims and their supporters. The local parish priest commented, "I had never seen people cry openly for their lost loved ones before."

Prominent during the exhumation were CONAVIGUA and also the National Coordination for the Displaced in Guatemala (CONDEG) and the Mutual Support Group (GAM) who gave support to and helped organize the family members to identify the remains, make public statements and prepare for the burial.

Since the Río Negro exhumation there has been one other exhumation, this one at Plan de Sánchez where 268 people were killed on July 18, 1982 by the Army and patrollers. The Plan de Sánchez exhumation began in June 1994 and since then there have been requests for at least six more. The Río Negro community has petitioned for exhumations in the sites of the three other massacres of their community, including in the village of Xococ (73 Río Negro residents were killed by the patrols in Xococ on market day), an action which would be a direct challenge to the authority of the existing civil defense patrol in Xococ and to its sponsor, the Guatemalan Army.

The challenge by the family members of the victims does not stop there. Massacre survivors also are organizing quietly to press legal charges against the commanders of the patrol in Xococ and against Army officers who directed a number of the massacres, including the massacre at Plan de Sánchez. Aiding the victims in the effort are the popular organizations which make up the *Sectores Surgidos* group, the Archdiocesan Human Rights Office and the regional office of the Human Rights Procurator (a government institution). In interviews, survivors of the massacres state clearly that their goal is not revenge but justice. Said one, "This is nothing to do with vengeance. The names of the dead are the proof of the massacre. Vengeance is not the same thing as the truth."

Whether or not the local judges are willing to investigate and to hear the cases against the patrollers and the Army, the wall of impunity has been partially dismantled in Rabinal. The terror and pervasive fear, though still prevalent, is no longer the only possible response. While the effects of the internalized trauma and collective psychosis continue to exact a high toll on the population (14 people committed suicide in 1993 when previous to the violence suicide among the indigenous population was unheard of) and continue to impede freely-formed, independent community organizations among the indigenous, the presence of organized groups asserting the truth and demanding justice represents a serious challenge to the military.

The military's control over the population is no longer total, and military and paramilitary structures are no longer the only organizations in Rabinal. Informal work groups, newly formed cooperatives, committees of widows, parish councils and victims' associations are opening new spaces that allow people to survive economically and to assert the truth about the violence. With the support of the international community, forensic teams, popular organizations and courageous judges, justice may prevail and the bones of Rabinal may finally rest in peace, having spoken the truth.

FOOTNOTES:

[1] The Achí language is spoken in the municipalities of Rabinal, Cubulco and San Miguel Chicaj of the Department of Baja Verapaz. It is considered a variant of the Quiché language.

[2] Instituto Nacional de Estadistica (INE), *Estimaciones de población total segun municipios (1985-1990), Guatemala, 1985. p. 185.*

[3] Hugh Arnold Conde Prera, *Pequeña Monografía de Baja Verapaz*, 1987. Monograph.

[4] Dirección General de Estadistica (DGE), *III Censo nacional Agropecuario* (Guatemala: 1979).

[5] For example, in 1992 the average salary of an agricultural laborer was 5 *quetzales* (US$0.98) for a day's work (10 hours) in the Rabinal municipality or surrounding areas, while in the southern coast it was approximately 8 *quetzales* (US$1.56). As a general rule, women receive between 50% to 60% of the salary of a man for rural labor.

[6] This calculation is based on the information provided to us by artisans. For the palm leaves (the only material used), the women paid Q75.00 (US $15.00) with which they could make 72 mats at a pace of one every two days. They took their mats to Rabinal and sold them to a middle man who paid Q2.00 (US $0.40) for each one. The Rabinal market price for a mat is Q2.50 (US $0.50).

[7] A soldier would receive Q.200 (US $40) monthly salary and his family would receive a "compensation" of Q.100 (US $20) monthly, which, combined, is a greater salary then a peasant laborer would earn according to the 1990 minimum wage.

[8] Although the possibility exists that currently one *cofradia* would still retain political functions and control certain economic aspects of the community, no *cofradia* member admitted it; state-sponsored counterinsurgency policies forced the *cofradias* to take on only purely spiritual matters.

[9] George Black, *Garrison Guatemala* (New York: Monthly Review Press, 1984), pp. 29-30.

[10] Several of the witnesses used this phrase to refer to incidents which are mentioned later in this section.

[11] Author's interview with a resident of Río Negro who was living as a displaced person in another community of the municipality of Rabinal. August, 1990.

[12] Principally, border and property conflicts.

[13] Days after the massacre in Rabinal, the Army unleashed an offensive against communities located to the north of the town. The communities were bombed and the residents machine-gunned. The communities hardest hit were Xococ, Buena Vista, Panacal, Vegas de Santo Domingo, Pachicá and Pichec. See Shelton Davis and Julie Hodson's *Witnesses to Political Violence in Guatemala* (Boston: Oxfam America, 1982).

[14] Residents of mainly Rio Negro but also Canchún and Chitucán were deceived into going to Xococ where they were assassinated.

[15] In this village the residents of Concul and Raxjut as well as Plan de Sánchez were massacred. An informant accused the civil defense patrol of Xococ as well as the Army as responsible.

[16] This village falls under the jurisdiction of Uspantán, El Quiché. Because of its proximity to Río Negro, it was chosen by the survivors of earlier massacres as a refuge. Nonetheless the displaced were identified and assassinated. The majority of the victims were the elderly, women and children. The crime is attributed to the patrollers of Xococ.

[17] Cited in *¿Donde está el futuro? Procesos de reintegración en comunidades de retornos* (Guatemala: AVANSCO, July 1990).

[18] The headline of an article published in *La Prensa Libre* (10/10/1981, p. 12) read, "Neighbors of Rabinal Alarmed: 200 *Ladinos* Kidnapped." The article read, in part

> Two hundred persons which lived in the villages of Rabinal and Salamá were kidnapped by subversive groups that operate in the region... *Ladinos* were taken from their homes into the mountains... Only those who were indigenous were left behind. The Army, at the request of the residents, began a military sweep operation.

The article described the specific village as La Esperanza. None of the residents in Rabinal who were interviewed had any knowledge about this massive kidnapping. Furthermore, there is no community with the name of La Esperanza. The incident never happened. These kinds of incidents were part of the Army's disinformation campaign with the civilian population.

[19] The involvement of entire communities as the executors of violence against neighboring communities can be explained. The Army used local rivalries and conflicts between communities and between family groups, adding the accusation of "communist" to the victim group, to incite the violence by one community against another. In Guatemala, since 1954, the accusation of "communist" was equivalent to being condemned to death.

[20] Becker, David and Hugo Calderón. "Traumatizaciones extremas y procesos de reparación social, crisis política" in *Era de nieblas: derechos humanos, terrorismo del estado y salud psicosocial en América Latina.* Edited by Horacio Riquelme. (Caracas: Nueva Sociedad, 1990). pp. 67.

[21] Interview by author during on site investigation, July-August, 1990.

[22] Interview by author during field investigation, July-August, 1990.

[23] Arturo Arias, *Guatemala: Polos de Desarrollo: El Caso de la Desestructuración de las Comunidades Indígenas, Vol. I* (Mexico City: Editorial Praxis, 1988).

[24] It is thought by some of those interviewed that Xococ hangs on to the patrol as a mechanism of defense against those who might seek a vigilante retribution or who might attempt to press a legal prosecution of the patrollers for their crimes.

[25] Interview with a pastoral worker in Rabinal. June, 1994.

"Poor people, indigenous and ladino *alike, want peace and justice"
reads the wooden sign lying in front of three Mayan men in the
Department of El Quiche.*

Weaving Our Future: Campesino Struggles for Land

Rigoberta Menchú and the Committee of Campesino Unity (CUC)

The history which we narrate here is one of suffering and pain, but also one of joy. We will speak of aggression and abuses, not to seek sympathy but rather to invite reflection. The Committee of Campesino Unity (CUC) has a history of more than two decades of struggle but our roots go back much further.

In Guatemala the state and its security forces--from the whole Army to every last gun man for hire--guarantee that the labor force remains docile in order to meet the demands of an agro-export economy which produces principally coffee but also cotton, sugar cane and cardamum. Under this system, we, as campesinos, are the most important source of the country's income, but we have no control over this income. Through our labor, the wealthy eat, and eat very well, as do the police and the government employees and officials.

How does this system of oppression work? The root of the problem is land. The terrain of Guatemala covers a number of geographical regions: the central highlands, the southern coast, the Atlantic coast, the volcanos, the jungles in the north, and the arid area in the east. Despite the fact that our forefathers occupied all of what is today Guatemala, the Spanish conquistadors and later the *ladino* landowners expelled us from the most fertile region of the country, the southern coast. With the passing of time, the greed of these usurpers of our land resulted in our being forced from our communally-owned land in the south and confined to the cold mountainous regions. Thus, almost all the indigenous people were concentrated in the highlands. Despite our love of the highlands, the land there is not fertile, nor is there enough for all of us. Even if most families have a small plot of land to farm, it is seldom enough to sustain a family. We have little choice but to journey to the southern coast in search of migrant labor.

The cultivation of coffee requires an enormous amount of farm labor during two periods, the preparation and the harvest, but not at other times. Each coffee plantation has a small number of year-round workers who maintain the coffee trees, but during the preparation and harvest seasons a large number of outside workers, mainly indigenous people from the highlands, are brought in. The plantation owners use labor contractors to enforce a system of exploitation. The contractor will often recruit laborers in an indigenous village during the days prior to a significant feast day when people need money for the feast day. Poor people borrow from the contractor and promise to repay by working on the coast. Much of the money is squandered on drinking sprees. On the specified day, the contractor's truck arrives to collect the indebted workers who are known as *cuadrilleros*. There is no escape as the contractor knows everyone in the village personally and few break the obligation.

After a journey of several hours during which the people are packed into the truck like cattle, we arrive at the plantation and are housed in large barracks or under a *ceiba* (cottonwood) tree. Although it is far away from our homes, the plantation takes on a central part in our life. From the time we are newborn babies, we are taken there on the backs of our mothers and carried in the fields during long work days. The plantation steals our childhood, and many children die from the thousands of diseases which the rich in the country will never know. There is no potable water, and usually no wells or rivers nearby. We are given a grinding stone so that we can grind corn to eat. There is no firewood nor medical facilities. The only food we receive is a few pounds of corn per week which is deducted from our wages. This is a trap because the plantation owner buys the corn at a cheap price and sells it to us at a high price. Often the corn is from the previous year's harvest and is rotten and infested with insects.

Work on the plantation begins early. The *cuadrillero* rises at four and by five is in the fields. All day we work under the burning sun, harassed constantly by swarms of mosquitos. Women, often carrying their children, are the ones who suffer the most. The coffee beans are weighed by the owner's men who steal as much as 20 pounds per bag from the workers (a good worker, with the assistance of one of his children or his wife, can pick only about 100 pounds of coffee a day). On pay day, the original debt to the contractor is deducted as well as the cost of everything purchased on credit at the plantation store where the prices are exorbitant. Little is left from the workers' wages. During the preparation season, the system is the same except the fraud is perpetrated in terms of calculating the area cleared.

When the season is over, we return to our villages suffering from illnesses because of the living conditions and just as desperate as when we left. Usually there is enough money only to buy the seed corn for our plots. There is nothing for school expenses, medicine, clothing or recreation.

Tourists rarely see this side of Guatemala: the systematic dehumanization of the indigenous people. The economic system in Guatemala is based on maintaining a cheap labor supply. In order to legitimate the exploitation of indigenous, we are characterized as lazy, cowardly, submissive and inferior. In this way, the *criollos* and rich *ladinos* have for centuries organized Guatemalan society as if five million indigenous people did not exist. This myth helps the dominant classes believe that we are dispensable.

On the plantations of the southern coast of Guatemala, child labor is heavily exploited. Here two children, under the age of ten, work on a sugar cane plantation.

The Founding of CUC

In the late 1960s the impoverishment deepened as the erosion of the steep farmland worsened. Cheap fertilizer, which cost Q2.50 per 100 lbs. (Q1 = $1), became available and was seen as the answer to our problems. At first, production of corn increased so that people had enough corn for themselves and to sell. Then after two years, our good fortune reversed; there was too much corn, and it could not be sold at any price. People turned to plant potatoes, but the result was the same: too much product and no market.

In 1973 the international oil crisis hit and the price of fertilizer (which is petroleum-based) jumped. What cost Q. 2.50 per sack then rose to Q. 18.00 and we didn't have the money to pay for it. Representatives of the Development Bank came to our community offering loans to pay for the expensive fertilizer. We borrowed and began to buy fertilizer again. Our problems continued. The soil quality deteriorated and the land did not give the same yield even with fertilizer. The land needed more fertilizer for the corn and now fertilizer for the beans. For our small plots we had to buy two bags of fertilizer. What used to cost Q. 2.50 now cost Q. 36. Many of us could not meet the payments on our loans and after five years, the banks took our lands.

People began to migrate from the villages as never before to the southern coast and to the capital. Before we would come down to the cities to buy a pound of salt and tomatoes, but that's only when we had corn to sell. Now our children were forced to the cities or to the plantations in search of year-round work, and they faced discrimination as never before. We saw how they began to shed their traditions and become ashamed of their indigenous identity.

In 1972 a group of campesinos, a few professionals and priests and nuns began to meet together to discuss the problems of the poor: the discrimination, the exploitation and all the injustice that exists in Guatemala. The idea arose of taking some kind of action, though no one knew what. People began to discuss and reflect more. Different study groups formed and discussed a variety of themes, from the Bible to the Guatemalan Constitution. Although the priests and nuns never talked about revolution, they did make us aware of the level of injustice in the country. Centuries of discrimination had instilled within us an acceptance of abuse. Little by little we changed. One campesino said, "It is not right that we are mistreated, that we are overworked and paid salaries that are so miserable that we cannot even feed our children." We realized that it is not just that we are poor meanwhile the plantation owners grow rich from our labor.

The priests and nuns, through use of the Bible and their own example, showed us how to say "no" to those who treated us like mules. They showed us the way to liberate ourselves, the path to our own awareness of our rights as human beings. Simultaneously, the clergy learned too that saying mass is not enough and that religion by itself cannot solve the problems of our communities. We must look for other ways, other solutions.

We also realized that we could not expect compassion and concessions from the powerful and from the government. Jesus came to the same conclusion during his time. We also saw the authorities for who they were: ambitious men who did not serve the nation but rather defended the rich and repressed the poor who attempted to defend their own rights. The development projects, such as fertilizer projects, had failed us and were being used against us.

This kind of formation work in groups took place in the departments of El Quiché and Chimaltenango and in various towns on the southern coast and were the seeds of what later would become the Committee of Campesino Unity (CUC). From the beginning, there was great enthusiasm; we were convinced that we were moving in the right direction. Now twenty years later, those of us who survived can recognize that we were not fully aware of how difficult and long the path was that we were taking.

In 1976 the earthquake struck. Nearly all of the 26,000 dead, 70,000 wounded and one million left homeless were poor people. The most heavily affected areas were indigenous communities: Chimaltenango, San Martín Jilotepeque, Patzún, Patzicia, Tecpán, San José Poaquil, San Juan Comalapa, Joyabaj, Salcaja and others. Most of our people interpreted the calamity as God's punishment for our sins. But then we began to ask ourselves, "Why would divine judgement take such action against the most poor and simple people?" Some said that it was because we didn't pray enough, but others responded that they prayed regularly yet their entire family had been killed.

A pastoral letter signed by progressive Catholic bishops also analyzed the reasons of the catastrophe. People died, said the bishops, because their houses were poorly constructed and they had no money for better homes because the wealth of Guatemala was in the hands of the very few. We said the same, yet as poor people we did not have the same authority to speak of exploitation and class differences. So despite the suffering, the earthquake brought a ray of light.

International donors sent money to Guatemala to aid in the reconstruction. Parishes organized the communities for the rebuilding, and people realized that if their community was well organized they would receive more money and would be better able to rebuild. The reconstruction brought people from different communities together, and we exchanged experiences. Many *ladinos* began to see indigenous people in a different light, that we were not only the malnourished people working for starvation wages on the plantations, but in our home villages--despite our poverty--we had a rich culture and traditions worthy of respect and that we were organized. In the same way we began to see the need to differentiate between *ladinos* who were exploiters and those *ladinos* who were sympathetic with our struggle or who were in situations similar to our own.

Though these ideas had begun to ferment and even take shape, the difficulties were overpowering. After the 1976 earthquake the community groups had just begun to address their needs when the Army started selective repression. The Army viewed reconstruction as the work of the guerrillas and began kidnapping and assassinating defenseless campesinos. The most active members of the committees were captured and their mutilated bodies appeared subsequently on the roadsides. The sinister death squads which had been operating in the eastern part of Guatemala since 1966 became active in the highlands now.

Throughout this period we had been very cautiously experimenting with different models of organization, but so far none had met our needs and situation. The *Ligas Campesinas* (Peasant Leagues) which organized to defend the rights of small property owners were attempted but later discarded as a model because many of our people were landless. Much of the leadership of the *Ligas* also sought personal gain rather than the well-being of the membership, and corruption led to the organization's demise.

Models such as traditional labor unions were also limited in their effectiveness because labor law prohibits unions for workers who do not have a work contract, an important distinction since the bulk of the labor force on the plantations, the indigenous migrant laborers (*cuadrilleros*), rarely had work contracts.

The strategy of the plantation owner is to play off the year round workers known as *rancheros*--often *ladinos* or ladino-ized indigenous who are legally entitled to unionize--against the *cuadrilleros*. Through the 1970s the growing migrant labor surplus allowed the plantation owners to fire the *rancheros* who because of their right to organize unions received somewhat higher wages. Driven from the plantation lands, the *rancheros* often bought small plots, erected tiny shacks and continued to seek work on the plantations not as contracted year-round workers but as *voluntarios*, local day laborers who had no contract and little rights just as the *cuadrilleros*. So the vast majority of the plantation's work force had no right to unionize and that tendency was increasing. For us, neither the *Ligas Campesinas* nor the labor unions served as models for organization. We needed another way.

In November 1977 a watershed event in the development of our movement occurred in an isolated region of the Sierra Madre mountains in the department of Huehuetenango. The tungsten mine in San

Idelfonso Ixtahuacán fired 300 workers who were labor unionists. The workers, who were almost entirely Mam and were dependent on the mine for their livelihood, even living on the mine's property, saw few possibilities for protest. A visiting cooperatives expert, Mario Mungia Guigui, proposed to the laid-off miners that they borrow the strategy of a march that recently took place in Argentina. The miners agreed and mobilized to march 300 kilometers from San Idelfonso to Guatemala City.

When we learned of the march, we organized support along the route so that they never lacked coffee or *tamalitos* (a traditional food of corn flour and meat cooked in banana leaves). In Santa Cruz del Quiché we organized a tremendous demonstration to support their cause. When the marchers had reached Tecpán, two-thirds of their route completed, the mining company gave way to the demands of the miners. The Laugerud government had pressured the company to rehire the fired workers and end the strike before the marchers could enter the capital. But the miners kept marching and triumphantly entered Guatemala City in the largest demonstration since 1954. Thousands of people, indigenous and ladino, campesinos, students and workers lined the streets in a tremendous show of solidarity. It is difficult to exaggerate the march's significance during this time. Campesinos, who previously were reluctant to organize, saw that through unity they could triumph and began to join organizing efforts. The success of the march also showed that at a national level a broad-based mass movement could triumph in a country as desperately oppressive as Guatemala. What was needed, we realized, was to lay the groundwork and build that movement.

The time was ripe. On April 15, 1978 a national assembly of grassroots leaders of different groups from many regions of the country officially founded the Committee of Campesino Unity (CUC). All of the delegates were rural people who had been oppressed and exploited and who looked to unite with other groups of workers in order to end injustice and build a better society. We reached the conclusion that we needed to consolidate our efforts and proposed a broad-based organization of thousands of members made up of *cuadrilleros, voluntarios, rancheros,* renters, artisans and sellers--indigenous as well as *ladino,* men as well as women. We had learned that our rights are won through the strength of organization.

The enemy, however, had sharpened its long knives in preparation for confrontation. After the miners' march, the number of disappearances and violent deaths rose. From the beginning we were aware that CUC would have to be a semi-clandestine organization and that we would have to take severe security measures. We knew that the government would attempt to eliminate all of us. For these reasons we did not seek legal recognition, and we kept hidden the identity of our leaders.

On May 1st, 1978, eager to publicly make known the foundation of CUC, we participated openly for the first time in the Worker's Day March in Guatemala City. Our chant for the demonstration–"Clear head, strong heart and combative fist of Farm Workers"--became the motto for the organization. That march was the largest concentration of indigenous in the modern history of Guatemala. For the first time, rural people took over the streets, marching for their own demands and in their own style, carrying straw mats painted as banners, machetes, hoes, *huipiles, morrales* and sombreros.[2] In the rally which took place in front of the Presidential Palace, the leading speakers were CUC activists.

The Consolidation of CUC and the Massacre at Panzós

Our work spread throughout the country. Within a year we truly became a national organization working in the departments of Quetzaltenango, Alta Verapaz, Baja Verapaz, Izabal, Huehuetenango, San Marcos, Tetalhuleu and Totonicapan. The moment was still not opportune for us to press our demands, but we continued to denounce the repression and promote discussion among the workers. One of our first communiques called for opposition to the forced military recruitment. We tried to maintain a high level of visibility by painting murals and graffiti, displaying posters in public places and handing out leaflets. From the beginning our message was clear: exploitation and discrimination must end and that is possible only by building an organization of working people. Throughout our campaigns we projected the vision of building a new society, and we asked the people for direction.

Our organization grew because it belonged to--and continues to belong to--the campesinos. Our power resided in the strength of our grassroots structure. In every community where the CUC was present we organized a Coordination Commission which held local assemblies to direct the work of the organization; the Coordination Commission was the heart and foundation of CUC, it was work at the base with our feet firmly planted on the ground. CUC community leaders were not bosses or supervisors but rather servants to the people.

One event in particular was decisive in incorporating more people into our movement. On May 29, 1978 a demonstration about a land dispute in the town of Panzós, department of Alta Verapaz, which involved more than 800 Kekchí men, women and children brought the crisis to a head.

The Kekchí people had farmed the lands in the region for as long as anyone could remember, yet they were being systematically driven off the land and forced into migrant or wage labor on large plantations or forced to work in mines. Without land, they faced losing everything.

The march to Panzós was an attempt to resolve the land evictions through peaceful means. On this day indigenous people from Panzós, Sepón, Secocopo, Coboncha, Semococh, Tabetzal and other villages participated in a march in order to hand-deliver a petition to the town mayor. When the marchers arrived in the town center, the mayor was absent; hiding in the town hall, however, were 150 *kaibiles* (Army special forces). When the marchers filled the park, the commandos opened fire raining bullets on the people. The marchers threw themselves to the ground and then the *kaibiles* threw grenades on top of the unarmed people. When the guns stopped, more than 100 people lay lifeless on the ground. A few people, in a futile attempt to save themselves, had thrown themselves into the waters of the Polochic River and drowned. The exact number of victims was never known.

The massacre had been ordered by the High Command of the Army, some of whose members were *latifundistas* (large landowners) in the region. News of the massacre eventually reached the people of Guatemala and in the days following thousands of our machetes were seen once again marching through the streets of Guatemala City as campesinos joined with other groups to repudiate the crime and demand an end to governmental repression in the indigenous communities.

In Panzós, however, the problems of land persisted and the Army continued its military occupation of the town. The massacre and subsequent violations only furthered the politicization of the rural population, and across the country, many campesinos joined the ranks of our organization. We were not frightened, instead the massacre made us more determined. We took on more tasks inaugurating a clandestine "people's newspaper" known as "From Sunup to Sundown" (*Del Sol al Sol*).

The international situation influenced us as well. We paid close attention to the situation in Nicaragua when the then Sandinista guerrilla force took over the National Palace in August 1978 capturing all of the deputies and holding them in exchange for the release of political prisoners. Their success helped us realize that the people do not always lose when they fight. That incident also helped us learn something about our own country; in Guatemala, there are no political prisoners, only political disappearances.

Our activities multiplied. During October CUC joined the fight against the rise of bus fares in the capital, our first action which was not strictly associated with rural issues. On October 7th, one hundred CUC activists paralyzed traffic on the highway between Chimaltenango and Sumpango and also near Los Encuentros. On the southern coast in Escuintla we distributed leaflets in the bus terminal and in the buses. This action helped us connect the problems of workers in the city with our problems in the countryside and helped us realize that only a broad-based movement could bring about substantial change. Our vision of social change was becoming more open-ended.

In the countryside the regions that were most conflictive were the *Franja Transversal del Norte* (a large stretch cutting across the departments of Alta Verapaz, El Petén, El Quiché and Huehuetenango) and the western highlands. Nearly everywhere the problems were the same. Agro-industrial projects and modernization efforts demanded better lands and a cheaper labor force. Plantation owners and cattle ranchers sought to expand their holdings at the cost of the campesinos who had cleared virgin land or who had owned their land for generations. Their means were varied: deceit, legal traps, bribery of the authorities, or outright violence.

Our movement grew and in order to evade repression took unusual steps. The towns were full of government collaborators and so CUC meetings had be held secretly or at least discretely. We resorted to whatever cover we could employ. In one village, we used the *cofradia* (a parish committee in indigenous communities) as the cover, in another it was the local soccer team, in others it was the local parish or even the evangelical church. Patron saint day feasts provided the opportunity for CUC activists from different areas to meet and to pass out anti-governmental material. We infiltrated the local structure of political parties in order to nominate candidates that were CUC members for local elections. In some cases, an entire slate of candidates would be CUC members.

We also confronted problems of a different nature. In Santa Cruz del Quiché, for example, thieves and rapists were terrorizing the community. CUC organized the people to capture the suspects and instead of turning them over to the local authorities, we turned them over to the elders of the community. The elders held a public trial where it was decided to punish the offenders according to traditional ways: beating them with a chicote stick. The incident exposed how the authorities disregarded the complaints of the local people who undergo ongoing abuse. By initiating effective ways of protecting the lives and possessions of people in the communities, the CUC gained prestige.

With the help of the Church, we undertook literacy campaigns specifically designed to encourage discussion among the poor about our situation and ways to change it. For example in the literacy courses, we would discuss the news reported in the newspapers. *El Gráfico* once reported on the widespread poisoning that occurred at Olga Marina, a plantation in Tiquisate. One infant died and 28 other people were hospitalized. In the course people commented that this was not an isolated incident but rather a common occurrence because of the poor health conditions. Particularly in the cotton plantations such as Olga

Marina, enormous quantities of insecticide were sprayed by crop dusting planes and the airborne poison stuck to the skin of those people who were picking the cotton (this practice continues today in Guatemala). We also discussed how Guatemalan plantation owners would buy from U.S. companies chemical pesticides which had been banned in the U.S. and other countries. For us, this was another front of the war.

In April 1979 the CUC completed its first year as a popular organization. During an evaluation session of our successes and failures we outlined for the first time our demands. They included the right to life, the right to access to land and an end to the abuses of money-lenders, the right to year-round work, fair pay and overtime on Sundays and an end to unjust layoffs and fraud in weighing and measuring for piece work, the right to fair prices for the purchase of fertilizer, insecticide, tools and other necessary items for campesinos, the right to fair working conditions on the plantations, including an eight hour day, safe transportation, adequate housing, food, medical attention and safeguards in application of insecticides, the right to organize when and how the workers determine, respect for culture including the right to speak different languages and to practice indigenous customs, respect for equal treatment of *ladinos* and indigenous people, and the right to receive a sufficient education that allows for a dignified life and work.

We Will Not Be Silent

In December 1979 in the village of Chajul, department of El Quiché, the Army rounded up 500 people and forced them to witness a spectacle of torture. Seven campesinos had been captured and were accused of being guerrillas. They had been badly tortured, but were still alive. One Army officer described in detail to the terrified crowd how these "guerrillas" had been tortured: fingernails removed, electric shocks, poked by needles, burned. Their bodies were badly swollen. Ending his speech, the officer warned the crowd that they should give up all ideas of rebellion, and then he bathed the seven men in gasoline and burned them alive.

The Army atrocities against the civilian population continued to radicalize more and more campesinos who were determined that the Army withdraw from their communities. Beginning in mid-January groups of campesinos from the highlands journeyed to the capital to protest. More than one hundred indigenous brothers and sisters from Uspantán, Chajul, Cotzal and Nebaj made every effort to denounce to the municipal authorities and to the newspapers the atrocities which were taking place, but their voices were ignored. Perhaps the newspapers and even the local officials feared violent reprisals if they took action in behalf of the villagers. The government itself accused the campesino groups of being guerrillas and threatened to take action against them. Despite the obstacles, the campesinos made visits to leaders of popular organizations, the University, progressive political parties and other institutions and in that way were able to build support. Some of those who offered to help, such as Lic. Abraham Ixcamparic of the United Revolutionary Front, were brutally assassinated for their gesture.

Seeing little other option, twenty-eight persons, mainly indigenous people (Ixiles, Quichés as well as of other ethnic groups and *ladino* laborers and students) decided to peacefully occupy the Spanish Embassy on January 31, 1980 in order to make their voices of protest heard throughout the world. Within minutes of the occupation, the government militarized the Embassy with 400 agents despite the fact that the occupiers were meeting peacefully with the Spanish Ambassador and his functionaries.

When the security forces crossed onto the soil of the Spanish Embassy, Embassy officials asked them to withdraw. After a standoff for several hours, special commandos broke down the front door and set off an incendiary bomb. Amid the smoke and the confusion the Spanish Ambassador Máximo Cajal fled but not before suffering burns. The door was shut as first smoke and then flames poured out. From the outside people heard shouting, and then the shouting stopped. All but one person had been consumed by the flames;[3] thirty-nine bodies, including ex-Guatemalan officials and Spanish Embassy employees, were found.

The official version of the incident, reported by the president in a press conference, was that terrorists had burned the building with a molotov cocktail after the security forces had arrived, and that all had perished. This contradicts the evidence that the building had hardly burned and that the flames subsided within 12 minutes, both signs which point to the incendiary bombs used by the special commands.

On February 24th, more than 150 representatives of different indigenous groups met to condemn the massacre. Out of that meeting came the Declaration of Iximché, which was the most significant attempt of the indigenous people to proclaim their hopes and demands for a "society of equality and respect." The indigenous peoples of Guatemala struggle for, as the Declaration read in part,

> the right of indigenous people to develop our culture which has been ravaged by the colonial invaders; for a just economy where no one exploits anyone else; for land to become communally held as was the practice with our ancestors; for a society without discrimination...For this present infamy to end, the union and solidarity among indigenous and ladino is indispensable, a solidarity which has been sealed with the sacrifices of those in the Spanish Embassy.

Labor Strike on the Coast

Beginning in February 1980 the southern coast was the scene of the most bitter labor struggle in the history of Guatemala. CUC's work on the plantations had been expanding, but with the massacre in the Embassy, this was the time for the final push. A new labor code passed in October 1979[4] had already deepened the dissatisfaction among laborers on the coast. In elaborating the bill, the Ministry of Labor had consulted with pro-government labor unions and representatives of the plantation owners leaving out CUC and other popular organizations which represented the rights of the migrant labor force. Working people began to realize that the laws are made for the rich to defend their interests.

For years we had worked raising consciousness of the plantation workers, and the combination of the economic situation, the onerous labor code and the brutality of the Spanish Embassy massacre sparked a commitment to act. The years of organizing, raising awareness and other preparation had already built the base. We began to distribute flyers and paint graffiti on walls throughout the southern coast demanding that the basic wage be raised from 1.12 *quetzales* (1 *quetzal* = U.S. $1.00) to 5 *quetzales* per 100 lbs. of cotton picked–which was the average amount one could harvest in a day's work. CUC had elaborated a daily food budget for a family of five that was based on rice, beans and tortillas plus a single banana per person and a cup of coffee per adult. Daily food expenses reached Q3.95 which did not even include the costs of medicine, clothing, tools, school supplies, or other necessary items. We felt that Q5.00 was the minimum wage of survival. Moreover, since 1972 the purchasing power of the *quetzal* had dropped by 45%. For plantation owners, the economic situation was anything but deteriorating. The price of sugar on the international market had tripled since the year before, and the selling price of cotton had risen from $65 per 100 lbs. to $88, and the 1980 harvest looked to be a bumper crop.

We chose the sugar cane plantation, Tehuantepec near Santa Lucía Cotzumalguapa, as the site of action. On February 18th, seven hundred workers–*voluntarios* and *cuadrilleros*, indigenous and *ladino*, men and women with children–began a strike demanding five *quetzales* per day. The overseer only ridiculed us believing that we would return to work the following day. But the next day CUC led a march to surrounding plantations and the strike spread to the La Florencia, Cristobal and La Guanipa plantations.

To keep enthusiasm high, we held meetings continuously and continued the marches. Our chant was: "IF WE STRUGGLE TOGETHER, 5 *QUETZALES* WILL BE WON!" (*"¡Si luchamos organizados, los cinco quetzales serán logrados!"*). It was the needed spark. People received the marchers with applause and offered us food and drink. In the following days more and more plantations and several refineries struck. Within the first week, sixty plantations went on strike. Without food, some strikers returned to their villages, but most held out on the plantations, committed to lasting until we triumphed.

The strike took on greater force, and to show our resolve, we undertook acts of sabotage halting the transport trucks that hauled sugar cane, sometimes puncturing the tires or burning the truck. We also blocked the buses that carried other workers and tried to convince them to join our cause. On other occasions we burned the large packs of raw cotton or piles of cut sugar cane.

The workers at the sugar cane refineries joined the strike in part because there was no cane to process but also out of solidarity with the workers. From Santa Lucía the strike extended to Escuintla where mainly women worked in the cotton fields. By the end of the month more than 80,000 persons throughout the southern coast were on strike with women, their machetes in hand, leading the way.

Our combativity was met by the repressive hand of the powerful. Specially trained military police, departmental police, and soldiers from the military base of San José filled the transport trucks and tried to force their way through our blockades. Some CUC members were attacked with tear gas but they defended themselves with stones, sticks and machetes and held their position.

In the La Papelera factory the head of the Military Police threatened the striking workers and shot at their feet with his machine gun. When he tried to enter the factory, the workers with their machetes held high surrounded him and forced him to withdraw. Then Gen. Germán Chupina arrived and threatened the workers that he would order his troops to fire on the workers if they did not clear the premises. The workers did not scare easily and retorted that they would blow up the boilers which would take with it a number of the General's henchmen. Only when the General threatened to kill some of the captured workers did our people retire from the scene.

At the Pantaleón factory owned by the Herrerra family (a member of the Herrerra family later became Minister of Foreign Affairs), a striking worker was assassinated. Members of CUC were able to capture some of his assassins and punish them.

The expanse and strength of the strike on the southern coast deeply concerned the government. Spies infiltrated our movement to obtain information of our organization and to identify leaders. Under the pretext of offering CUC legalization, the government tried to get lists of those affiliated with our movement which of course we never released. The plantation owners spent thousands of *quetzales* to publish communiques which falsely accused us. We knew some newspapers were sympathetic with our struggle, but they were terrified to even publish our communiques. Nonetheless, notice of our struggle reached the international press, and we learned of democratic governments which mobilized to suppress the possibility of a massacre against us.

By March the government was looking for a way to end the strike by convincing the workers to return to work. On March 3, the Minister of Labor announced that the government would authorize a minimum daily wage of Q 3.20 for workers on sugar cane, cotton and coffee plantations. CUC responded the next day that even though their offer was inadequate, it was a recognition of our strength and accepted the offer.

On March 5th, the 17th day since the strike began, people returned to their work. The significance of the strike was not only in the numbers of workers mobilized, but also the qualitative change in the popular struggle. The combativity of the strikers–facing down the Army, police and armed paramilitary forces of the owners--and the participation of the indigenous as the bulwark of the movement were momentous in the Guatemalan popular movement. The machete, a tool normally used to earn a living, was converted into symbol of the defense of life. For the first time, the *cuadrillero,* who previously was seen as the servile *peón* of the plantation owner, shed the role of a strikebreaker and joined fully the class struggle.[5] The high level of maturity of the movement enabled the strikers to avoid provocations and to reduce the number of victims. At the conclusion of the strike, in one more show of coordination, the workers throughout the coast all returned to their work places at a designated hour.

The Disarticulation of CUC

Following the 1980 coastal strike, repression against the most active CUC members and the region's pastoral workers escalated. Some of our members were kidnapped from the hospital and then assassinated in front of their family members. We also learned that many plantation owners were refusing to pay the newly established minimum wage. Army officers supported the owners saying that no one would obligate them to pay.

By this time protesting the landowners' intransigence would have resulted in widespread repression. The situation since the strike had deteriorated further. On May 1st, the last major demonstration on International Workers' Day took place amid police kidnapping of several organizers of the demonstration. The leaders of the popular movement did not call another large demonstration as the political space for the mass movements was closing.

Throughout 1980 the face of genocide was becoming more and more clearly seen. While before the repression had targeted the most active members, the uncontainable growth of the movement obliged the government to change tactics. Killing just the leaders did not contain the movement; it was necessary to declare a war against the people. The period of large-scale massacres, blind fury and ritualistic killing began. Scalped cadavers, cannibalism, raped children, pregnant women with the head of her husband thrust in her belly, pyres of people burned alive in their village plaza: these are just a few of the atrocities committed by the Army in the early 1980s.

Repression fell on any village that the Army believed was organized. The killers attempted to annihilate whatever form of protest or resistance in the highlands. CUC had one advantage over other organizations. Born in conditions of semi-clandestinity, our structures were more difficult to detect. Unable to eradicate the "subversion," the army's brutality turned random. In El Quiché, San Marcos, Quetzaltenango, Totonicapán, Sololá, Chimaltenango, Huehuetenango and along the southern coast and northern belt of the country, military assassins set up posts on the edges of town and robbed, harassed, and intimidated people. All actions were viewed with suspicion. The army threatened--and carried out their threats--to poison the village's water supply, bomb the central plaza and destroy the fields.

Facing such a situation, it was practically impossible to continue functioning as a mass organization, even semi-clandestinely. We doubled security measures and, outside of small strikes on the coast to demand the compliance of the March wage accords, we almost exclusively acted under cover: painting graffiti, distributing flyers and committing acts of sabotage. To counterattack the government's lies and to keep our people informed, we continued to release our publications *la voz* and *De Sol a Sol* despite the attacks on those who published them. These newspapers were the only periodicals in Guatemala not subject to controls by the Army.

In February 1981, we took the risk of organizing on the sugar cane plantations again. We presented a list of demands to the plantation owners that included a minimum wage of Q 6.00, overtime pay for work on Sundays and extra hours, safe spraying equipment, free transportation to and from the worksite, adequate year round housing for the *cuadrilleros*, indemnization in case of layoffs and elimination of abuses by the labor contractor. Prominent on the list was the demand that the security forces should be prohibited from militarizing the plantations. All were reasonable demands that would ensure decent standard of living.

However this year was not like the year before; the conditions which led to our success in 1980 were no longer present. The assault on the popular movement had reached new levels of barbarity. Our struggle was becoming increasingly politicized to the point of becoming a direct confrontation with the government and the Armed Forces. Many *compañeros*, seeing that the space for political protest was closing, chose the mountains: that is, they joined the guerrilla movement.[6] There, at least, one had the possibility of defending oneself. However, most of us did not possess arms and had to prepare ourselves to face the Army as we could. We used ingenuity and street-wise creativity. We sought new forms of resistance.

It is impossible to retell the torment which our people suffered in those years. In terms of brutality and number of victims, that period could only be compared with the conquest 460 years previous. Each time that the Army learned of the sighting of the guerrillas in an area, the government forces scorched the nearby villages and massacred innocent people. The names of the villages were etched in the collective memory of Guatemala as a testimony to the fury of killing: Comalapa, Chubajito, San Mateo Ixtatán, Chupol, Zaculapa, El Arbolito, Chisec, Chajul, San Martín Jilotepeque... By the end of 1981 Guatemala was a country in a permanent state of war with hundreds of people assassinated every day.

After Gen. Efraín Ríos Montt's military coup in March 1982, the situation worsened still. The genocide reached unprecedented levels. Meanwhile, the junta hid the evil of its own actions under the cloak of a holy war: the good against the evil.

After the CUC occupation of the Brazilian Embassy in 1982,[7] the risk of repression made our work ineffective for the next four years. The repression did not destroy us, but it did hit us hard. The National Coordination Commission (CONACO), our highest decision-making body, was not able to receive the information necessary in order to orient the organization's activities. CUC's publications were discontinued. The lack of security did not allow for the existence of an organization such as CUC. The conflict had taken on an exclusively military dimension and political work through a mass movement such as CUC was impossible. In spite of the extensive base of support for CUC inside Guatemala, our work was restricted to the international field. Of the approximately 30 *compañeros* which had founded the organization in 1978, by this time no more than six had survived. Some of our members fled the country while others undertook incredible measures of security and self defense so that they could remain alive inside Guatemala.

The Resurgence of CUC

By 1984 the results of "scorched earth" policies were staggering. The government had eliminated the leaders of the popular movement and forced a million Guatemalans to seek refuge outside the country, to hide in remote regions or to lose themselves in crowded shantytowns of Guatemala City. The massive displacement of population, in addition to the psychological trauma, caused enormous social dislocation. In the capital, the level of unemployment escalated, and in the highlands the destruction of the crops by the Army caused hunger and malnutrition.

On the southern coast, the daily wage of plantation workers dropped to Q 2.00 and then to Q 1.00 (with the *quetzal* then worth only US $0.50) as displaced people flooded the coast seeking work. Of every 100 *cuadrilleros* which went to the coast, forty could not find work or would lose their jobs because of persecution. Plantation owners, too, faced losses because of the decline in export agricultural prices. Some owners withdrew their money from the plantations choosing instead a safe investment in Miami banks; others switched to planting corn which they sold at exorbitant prices in the highlands.

The government was becoming increasingly isolated both outside of and within Guatemala, and the spirit of struggle of the people never broke. Despite the repeated declarations of the government about their impending triumph over the guerrillas, 1984 was a year of war and economic crisis. Despite the continuing repression, the year marked a resurgence by the popular movement in the capital. The poverty and the resentment of the people against the government were more powerful motivations than the fear of the death squads. In July the Mutual Support Group (*Grupo de Apoyo Mutuo* - GAM) was founded by family members of the disappeared and mobilized people from the marginalized communities in the periphery of Guatemala City including many CUC members who had taken refuge in those communities. Those *compañeros* and *compañeras* wasted little time in showing their courage and combative spirit when in November they peacefully occupied the building of the National Assembly in order to make their voices heard.

On January 14, 1986, after three mournful decades of military dictatorships, a civilian government under the Christian Democrat Vinicio Cerezo was elected. The electoral process itself was declared by the Guatemalan Bishops as one "not open to all citizens." In reality progressives had already broken from the Christian Democrats which reorganized to become acceptable to the military. The architect of the reorganization was none other than Cerezo himself who, once in power, oversaw the continued militarization of Guatemala (through "model" villages, "development poles" and the civil defense patrols). The first phase of the civilian rule achieved the primary goal sought by the Army High Command: the strengthening of Guatemala's international standing in order to receive international aid--without losing control of the country.

At the beginning of March 1986 a group of CUC members who had remained active, albeit clandestinely, met together. The meeting went on for days and under tight security measures; on March 14th, a historic day for our organization, we decided to raise the flag of the CUC once again and rebuild our organization within Guatemala.

We elected a new coordination commission (again known as CONACO) which had the difficult task of rebuilding the pieces of the organization and re-connecting CUC members who had dispersed across the country. Time was short as we tried to take advantage of the limited political opening brought about by the change in government, and expectations of the thousands of CUC members were high. We operated only under the most strict measures of clandestinity. Guatemala remained under a harsh military control and despite a relative decrease in massacres, kidnappings and disappearances, the repression was far from over.

The re-organization of work in the villages began in 1987 with political formation workshops for CUC members. The exchange of ideas and experiences helped the CUC members to overcome their fears. Discussions among the membership were long and heated, no doubt motivated by the fear of committing an error which would have drastic consequences for their community. We stressed the need for a broad national vision, which was important since most of our members had little contact with other groups in the resurging popular movement.

After 15 months of Christian Democrat administration, none of the government's promises had been fulfilled; the economic situation was deteriorating, and the war continued. At the beginning of 1988 the CUC joined an umbrella group of labor unions known as the Social and Popular Unity of Action (UASP). With CUC's participation, the UASP broadened its focus and began to address the concerns of campesinos and indigenous people, for example, by demanding an across-the-board minimum wage of Q10.00 per day (for the countryside and the urban areas). We convoked our bases to participate in UASP demonstrations of 50,000 then 80,000 persons on the 13th and 18th of January, respectively. The Minister of Government Rodil Peralta,[8] when he learned of CUC participation in the march, threatened to arrest all the participants and hold them responsible for the massacre in the Spanish Embassy. The charge was cynically repeated by Cerezo who also called the CUC a guerrilla organization, an accusation which would be repeated over the years. The purpose of the defamations was to isolate the CUC and disrupt the unity of the popular movement by sowing fear and division.

On March 8th the UASP signed an agreement with the government after the rounds of protest which guaranteed, among other things, the legalization of the CUC.[9] This signified for us, at least in paper, an end

CUC members lead march in Guatemala City.

to an era of clandestinity and the beginning of open work. The legal right to exist and implicit recognition of our ten years of work with campesinos, however, did not deter the kidnappings or repression against us. The agreement opened a legal space, and we accepted the government's offer insisting, though, on protection for the families of members of CUC. Without being overly optimistic of the implications, we began to take more risks, making more public appearances as CUC representatives.

In April we celebrated the tenth anniversary of our organization together with the labor unions and the rest of the popular movement. For the first time since the Spanish Embassy massacre a large number of CUC members marched in public carrying banners. In *la voz* we editorialized:

> This anniversary marks ten years of struggle, of organization and self-defense for the CUC against the extermination policies of the enemies of the people. We survived the years of genocide, we were persecuted, we were obliged to hide ourselves, but we found strength in the secret ways of organizing our people, with the wisdom and experience that for centuries our predecessors have guarded. This historical legacy is present in the CUC and it gives us courage and resolve. After ten years, the situation has worsened: there is more poverty and more hunger, deception, no land, low salaries, violations of our rights, discrimination and margination. For all of these reasons, our struggle not only continues, but it seeks different forms and alternative paths. We have the right to construct a true democracy and to live in peace.

In the Workers' Day demonstration on May 1st, CUC members marched once again, this time for the first time with signs, straw mats (painted with slogans) and chants. The march was largely made up of indigenous people (and mainly women). The UASP carried CUC banners as we, still skeptical, bore posters and chanted slogans which were not our own. This demonstration had tremendous psychological importance for the popular movement. Despite all of the accusations against CUC, our organization had gained a prestige almost legendary among the people of Guatemala after having survived the most difficult years in the recent history. We were once again "with the combative fist and heart of solidarity."

The next months were filled with intense work and great hopes. Commissions were formed in different parts of the country to dialogue about the land problem with popular organizations, unions and Christian groups. We again took up the struggle against the civil defense patrols. We demanded the reduction of the hours in a work day, and fought against unfair taxes, fraudulent weigh scales on the plantations and the high cost of living. By pressing these issues we gained a larger following of new people and organizations, particularly among women and widows (whose husbands were killed in the violence).

The slow but sure reconstruction of the popular movement brought another cycle of state repression against the communities. The first targets were 21 campesinos from El Aguacate (near San Andrés Itzápa, Department of Chimaltenango) who were found murdered after being brutally tortured. The massacre did not slow the movement as in mid-January 1989 the CUC and the UASP took up the clamor of the campesinos in their demands for Q 10.00 per 100 lbs. of picked coffee or cotton, ton of cut sugar cane or 8 hour work day. We also insisted on a daily ration of three meals, tools, overtime pay for the seventh day of work, and fair credit on advances in accordance with the labor laws. At the time, the salaries varied between Q 2.00 and Q4.50 depending on the plantation.

With no response from the plantation owners, on January 23rd we struck paralyzing 15 plantations, including seven sugar cane refineries, with the participation of 15,000 workers. Within a day, the strike had grown to thirty plantations and 50,000 workers. The following day anti-riot police squads and Army troops forcibly evicted the strikers. The entire region where the strike had commenced was put under strict military control with roadblocks controlling the highways and prohibiting access to the national and international press.

The Minister of Government issued the old accusations that CUC was an illegal organization and that, according to then Foreign Minister Alfonso Cabrera, CUC had been infiltrated by people of the extreme left, an accusation which in Guatemala is tantamount to condemnation to death. The government was plainly reneging on the March 8th agreements, which included our legalization, and showing their true face which to us looked very much like the previous military regimes'.

On February 2nd, sixty-seven labor unions, religious groups, academics and human rights activists expressed their support for the strike classifying the salaries paid on the plantations as "inhumane." On the 9th the National Agriculture and Cattle Union (UNAGRO), the most powerful agricultural association of the plantation owners, accepted the UASP proposal to negotiate. One CUC member joined the negotiations. It became clear that the objective of UNAGRO was not to genuinely discuss the issues at stake but rather to delay the negotiations until the crops had been harvested.

For us, after so many years in forced silence, the principal issue was that the struggle for a decent wage, a fight begun in February 1980, had been re-activated in 1989. Independent of the results, the most important gain was the ability to mobilize so many people under conditions which rivaled a concentration camp. With almost all of the *cuadrilleros* integrated into the civil defense patrols, that is, under direct military command, and given the level of terror which the memories of the last decade had evoked, the plantation owners had counted on a submissive work force. Nonetheless, they were faced with a massive work stoppage in the cane fields, coffee and cotton plantations and now also by rubber workers who had always been on the margin of the movement. Thirty plantations had been paralyzed and nearly 50,000 campesinos on strike; the illusion of the plantation owners that they could simply ignore the inhuman working conditions had been burst.

In preparation for the January 1990 harvest on the coast we sponsored a march from Chimaltenango to the capital in coordination with labor unions and other popular organizations such as CERJ, CONAVIGUA, and GAM. By the time we reached the outskirts of Guatemala City on December 8, 1989, ten thousand campesinos had joined in the demonstration. After this, we intensified the work on the southern coast in preparation for the upcoming struggle. The task of organizing the plantation workers fell to us; only if the workers on the coast were well organized and firm in their resolve could other organizations assist. The situation on the southern coast had become even more desperate since the year before. UNAGRO had been successful in delaying the negotiations so that nothing had been achieved. The value of the *quetzal* on the international market had dropped even further (from Q2.50 for the US $1.00 to Q3.41 for every dollar) causing prices to rise drastically. The yearly expenses of a family of seven for food, clothing, school supplies, cooking instruments, and tools came to Q5,864 (or approximately US $1720) on the average or approximately $4.20 per day. Yet the minimum wage in 1990 was only US $0.93, less than a third of its value in real terms of the wage in 1980. The following table illustrates the deterioration of income for the Guatemalan worker.

TABLE 1: WAGES OF WORKERS

Minimum wage in 1980 (daily):	Q 3.20	$3.20
Min. expenses for family* in 1980 (daily):	Q 3.95	$3.95
Minimum wage in 1990 (daily):	Q 3.20	$0.93
Actual wage in 1990 (daily): between	Q 2.20	$0.57
and	Q 5.00	$1.31
Min. expenses for family" in 1990 daily:	Q16.06	$4.20
Minimum wage demanded in 1990 (daily):	Q10.00	$2.63

*Note: * for a family of five; " for a family of seven.*

Work stoppages on the plantations broke out on January 30, 1990. About 60,000 workers participated in the strike involving 37 plantations in the departments of Suchitepéquez, Retalhuleu and Escuintla. Our demands were similar to those of the year before except now we were demanding Q10.00 as a minimum wage which still did not cover the minimum basic needs of a Guatemalan family.

In the capital UASP communicated immediately with the government and with UNAGRO to open negotiations. The Army acted rapidly to contain the movement, however, and began searching and detaining thousands of *cuadrilleros* upon their arrival from the highlands. Other plantations denied access to the migrant workers for fear that resident workers would join the movement. The southern coast was once again the scene of military presence with the workers surrounded and cut off from the rest of the people.

Despite the threats and abuses, the strike was a success given the number of workers participating and the high level of organization and discipline. On January 31st we lifted the strike for ten days as a gesture of good will to the government and to UNAGRO. The plantation owners never showed a willingness to dialogue but rather once again pursued delay tactics until the end of the harvest. When the first tripartite meeting between the government, UNAGRO and UASP did occur on February 12th to discuss wages, several UNAGRO members did not show up for the meeting and others walked out after several minutes as an insult to the organization of workers.

On the 20th of February we organized a march of ten thousand persons which ended with a large concentration in the central plaza of the capital. There we handed a petition signed by eight thousand people to the Procurator of Human Rights appealing for the intervention of the President and of Congress to resolve the situation through legal means. Given the attitudes of UNAGRO and the prices of basic items spiraling, we increased our minimum wage demand to Q15.00 per day which provoked a boycott of the negotiations by UNAGRO. Months later, the government fixed a new minimum wage of Q10.00 per day, our original demand. The victory, however, was a shallow one as the plantation owners ignored the legal minimum wage, and rising inflation made the increase meaningless.

The rest of 1990 was dominated by the peace talks and the URNG-government dialogue. Peace became the major demand of the people. In March we met again with the Human Rights Procurator Ramiro de León Carpio to express our point of view on the unconstitutionality of the civil defense patrols and about the military aggression against the communities of El Quiché and in other departments. On March 30th, against all expectation, the URNG and the National Reconciliation Commission signed a Basic Agreement for Peace which opened a new path for peace.

We publicly expressed our enthusiasm and good will for the peace process. We warned, however, that a lasting solution would entail not only an end to the war but also would address social injustice, poverty and exploitation which had been the origins of the armed conflict. We called on the President to take concrete actions to respect the Agreement and to end the blood bath. Ironically, just a few hours after the signing of the agreement, society was shocked by the news of new acts of terror: four students had been captured and assassinated. Within days another incident occurred in Parraxtut, department of El Quiché, when the sub-procurator of human rights was attacked by the civil defense patrol. Both were reminders that Guatemala was far from the desired peace.

So what does the future hold for Guatemala? There are hopeful signs. One of them occurred in October 1990 when a delegation of popular organizations and labor unions met with the URNG in Metepec, Mexico. The meeting included ourselves, CONAVIGUA, CERJ, GAM, AEU and the Permanent Commissions of Guatemalan Refugees in Mexico. We all agreed that the unequal distribution of land was one of the fundamental causes of the internal war which has raged in Guatemala. The political opening had been won at the cost of sweat, pain and blood, but sudden acts of repression were closing political space. We ratified a common statement declaring that a firm and lasting peace will be achieved only through changes in the unjust social structures. In addition to democratic partisan politics and legitimate elections, conditions need to be established which raise the welfare of all citizens. This means to suppress the repressive military structures and discriminatory laws which impede peace, threaten life, make human dignity vulnerable and act as a brake on full development, happiness and creative realization. Guatemala needs to create new institutions which represent the interests of all the people and to achieve a national consensus which can help fulfill the aspirations of the people which have been denied for centuries.

The Declaration of Metepec, as it came to be known, set the framework and outlined the goals around which a new Guatemala can be built over the next few years. It will be a gradual process with contradictions, victories and reverses. We know that a counterinsurgency state cannot be dismantled with declarations. Nonetheless, after so much violence, these kinds of ideas open a path which gives us hope and is worth the struggle.

FOOTNOTES:

[1] *Criollos* refers to Guatemalans of European ancestry with few or no indigenous ancestors. Often *criollos* make up the economic and political elite of the country. *Ladinos* refers to people of mixed ancestry, European and Mayan, who are thoroughly western- ized and speak only Spanish. Indigenous people, generally wholly of Mayan descent, will speak primarily their indigenous language (though may speak Spanish as well) and constitute the majority of the working poor.

[2] *Huipiles* are the traditional blouses of indigenous women and *morrales* are the woven shoulder bags usually carried by men.

[3] The survivor, Gregorio Yujá, was hospitalized in a bed adjoining the hospital bed of the Spanish Ambassador at the request of the Ambassador in order to lend protection to Yujá. Notwithstanding the Ambassador's offer, Gregorio Yujá was kidnapped at the hospital in full view of police units. He was later assassinated and his body dumped at the rectory of the University of San Carlos. The government prohibited his burial in the public cemetery.

[4] In October 1979 the government debated a new Labor Code which later was passed into law. CUC sent an open letter addressed to the Labor Minister Lic. Carlos Alarcón Monsanto where we petitioned our demands.

Why do the authorities continue to allow unjust firings by plantation owners? Why do *voluntarios* and *cuadrilleros* not receive the first penny of indemnization? Why do our workers not enjoy a Christmas bonus, or even more, paid vacations? Why are we not eligible for Social Security [is this hospital care?] Why do we not have safe and decent equipment? Why is it prohibited to call a strike during the harvest season (we are permitted to strike only when we are out of work which is the most cynical way of ridiculing the working class)? Will the present situation change with the passage of labor code reform? Why are campesinos, who produce most of the wealth in the country by the sweat of their labor, not consulted about the proposed legislation? Why are we repressed and treated as criminals by the military? These and many others were our questions. And similar to petitions before this one, we received no answer.

[5] One journalist with *La Nación,* after visiting the southern coast after the strike, reported

We visited a different scene and different people than the indigenous of before who removed his sombrero and meekly placed it on his chest to ask the *patron* for a few cents more, thanks to God.

[6] In 1982 the separate insurgent factions unified under a single command known as the *Unidad Revolucionaria Nacional Guatemalteca (URNG).*

[7] In 1982 in order to break the blockade of information out of Guatemala, we decided to occupy peacefully an Embassy in protest. The decision was not an easy one because the memory of the recent Spanish Embassy tragedy was still fresh. Nonetheless, we calculated that the political situation was in our favor. The government could not afford the political cost of another massacre in the capital, particularly since part of its international image was its facade of concern for human rights.

The action was organized by FP-31 with the participation of CUC. We chose the Brazil Embassy because of its central location and visibility; we deliberately limited the number of *compañeros* because of the danger. Once the activists were inside the Embassy, there were difficult moments. The Army occupied two adjacent buildings and surrounded the

occupied Embassy. Constantly an Army spokesperson shouted threats that the o*
would be burned alive if they did not evacuate at once. The Brazilian Ambassador, an
older man, fainted twice fearing the worse. On this occasion, everything turned out well.
The *compañeros* negotiated their departure from the country and were able to give a
press conference at the airport to denounce the military abuses which were being hidden
from the world's attention.

[8] From 1992-94 Rodil served as President of the Supreme Court.

[9] Other aspects of the agreement were of even greater interest as the government
agreed to review and update laws regarding fallow land, recuperate lands for development programs and promote credit for small and medium-sized farmers whether
organized collectively or individually. The government failed to fully live up to its
agreement on any of these issues however.

For years the Communities of Population in Resistance have lived in hiding, evading the Army ground sweeps. During more than a decade of resistance, the communities developed a strong internal cohesion. Here, a community in the Ixcán jungle holds an open air meeting.

Faith, Community and Resistance in the Guatemalan Highlands

Minor Sinclair

Hidden under the protective jungle canopy in the Ixcán region of northwestern Guatemala, a handful of indigenous communities have been quietly resisting the Guatemalan military since 1982 when Army troops massacred thousands of innocent people in the region and destroyed their agricultural cooperatives. Cut off from the rest of Guatemala and the world, the survivors, numbering in the thousands, have organized local self-government councils, an educational system for children and adults, basic health care and a communitarian system of production which ensures that no one, including the hundreds of widows and orphans, goes hungry. The communities have banded together in a loose network and call themselves the Communities of Population in Resistance (CPRs). In other remote areas of Guatemala, dozens of similar communities have survived as well.

The people's resistance lies in their refusal to abandon the land which they had cleared and farmed even though now the jungle has reclaimed the land. They refuse service in the Army or to join Army-imposed civil patrols; in fact the people flee when the Army approaches their communities. For the past ten years the Army has claimed that the civilian communities serve as guerrilla camps and has bombed and invaded them regularly. The communities assert that their defense has been largely non-violent, outside of an occasional shotgun volley fired in self-defense or the use of traps (camouflaged pits concealing sharpened bamboo points) laid for invading Army troops.

On one afternoon in 1987 in a community in the Ixcán nearly a hundred people gathered to celebrate the word of God. Most stood, while a few people sat on stumps or on the ground. There were no benches, nor walls. Only the dense jungle foliage overhead served as a roof. One man, whose clothes were patched in a dozen places and who was one of the few people in the community with glasses, began to preach,[1]

> Be at peace, friends. Our trust is in the Lord. Just as the first Christian communities lived together, worked together and ate together, so we too live, work and eat together. The first Christian communities are our teachers. Their cause is our cause and for that we are persecuted just as they were persecuted.

People nodded in affirmation and understanding. The early Christian communities in first century Palestine lived in a society in some ways similar to the indigenous communities in the Guatemalan highlands: domination by a foreign power, prolonged military occupation, racial and class division and a grossly unjust distribution of land and wealth. Whether or not the people in the Ixcán communities understood the similarities between the two societies is not important; what is important is that they understood that their cause was just and that God sided with them, just as God sided with the early Christian communities.

The experience of the Church in the Communities in Resistance is an example of how pastoral work can validate and strengthen the resistance of the poor to their oppressors. Pastoral work in the CPRs has ordained their struggle with religious significance and justified in biblical terms their communitarian system in which the community's goods and responsibilities are shared as equally as possible. The daily pastoral work of catechism, prayer, Biblical reflection and celebration serves as the theological underpinning of an alternative social, political and economic system which government authorities perceive as a threat.

For the past thirty years progressive pastoral workers--priests, nuns and lay people--in the highlands of Guatemala have conscienticized, motivated and radicalized people to join in the struggle for liberation. Of course the struggle for liberation has taken different forms: Some people formed community cooperatives, and others joined political parties in the hope of gaining political power. Still others saw little other option than to join the guerrilla insurgency. Over the last thirty years, liberating pastoral work has faced difficult periods--the challenges of institutionalization, radicalization, cooptation, de-legitimation, clandestinity and legalization--yet a consistency has prevailed in the way in which Christian faith has opened the eyes of the poor to their oppression, restored their dignity, motivated them to organize to change the structures which oppress them, and helped them discover the faith to resist a brutal enemy.

This article examines pastoral work in the highlands of northwestern Guatemala, particularly in the department of El Quiché, during the last forty years. In the first period, beginning in 1954, traditional models of pastoral work were promoted heavily by conservative sectors of the Catholic hierarchy, but around 1965 the direct work of pastoral action in the communities underwent a radical transformation. Instead of a highly hierarchical model of priests directing the pastoral work under the supervision of the bishop, lay people, particularly community catechists, assumed leadership in the movement.

Pastoral work showed tremendous potential for empowerment, as the Catholic Action groups in the Quiché communities began to build schools, churches, clinics, and cooperatives. Rather than the bulwark against the spread of Communism that the bishops had envisioned Catholic Action, the evangelization program led to the radicalization of large sectors of the indigenous population. This period came to a close in 1978 as the level of government-sponsored violence escalated and targeted the church workers involved in community development.

Fernando Bermúdez, a Spanish priest who worked in the department of El Quiché, described the experience of the faithful in the highlands in the early 1980s as the "Church of the Catacombs,"[2] which we consider the second period of the pastoral development. Throughout the highlands, the Army and its paramilitary organizations blamed the Church for giving birth to the guerrilla struggle and heavily repressed all aspects of religious faith, even many fundamentalist churches which were avowedly pro-Army. The Catholic diocese of El Quiché was closed down, and 91 religious men and women fled the country. Christians, unable to practice their faith openly, worshipped in clandestinity. The Church became an underground Church.

Progressive Guatemalan Christians have articulated that their work roughly from 1984 until the present has been to help build the church of the poor, to rebuild the sense of community and to strengthen resistance among the victims of the government's counterinsurgency. We consider this the third stage. In the refugee camps, in the Communities of Population in Resistance, in isolated indigenous communities and among the displaced population, people have found a renewed strength in the Gospel call to seek justice, and they have grown bolder about openly combining their faith with political struggle.

The experience of church as one of living in the catacombs or as one of rebuilding the church of the poor are not entirely distinct experiences. Presently in Guatemala many progressive Christians fear persecution, but are intent on building the church of the poor. For our purposes here we make a distinction between the 1978-1984 period of the church of the catacombs where persecution forced people to conceal themselves and the practice of their faith and the 1984 to the present period of the church of the poor where people look to openly express their faith and dare to build a national Christian movement for justice.

The unique circumstances of the refugee camps and the CPR communities have allowed the church of the poor to take root and even flourish in those areas. That experience has not been replicated to the same extent elsewhere for a number of factors considered below. New pastoral approaches in the marginalized communities in Guatemala City and within sectors of the popular movement offer promise however. Moreover, in the last five years progressive Christian organizations have gained a significant degree of coordination at a national level.

TRANSFORMATION OF CATHOLIC ACTION (1954-1980)

The post World War II period in Guatemala was turbulent. Juan José Arévalo, elected in 1944 by popular vote in the first fair election in Guatemala's history, subscribed to what he called "spiritual socialism" and passed reformist legislation which guaranteed the right to vote for illiterate males and literate females, legalized rural unions, and established a social security system. His successor, President Jacobo Arbenz, elected by a vast majority of the vote in 1950, likewise maintained that capitalism had a social function and that marginalized groups should be integrated into a national economy. Arbenz worked to deepen Arévalo's reforms, pushing through a minimum wage law, strengthening the rights of farmworkers' unions and working to deed land to the impoverished peasantry.

The landed oligarchy was outraged by the land redistribution law, and the Catholic Church, one of the most conservative in the region, rallied to the defense of the rich. In 1954 in the Church's Pastoral Letter on the Advance of Communism, Guatemalan Archbishop Mariano Rossell Arellano called Christians to "rise up as a single body against the enemy of God and the Fatherland." The Archbishop's denunciation of supposed Communist influence in the Arbenz government helped pave the way for the CIA-sponsored coup later that year. The decade of democracy which had sprung up with the election of Arévalo ended just as abruptly.

A decade earlier the Guatemalan bishops had introduced Catholic Action, a world-wide evangelization program sponsored by the Vatican, into remote areas of the countryside which previously had been outside of the Church's reach. Implicit in the campaign was the assumption that if indigenous people were involved in the Church, they would be less sympathetic to the movements for social change that were seizing Guatemala. Catholic Action, which by the coup was just beginning to set down roots in the countryside, had little chance to make its mark against communism, the so-called enemy of God. Nonetheless, the evangelization campaign earned words of praise from the conservative Archbishop as "one of the greatest comforts in these hours of enormous distress in the presence of the Marxist advance that has invaded everywhere."[3]

In the year following the 1954 coup, the new military junta returned 99% of the expropriated lands to their former owners, abolished 533 newly-formed unions and arrested an estimated 9,000 "Communists," many of whom were tortured. The pacification goals of the new junta and the evangelism goals of the Catholic Church coincided to a large extent, and Catholic Action came to be seen as an integrated social, political and religious plan to re-establish authoritarian control in the countryside. Responding to Pope Pius XII's call to "save Guatemala from communism," the first group of Spanish missionaries of the Sacred Heart of Jesus arrived in El Quiché in 1955. From the mid 1950s through the mid 1960s the work of Catholic Action multiplied with more than a hundred new priests taking up residence throughout the highlands. New parishes were formed and new dioceses were created. Thousands of new converts joined the Church.

Twenty-five years later, Catholic Action organizing (led as much by lay people as by priests and nuns) in El Quiché had led directly to an awakened peasantry and the formation of the largest grassroots opposition movement in the country. Several priests joined the guerrillas. In reprisal the military and its agents assassinated 15 Catholic priests and hundreds of catechists. In protest, the Church closed down the Diocese of El Quiché. A dramatic transformation had taken place: an official program of "Christian resignation," as Archbishop Rossell characterized Catholic Action, had helped give birth to a movement of national liberation which led, in turn, to heavy repression of Catholic Action at the hand of a government it originally supported. How did Catholic Action, with its reactionary roots, become transformed into a progressive agent of change?

A Traditional Approach

The steep mountain regions of northwestern Guatemala had long resisted the forces of modernization which had changed the rest of

Guatemala. A few miles outside of the departmental capitals, the frontier began where the Mayan people spoke 22 different languages and over a hundred different dialects. They practiced largely subsistence agriculture and remained relatively excluded from the national economy. The few newspaper copies which circulated in the towns and villages of indigenous Guatemala ignored the reality of rural, indigenous Guatemala. The forces of modernization had erected, and to this day maintain, cultural, linguistic, economic, social and political barriers which have prevented the inclusion of all but a few indigenous people. In areas such as the department of El Quiché, where 98% of the population was indigenous, the worldview of the population was largely focused on the immediate concerns of work, family and community.

Before Catholic Action, the region had long been neglected by the Catholic Church. One diocese and just a few priests were the caretakers over most of the region of the highlands and campesinos could pass their whole life without a mass being held in their village or anywhere within a day's walk. Most people claimed Catholicism as their religion, yet many would find difficulty in describing their religion in terms other than prayers to the saints, feast days and the final judgement. For most of the faithful, their religion was an overlay of Catholic beliefs superimposed on traditional Mayan beliefs.

Catholic Action brought the mass and the celebration of other Sacraments to many villages for the first time. Unlike before, now the priests and nuns came and *stayed.* Initially, their ministry focused on recruiting active members and building churches. Later, the longer term plan of Catholic Action called for an elaborate organizational structure to insure that with the incorporation of thousands of newly active members, the Bishop would still retain control over his flock. Priests organized their parishioners in a tier structure of town-level Parish Councils, Parish pastoral teams, village-level parish councils, and catechist groups.

In the first twenty years of work in the highlands (1946-1965), the pastoral work of Catholic Action was characterized by its spiritual emphasis. The explicit goal of Catholic Action was personal conversion-- of entire communities if possible. [The priests demanded that their parishioners renounce the *costumbristas* and the *zanborines* of the Mayan religion. Hostilities between Catholics and Mayan priests and their followers are only now beginning to subside.] A lay Catholic described life and worship in the village of Estancia near Santa Cruz del Quiché as Catholic Action was being introduced.[4]

> In 1945 I remember that there wasn't any kind of organization. People depended on themselves. They were individualistic; we didn't know what community was. There weren't any community buildings, not even a church. There were no schools--the few children who received classes took them in their homes...At this time,

the priests were traditional. They read the Gospel but didn't develop
the ideas. They only read. We left church the same as we entered.
We learned things by memory without understanding the meaning.

Like the traditional theology of the Church elsewhere, Catholic
Action's theology exhibited a strong anti-communist bias and held up
the authorities as legitimate figures to be respected and obeyed. The
difference between Catholic Action and other pastoral approaches lay
in the fact that Catholic Action encouraged the participation of the laity
in worship and in a limited range of other community activities
sponsored by Catholic Action (Bible study, catechism classes, and
literacy classes for example). Lay people became involved in the church
and took on leadership positions in church committees, direct ministry
and religious formation. This meant that the parishioners were no
longer dependent entirely on the ordained clergy as Fr. Luis Guirarán,
a Sacred Heart missionary from Spain recounts,[5]

> In my first visit to a rural church in El Quiché thirty years ago, I was
> surprised to find that there already about 200 or 300 people
> congregated in a small chapel. I asked, what were they doing, were
> they waiting for us? "No, no," they replied, "We have been reflecting
> on the Scripture for the past two hours." In Spain studying the Bible
> for two hours is not very common. They were reflecting on a
> passage in Luke where Jesus brings the good news to the poor. The
> good news that day was not the arrival of me as a new priest; it was
> their decision--before I arrived, to form a committee in order to build
> a community school.

In the second stage of Catholic Action, roughly beginning in 1965,
the reformist spirit which took hold of the Vatican II Council in Rome
affected the ministry of the Church in Guatemala. For the first time, the
Bible was made accessible to the laity (mostly indigenous) which had
a tremendous impact on the consciousness of the newly faithful. People
were encouraged to reflect in church and in their homes on the Bible,
particularly passages such as that from Exodus which recount the
liberation of the enslaved Israelites from Egypt and from Isaiah which
promise a new heavens and new earth to the poor and dispossessed.
After Vatican II, masses were held in Spanish or even in the local
language. In the absence of the priest, communities were encouraged
to hold celebrations of the Word.

In the 1970s priests described their work as a *pastoral de conjunto*,
a pastoral plan which combined liturgical reforms with social development programs.[6] Changes in the liturgy and the social ministry were
mutually reinforcing and validating. People were encouraged to "see,
judge and act" (Catholic Action's motto) in both the liturgy as well as the
social ministry. The process encouraged indigenous people to question
the political and social realities which kept them poor. Reflections such

as the following by Petrona Zapón, an indigenous woman from La Estancia, were common.[7]

> A priest came to La Estancia and began to explain many things which we hadn't known. We had been told that Christ was in heaven and that for us to be able to go to heaven we must act good and accept everything. Through the priest, we began to understand that Christ is on earth..that Christ is in our sisters and brothers and that we can change things to improve our living conditions.

As the people became more conscienticized, they in turn pressed the priests to become more aware of the desperate conditions of life in the highlands. Many priests began to realize the contradiction of promoting a highly spiritualized ministry when their congregation was literally starving between harvests. Father Angel, a Spanish priest involved in Catholic Action, remembers[8]

> We were impacted by the hunger, the misery, the deaths of so many children because of lack of medical care. The only doctor for the whole region was a drunk. At that point, we didn't really understand the problem in terms of power, in terms of domination, but more in terms of a humanitarian mission. Our response was: how can we help the people live better? We organized potable water committees, cooperatives for agriculture and cattle projects. The more we became involved in organizing, the better we understood the reality of the people because the people taught us.

As the social ministry grew so did lay participation in ministry. Lay catechists took on major roles in the implementation of pastoral work and gained greater control over its direction. The same priest reflects on the changes.[9]

> We had come to evangelize, to convert, to give the sacraments. With sword in hand we came to implant a totally westernized, European and Roman church convinced that this was the only form of religion. The people themselves began to change the nature of the pastoral work and it happened first with the catechists. They saw the church as the central part of a unified life, based on their experience as Maya where religion was the center of everything. There was no separation of religion from politics, from the economy, from social life. Everything is united for the Maya.

This process of using worship, Biblical reflection and church development programs to raise awareness, or to *conscienticize*, gave people dignity and the hope that life could change for the better. Some proponents of Catholic Action hoped that the *pastoral de conjunto* would improve the living conditions of the indigenous peasantry and thereby forestall any greater radicalization. As events later proved, these reforms were just the first steps towards a growing politicization that went far beyond what the early promoters of Catholic Action had conceived or desired.

Indigenous communities at first resisted Catholic Action, partly because of its frontal assault on traditional Mayan spirituality. Others found Catholic Action unappealing for other reasons.[10] Local indigenous leaders who benefitted from the unjust system resisted the changes brought about by Catholic Action and sought allies among the traditional Mayan religious leaders who were under attack from the Catholics. Even the poor were initially skeptical of the promises of Catholic Action because for them change so often meant a change for the worse. Fr. Luís Gurriarán recalls that at first,[11]

> The Indian world appeared to be hermetically sealed. It seemed to have a wall of defense which no one could penetrate. They defended their world through their [traditional] religious organization. It was as if they had cloaked their internal organization with a religious mantle to defend their ways.
>
> Their world was so closed. They didn't want schools. They didn't want community improvement projects. Why? Because these things represented a crack in the system of defense of their traditional ways. They rejected anything that symbolized a crack through which capitalism, Western ways, other traditions, could seep in.

Widespread resistance to change was gradually overcome as the indigenous people realized that they were involved in determining the pace and type of change. Only through widespread participation at the grassroots level was change possible, and once the people were convinced that the organization benefitted them, they flocked to join. In the department of El Quiché alone, for example, Catholic Action drew 80,000 members and organized 3,600 catechists. The municipality of Santa Cruz del Quiché is a good example of the dramatic changes which grassroots participation in Catholic Action brought. In 1960 in Santa Cruz and in the 33 surrounding villages there was only a single church and no roads to the villages. There were no cooperatives, and almost no indigenous children attended school. Just eight years later Catholic Action had formed 33 Christian community centers in the rural areas and three such centers in the town of Santa Cruz. Organized through Catholic Action, the people had built 35 chapels, 33 schools, 48 soccer fields, 16 cooperatives and passable roads to each village.[12]

Throughout these years, Catholic Action focused on projects and community development strategies which did not confront the economic and political structures of exploitation and poverty. Perhaps out of fear of repression or out of a genuine belief that "radical" solutions were not viable, Catholic Action leaders took pains to distance themselves from anything that resembled land expropriation or a minimum wage law for agricultural workers. In contrast with Arbenz' land *redistribution* measures twenty years earlier, the Catholic Church promoted land *colonization* projects in the virgin jungle territory of northern El Quiché and Huehuetenango near Zona Reyna and Ixcán Grande. Though these projects were sponsored by U.S. Maryknoll missionaries and not by Catholic Action, the colonization projects were inspired by the social development philosophy of Catholic Action.

Landless campesinos from the densely populated highland regions were attracted by the promise of good land, and altogether 30,000 people were organized in more than 25 cooperatives covering hundreds of thousands of acres of land. The names of the new cooperatives--*Resurrección, Pueblo Nuevo* (New People), *Samaritano* (Samaritan), *Los Angeles* (the angels)--reflected the utopian hopes of a religious people.

In the cooperatives the Church managed the finances, technical assistance, administration, internal coordination and even police duties. With the priests shuttling in purchased supplies aboard Cessna planes and the catechists serving as on site managers there was little separation between project management and Christian formation. The early problems were organizational and logistical: how to organize tens of thousands of indigent campesinos who spoke multiple languages and who lacked formal eduction into self-run cooperatives. Beating back the jungle, overcoming disease, building roads and finding water sources were no easy tasks.

After a few years, however, the cooperatives showed signs of self-sufficiency and even financial success as the market price of the cooperatives' chief product, cardamum, rose. More and more settlers arrived, and the seemingly limitless land became scarce and a source of contention even in the Ixcán.

Catholic Action and Political Change (1970-1978)

In the early 1970s the community development approach of Catholic Action was being questioned by a growing number of catechists who had been conscienticized through the Catholic Action experience. They disagreed with the Catholic Action practice of concentrating on self-help community projects and avoiding larger structural issues of poverty, such as grossly unequal land distribution, the forced migrations to the harvest, and starvation wages. These catechists argued that after ten years of organizing self-help projects, the communities were ready for the next step. The social improvements in health, education and community cooperation had reached their limits unless the structural issues were addressed. Catholic Action, they felt, had the potential to bring about broader social transformation; what the current movement lacked was more direct political action. One catechist involved with Catholic Action recalled,[13]

> There was a group of people within Catholic Action which was rethinking its commitment to the poor. As campesinos, they understood the commitment of a Christian and the path that the poor were taking. To share your possessions, your ideals, your work, to give up even your life. People who understood this were clear [about the struggle]. It was like a sieve which defined the different groups within the movement. Some moved forward and others, more reactionary, stayed behind. The core of Catholic Action split.

The developmentalists, the ones who "stayed behind," warned that Catholic Action was already becoming too political, and that by increasing the pace of change the movement risked an even greater reaction from the authorities who had been repressing Catholic Action catechists since 1964. The "radical" group argued that the military resisted any kind of change, without regard to whether it was gradual and developmental or sudden and political, and would use repression to block it.

The land cooperatives in the Ixcán were a prime example of the attempt at a politically neutral approach to development, and the Army attacks on cooperative leaders validated the position of the "radicals" within Catholic Action. The Church colonized the unclaimed virgin jungle in order to look for a solution to landlessness without having to confront the large landowner.

However, when oil was discovered in the Northern Transversal strip, an area which includes the Ixcán, the cooperative land became much more valuable. Various multinational oil companies, including Getty Oil, Texaco, Amoco and Shenadoah Oil, opened exploration sites along the Chixoy River and by 1974 had extended their drilling into the colonization sites in the Ixcán. The companies laid claim to the land which the new cooperativists had cleared, and soon the companies produced land titles granted to them by INTA (the National Institute of Agrarian Transformation), titles which had been long promised to the cooperatives but never delivered. When threats to throw the settlers off the land failed, the Army and paramilitary forces acted to back up the oil companies. During a three month period in 1975, twenty-eight catechists in the Ixcán cooperatives were disappeared. The priests, too, were regularly accused by the Army of aiding the fledgling guerrilla movement, and one priest in particular, Father Bill Woods, was threatened repeatedly by the local Army commander. In 1978 Father Woods and several other passengers were killed when his plane crashed while carrying supplies to the Ixcán. It is widely believed that Army agents had engineered the crash.

As the "developmentalists" continued their work in cooperatives, etc., the "radical" group within Catholic Action began to pull out of the organization and seek new allies. In the early 1970s they joined many of the newly-conscienticized indigenous leaders who were seeking a voice in the political process. In many towns and villages in the highlands they campaigned and won mayoral elections replacing the mixed blood ladinos. The newly-created Christian Democrat party welcomed the new indigenous leaders, particularly as the party geared up to challenge the military-led National Liberation Movement party in the 1972 presidential election.[14] The hopes by the indigenous people for change through the legal political process, however, were frustrated-- first by that year's presidential electoral fraud which cheated the Christian Democrats of victory and, secondly, by the Christian Democrat mayors who dismissed the concerns of the indigenous communities after the electoral campaign.

Disillusioned, the "radicals" of Catholic Action began to look for other methods. They initiated discussions with indigenous activists involved in the social analysis workshops of the Jesuit *Centro de Información y Acción Social* and with educated indigenous youth[15] on how to take Catholic Action one step further. That next step was the Committee of Campesino Unity (*Comité de Unidad Campesino - CUC*).

What began as a coordination of local actions in the Quiché developed into a broadly based popular organization known as the CUC. Operating throughout the highlands, the southern coast and in the capital, the CUC united poor ladinos and Indians in a class-based struggle against local as well as national structures of oppression. The CUC found its initial leaders among the most radicalized catechists of Catholic Action and its most faithful supporters among the community organizations promoted by Catholic Action. Because of Army threats and persecution, they operated clandestinely. The work of CUC spread, and CUC members began to organize workers on fincas, migrant laborers along the coast, and townspeople. The tactics of the CUC were daring and strategic against the oligarchy's power. The CUC organized land takeovers, demonstrations, marches, strikes, and other forms of resistance. In 1977 the CUC led a march of 100,000 people from Ixtahuacan to Guatemala City in support of striking tin miners. Three years later a massive strike called by the CUC during the harvest shut down the large agro-export plantations along the coast.

Despite its militancy, the CUC never entirely left behind the goals of Catholic Action or its Christian inspiration. Practically wherever Catholic Action had been strong, CUC was active. The town of La Estancia, located outside of Santa Cruz del Quiché, had been one of the first communities organized by Catholic Action and was a base of strong support for the CUC fifteen years later.[16] One of the catechists involved in CUC in La Estancia said[17]

> Within the CUC we would go back and forth on the importance of being a Christian. We would tell our non-Christian brothers and sisters that the organization grew out of the initiative of Christians, that the leaders of CUC are the lay leaders in the Church. Those of us who believe in God are convinced that it has been our Christian commitment which led us along this path.

It was no coincidence that the first victim of assassination (April 1981) in La Estancia was Fabián Pérez, a CUC member, a Catholic Action catechist and a founder of the cooperative movement in the area. Shortly thereafter two brothers, both members of the pro-development committee of La Estancia and both former Catholic Action catechists were assassinated by death squads. The community secretly debated among themselves on how they should respond. Should they flee? Should they join the guerrillas as some of the young people had already done? An organizer of the CUC from La Estancia relates[18]

> When Fabián Pérez was killed, people in the community became more aware of the injustices. The [Army] had repressed community leaders and committed massacres in other villages. People in the community started to come to us and tell us the situation was falling apart. They asked us how were we going to defend ourselves, how were we going to protect our children. Many, many people joined the CUC and the guerrillas.

In some areas, at first only a few people, as they became more radicalized through their experience with Catholic Action, the Christian Democrats and CUC, joined the guerrillas. In other communities the repression forced whole communities into guerrilla structures overnight. "Leonardo," a Catholic Action priest recounts[19]

> I saw all the people come and go, and felt clearly that they didn't want to know anything about guerrillas. There was no trust. We don't know anything [about them], the people said. Until all of a sudden the people realized that this [guerrilla] movement was for them. From one day to the next, everybody joined up at once. I felt like the ground was moving out from under me. What was happening? It was the decision of the community to take this option. This was their path.

For the people in these communities their decision to join the guerrillas was less ideological than practical; it was less based on the hopes of taking power than it was an act of survival and self-defense.

As an institution the Church maintained a commitment to non-violence and non-confrontation in face of the injustice and the growing abuses. Given the wide-spread government-sponsored repression, many Christians had grave doubts about the effectiveness of non-violence.

One incident in 1979 demonstrates the problem. During the inauguration of a new church building in the department of El Quiché, the bishop Mons. Juan Gerardi asked a group of 84 catechists, "What do you want? What do you need from the Church to help you in this desperate situation?" They responded that what they wanted was help in organizing their defense. "What we need are guns," they told Mons. Gerardi. His reply was that they should seek dialogue and not burn the bridges of reconciliation. Dissatisfied but obedient, the catechists followed his directions. Within two years sixty of the 84 catechists had been killed.

The experience of Catholic Action in the highlands from 1965 to 1980 has shown both the potential as well as the limitations of pastoral work in bringing about social change. After overcoming its earlier errors in confronting traditional Mayan beliefs, Catholic Action found greater acceptance among the indigenous people in the highlands. Catholic Action succeeded in engendering a critical consciousness in the people and offered models (even if limited) of community development. Catholic Action responded to and was rooted in the objective conditions in which the people lived. Over the decades Catholic Action transformed itself from, as one priest put it, a foreign ideology imported from Rome and imposed on the people to[20]

> filling an organizational vacuum in religion and social life. More than anything, Catholic Action responded to the cultural values which the Maya had preserved through centuries of oppression: the sense of community life and the mystical/religious interpretation of existence. The community was and continues to be the vital center of the indigenous people, like a large family, it was the vital nucleus of Maya society. While Catholic Action began as a Christian renovation movement, the indigenous converted it into a pillar of their community life, and consequently a potential instrument of transformation for a people marginalized from power since the conquest.

> The Maya people are deeply religious. They see divinity in life: in mother earth, in plants that grow, in women who procreate, in the forces of nature, in pain as a means of purification, in community life..For centuries, religion has been manipulated as an instrument of submission. Through Catholic Action, the people began to rediscover the religious values that had been dormant, restoring their original liberating power and re-establishing harmony between God and God's people.

Secondly, says Fidel Hernández, a Sacred Heart priest involved in Catholic Action, the activity of the Church[21]

> moved from the centers of power to the periphery where the people live. People were used to coming to the center to vote, to pay taxes,

> to buy and to pray. There was no power at the periphery. When Catholic Action built chapels in the villages--out of their own sense of the Church of Christianity[22] to be sure--they became elements of destabilization of the center of power. The village chapels weren't just buildings of prayer, but rather centers where people met, deliberated and made decisions affecting their lives. They became, in a sense, new centers of power. As a consequence, the liturgies acquired dimensions of an authentic revolution within the Catholic Church.

The shift from center to periphery as the locus of church activity was seen as an important strategy in order to reach the masses in the villages. Its effect, however, was to loosen the hierarchical control of Catholic Action. The priests could no longer control the lay-led pastoral work, nor, as some of them were realizing, was this desirable. Pastoral work, in the hands of the people, in conjunction with other factors brought about the awakening of the peasantry and the desire for social transformation. Pastoral work controlled from the top eventually stagnated; though it met little resistance, it brought little fruit. The shift from center to periphery affected the political and military terrain as well as the religious. With increased community activity occurring at the periphery, military, administrative, and judicial control lost its absolute power over people's lives.

The pastoral approach of Catholic Action made people aware of their social condition, but as a reformist vehicle it only marginally affected those conditions. Catholic Action was unable to affect the structural injustice built into land tenure and the wage system because of its reluctance to address political issues. The social ministry of Catholic Action concentrated on community development projects which were unable to overcome the harsh political realities. Direct political action was no more successful, however, as the CUC was met head on by a wave of repression including the massacre of dozens of CUC activists who were burned alive inside the Spanish Embassy. Neither Catholic Action, the Church hierarchy nor the people anticipated the levels of repression which would be unleashed by the government forces. In terms of their theology, the people were more prepared for the "promised land" or to usher in the kingdom of God than for the years of persecution. The open organizing of Catholic Action had publicly exposed its leaders to the military and to government-sponsored death squads which converted Guatemala into a "decapitated nation."[23] The possibilities for non-violent change had closed.

The Martyred Diocese of El Quiché

In the wake of two attempts on the life of Monsignor Juan Gerardi, the Bishop of El Quiché, the killing of two priests in El Quiché and the brutal repression of hundreds of catechists and thousands of indigenous people, on July 20, 1980 the Catholic Church responded with a *pastoral de denuncia* (pastoral statement of protest). The Church closed the Diocese of El Quiché and withdrew all of its personnel as a "protest against the authorities."[24] The Diocesan communiqué read

> In this tragic moment in the history of Guatemala, one cannot offer spiritual attention in the Diocese of El Quiché... Our forced absence should not be seen as renouncing or abandoning the Christian people of El Quiché. It has been a sincere discernment of faith which has shown us the only possible road to help our people.

The "tragic moment" had been developing for some time. The Army's response to the growing organized protest by the indigenous in the highlands was brutal counterinsurgency campaigns. From 1976 to 1978, one hundred and sixty-eight cooperative or village leaders were singled out and assassinated in the department of El Quiché. On May 29, 1978 in Panzós, department of Alta Verapaz the Army opened fire on a demonstration of Kekchí Indians who were protesting the usurpation of their land and the forced disappearances of three of their leaders. Over 100 people were killed in the massacre and their bodies dumped in pre-dug mass graves.

The repression only added fuel to the fires of social unrest as more and more Indians became organized in popular organizations such as the CUC or the Campesino Committee of the Highlands (*Comité de Campesinos del Altiplano - CCDA*). In a display of defiance to the Army, one hundred thousand people demonstrated in Panzós a year after the massacre. A 1982 Oxfam study by Shelton Davis and Julie Hodson about the violence in the Guatemalan highlands documented that public protest and popular organization were not the only form of resistance. Their study stated, "Increased guerrilla activity and Indian membership in the guerrilla movement are almost entirely a direct result of such severe government repression that people see no other alternative."

The repression reached even greater heights during the iron rule of coup leader Gen. Efraín Ríos Montt. On the day he took power (March 23, 1982), 23 campesinos were massacred in Chumatzatz, El Quiché. It is estimated that between 15,000 and 17,000 people were murdered during Ríos Montt's 18 months in power. The entire population of northern El Quiché, estimated at between 250,000 and 300,000 people, was either murdered, compelled to live under military control, driven into exile or forced into a clandestine life in the mountains or jungles. Natán, a Catholic Action catechist in the Ixcán colonization cooperative of Cuarto Pueblo, described the attack on his village[25]

> On Sunday, April 30, 1982 I was in the market in the center of the village when we heard that the Army was coming. The troops poured in from the north, east and the south, and then mortar after

> mortar fell on the market. Bullets passed in front of and behind me,
> and one passed through my sombrero. Somehow I was saved--I was
> one of two survivors--and climbed the hill overlooking Cuarto
> Pueblo. I saw the soldiers round up the women and rape them. I saw
> the soldiers force the living into an old wooden school and then drag
> in the dead bodies and set fire to the building.

> After the Army left others from nearby communities and I climbed
> down to the village again. In the evangelical church there were about
> 125 burned bodies. You could tell which were women because their
> braided hair was too thick to burn. The same was true in the Catholic
> church--piles of burned bodies and clumps of hair. In the school a
> few of us pulled out the bodies which hadn't burned entirely and
> tried to bury them. We didn't have the strength to bury them all.

Attacks were directed against pastoral agents and Church leaders. Fifteen priests were assassinated between 1978 and 1985, and during a 20 month period between 1980 and 1982 ninety-one priests and 64 religious women were forced to abandon the country. Forty-two religious schools and six Catholic radio stations were closed. Mons. Ríos Montt, a relatively progressive bishop (Diocese of Escuintla) and brother to the coup leader, was forced to resign his post due to veiled governmental threats against his life. Especially targeted were the catechists and pastoral agents who were involved in conscientization and Christian formation. Unknown thousands of them were disappeared, tortured or murdered. They were targeted not just because they were Catholic, but rather because their belief in the Gospel--where the poor were the chosen people of God and deserved justice--was considered subversive to the security of the state.

The persecution of the Church and the scorched earth policies of the Guatemalan government passed largely unreported in the Western press. The testimonies of survivors and letters of pastoral agents, however, have left a record to how the faithful can be repressed but their faith cannot be destroyed, and how pastoral work in the midst of mass graves and burnt villages can begin again.

Catholics who survived the Army ground invasions, the bombings and the night missions of the death squads, likened their experience to the Roman persecution of Christians. The Church of the Catacombs of the pre-Constantinian period had become, in Guatemala, the church in the jungle: *martyred, abandoned* and *exiled.*

For the Church of the Catacombs, the most obvious characteristic was martyrdom, the killing of the faithful. Bermúdez cites incident after incident of the Army's hatred of the Church, pastoral agents and the Bible.[26] One catechist from La Estancia witnessed the actual crucifixion of a fellow catechist.[27]

> I watched from a hiding place as a brother was seized by the Army
> as he was returning home from work in the fields. He was literally
> nailed through the feet and the hands to a wooden plank and

dragged inside his house. The soldiers set fire to his house and then the soldiers–several hundred of them–just laughed out loud as they heard his screams.

The response of the people was to conceal what the Army already viewed as subversive. They buried their Bibles. They met in secret to worship, to reflect on the Bible and mostly to pray. Liberating Christian faith became in the 1980's in Army-controlled areas of Guatemala what Maya religions had been for the past 450 years, a religion for all practical purposes illegal, rarely acknowledged in public but buried deep in the collective consciousness of the people.

The second characteristic was the inescapable fact that the agents of the Church had been forced to abandon the people. The Episcopal Conference of Bishops was vociferous in its protest against the authorities,[28] but that was no substitute for the direct pastoral accompaniment. All of the structure of Catholic Action, all of the priests and nuns, the Bishop, in short every Church employee, was removed from the department. Not only did their departure leave a vacuum in terms of pastoral work, but it also cut off the communities' access to the outside world. With the exception of two priests who had joined the guerrillas as combatants, the entire region was left without ordained pastoral agents or any other independent agency with contacts to the outside.

The Army's scorched earth campaigns meant that most people in the highlands were displaced from their homes at one time or another; according to a 1990 study on displacement by AVANSCO, eighty percent of the residents of the four departments of El Quiché, Huehuetenango, Alta Verapaz and Baja Verapaz were forced from their homes by the conflict. In addition to the loss of loved ones, the indigenous people lost their communities and, with them, their grounding in the sacred. For many Mayan people, the place where their ancestors are buried, where the sacred corn which sustains life grows, and where they will die, is their spiritual grounding. Many Mayans are as likely to speak about belonging to the land as they are to talk about the land belonging to them. Their community, in a sense their world, was destroyed.

Persecuted, stripped of land and community, and feeling abandoned by the Church, pastoral work as it was known previously came to a halt. There were no longer priests, program budgets or Cessna airplanes. The indigenous Christians had nowhere else to turn other than to themselves. A pastoral plan dependent on the outside was no longer viable. The people had to either take on the pastoral work in its entirety–the theologizing, the formation, the worship and the structures–or abandon it. It was a new juncture in their faith and in their lives.

The Emergence of a Church of the Poor

By 1984 the Communities of Population in Resistance inside Guatemala were emerging out of the "darkness of the night," observed Ricardo Falla, a Guatemalan Jesuit priest who later worked in the CPRs in the Ixcán. The indigenous communities have survived by keeping themselves hidden, cooking only during the night so that the smoke does not reveal their location to military spotter planes, walking carefully through the jungle so as not to create paths which the Army patrols could follow to their homes or farm plots. The communities have resisted, not by militarily confronting the Army soldiers but by evading them. Each community maintains itself in a state of permanent alert, prepared to dismantle its village and evacuate within twenty minutes, carrying the old and the sick and all of the community's possessions.

In political terms, the mere survival of the people continues to be an act of resistance to the Army and its policies of counterinsurgency. The strategy of the Army is to control the civilian population and to isolate them from the guerrillas. The Army has used "soft" tactics–beans-and-bullets pacification programs, Army-controlled model villages and the establishment of civil patrol units--as well as scorched earth policies to bring the civilian population under subjugation. By surviving and by remaining outside of the Army's domination, the CPRs have represented a major blow to the Army's counterinsurgency goals. The cost of resistance has been high, as one catechist from Amajchel wrote.[29]

> We are totally without clothing, medicine and machetes, and nearly without food, even without salt. Nonetheless, we are resisting because we are clear about what the word of God says in Matthew 5: "Blessed are those who suffer persecution; blessed are those who suffer hunger." The Gospel consoles us in our suffering, but it is with great sadness that we acknowledge that this is the only way.

The struggle for survival demanded strong community organization within the CPRs. The forced evacuations, which for some communities took place fifteen or twenty times over a six month period, required a high degree of coordination, internal discipline and unity. In the communities people worked cooperatively. While some people performed roving patrol duty, others farmed plots far away, while others taught school or tended the fowl, and others cared for the children. They shared the goods they produced without using currency.[30]

Facing a common enemy within a shared situation, the tendency among the Mayan people to unite is strong. Even traditional animosities between ethnic groups, for example between the Canjobal and the Kekchí, dissipated. Language barriers and other cultural differences were overcome gradually through community meetings, work projects and intermarriage.

The strengthening of the experience of community in the CPRs not only fortified their survival and resistance, but also provided the context in which people more systematically expressed their faith. Initially, people gathered to pray, to mourn their lost family members and to give thanks to God for their own survival. Some people believed that they had survived because of a miracle from God; others described their experience as being "resurrected"–even in a literal sense–in order to fulfill God's plan in their lives. The Guatemalan Church in Exile has printed dozens of letters of catechists reflecting on their persecution, including the following.[31]

> We give thanks to God for allowing us to live a few days more. God doesn't intend for us all to die; God wants us to live so that we can further the struggle and so that we can act in the way which our Lord Jesus Christ asks of us: that we may not only lift our heads to the heavens but also break the chains of injustice of those who are bound and for the oppressed, that we may live out the fast which Yahweh approves.

In an interview, Fidel, a former president of a Catholic Action cooperative and a catechist in a CPR community in the Ixcán, told how he had lost faith in God during the worst of the repression. Later, he found that "together again with the other catechists, we could remember the songs we used to sing, maybe someone would remember one verse and someone else another. We didn't have any Bibles–they had been buried–but people could remember the Scripture."[32]

The people's expression of faith, in turn, reinforced the strength of the community. For the people of the CPRs their religious experience was interpreted in light of living through war, and their pastoral practice was adapted to that reality. People more commonly read the Bible in groups rather than individually, and in doing so, they readily identified with characters in the Bible story. They identified with the persecuted Christ, with the members of the early Christian communities or with the people of Israel, no longer enslaved to Pharaoh, but wandering in exile for the forty years. Their daily struggles took on sacred significance. Their struggle against the enemy became a righteous defense of the sacred and assertion of the belief in a God of life.

Without the presence of clergy, lay people assumed the roles of religious formation, liturgical preparation and the administration of the rites of baptism, communion, marriage and last rites. In 1990, three hundred children were baptized in one community in the Ixil by a team of lay catechists from a community in the Ixcán. The theological reflection focused on themes which the communities were experiencing, for example, persecution, martyrdom and final judgement or victory. One catechist from Ixcán wrote the following in his journal during a forced evacuation.[33]

> 7:00 a.m. Nov. 2. We are still moving but we held mass yesterday regardless. We discussed the theme "Blessed are the persecuted." People reflected that no one can take from us this joy which the Lord has given. That's what the Army wants to do.
>
> Yesterday we also celebrated the Day of the Dead. At the mass we wrote the names of the dead on crosses decorated with leaves and wild flowers from each community and processed to the graves to bring the "supper" of the Eucharist to the buried dead and to make a pronouncement of "jubilee" about the triumph and the Last Supper.

Gradually, the pastoral work became more systematic within a community and between communities. Catechists from different communities began to meet, and the pastoral work became more coordinated. Head catechists would journey from community to community to meet with local catechists, oversee religious formation and worship with the people. The catechists in the CPRs began to communicate and then coordinate with the catechists in the refugee camps. The catechist teams even functioned as one of the principal channels for delivery of medicines and tools from Mexico to the Communities in Resistance.[34]

The pastoral work also helped consolidate social organization in the CPR communities. This functioned in a direct way, for example, when community assembly meetings would be held following the religious service. It also happened at an ideological level through pastoral formation. Through pastoral work the catechists instilled values of sharing, compassion and freedom from domination which greatly benefitted the community organization and deepened resistance to the Army.[35] During the initial years of the Catholic Action period, pastoral work was in the hands of the priest who gave directions for people to follow; now, pastoral work was a response of faith by the people to a God of life who accompanied them on their journey.

One of the foreign missionaries who worked in El Quiché in the 1960s returned in 1986 to the northern part of the department to work in the CPRs. He was one of two priests who have been working at different times in the CPRs; their involvement, however, has struck a different tone from the role of priests in the early years of Catholic Action. He considered his recent time there as "the richest experience of faith and life that I've had in thirty-three years as a priest." He found that the pastoral practice was not disengaged at all from people's day-to-day experiences; in fact, it would be impossible to differentiate the pastoral work from the community work. Though the priest worked mainly with the Catholic population, there was a significant presence of evangelicals and believers in traditional Mayan spirituality. According

to numerous reports, there is little animosity between the three groups
and at times even shared worship. The role of faith in their lives, as the
priest explains, is central.[36]

> The first thing I noticed was that, despite the fact that there were no
> pastoral agents, the people had grown in their faith and Christian
> commitment. Every day there was prayer and every weekend a
> morning of prayer, reflection and worship.

> Their experience can be compared to the primitive Christian
> communities where after the resurrection of Jesus people shared
> everything--prayer, bread, wealth, poverty. People had already
> realized that their motivation to share work collectively was very
> practical--it was their only form of survival--but during Biblical
> reflection they also understood its Christian significance. They are
> sharing the land, the work and the danger. They are sharing life as
> well as the possibility of death at any moment because the Army
> is always threatening them.

> It was a beautiful experience to see people become more motivated
> and participate more in the life of the communities, in their own
> resistance and in the revolution. They understood that it was not
> only politics which motivated their actions but also that Christian
> faith was a source of inspiration for their resistance.

Ricardo Falla, an anthropologist as well as a priest and author of *El
Quiché Rebelde* and *Massacres of the Jungle*, lived and worked in the
CPRs. For the five years that Falla lived in the Ixcán jungle, his mission
was to "be with the people," he said. "And to follow them. That means
even physically to go with them because when we leave the communities under emergency plans, I am not one who will lead. I am the one
who is behind them, who is going where they go. By myself in the
jungle, I would starve to death."[37] Inspired by Salvadoran Archbishop
Oscar Romero, Falla practiced what he called a pastoral of accompaniment offering hope and encouragement to a people experiencing
isolation and persecution.

For Falla, accompaniment also means to share the risk of

> the constant threat of attack where mortars explode like rays of light
> in the darkness; threats always at the edge of one's consciousness,
> even when there is a dance or a mass, everyone must always be alert
> for the sounds of planes which the people in the CPRs can detect
> five or ten seconds before someone who is not used to the sounds
> can hear them.[38]

Falla also worked with the CPR communities in developing a
"*pastoral de la resistencia*" (a pastoral plan of resistance) which to Falla
means responding to the questions of "How can the word of God be
preached as bombs fall? How can catechists be formed in the midst of
war? How can a living church grow when the people constantly have
to flee?"[39] Falla has discussed elsewhere how the CPR catechists found

The CPR communities have been bombed, attacked by ground troops and had their homes razed to the ground. In the photograph, a girl with her sister, both members of the CPR community of Cabá, holds an exploded mortar shell found near the community.

parallels between stories of resistance in the Bible with their own experience of resistance; for example, the birth of Jesus during a journey and women in the CPRs who have given birth while fleeing.

Falla's time in the CPRs was cut short by a military offensive in November 1992 which forced three CPR communities (more than 700 people) to flee into Mexico. Along with hundreds of others, Falla fled deeper into the jungle. However, the Army discovered his personal papers and church documents which attested to his presence in the communities. Though the Army destruction of three communities and the burning of 20 tons of stored grain never made headlines, the Army's ludicrous accusations that this 60 year-old balding Jesuit priest was actually a URNG commander did. The Catholic Bishops both defended Falla publicly and defended the right of the CPR communities to receive pastoral attention.

Throughout 1993 the CPRs have grown bolder in asserting their demands and confronting the military's counterinsurgency plan. In February 1993 the CPRs organized an international delegation numbering more than 400 people and which was led by two Guatemalan Catholic Bishops in order to call attention to their cause. When the military responded with another offensive in March forcing more CPR communities to flee their homes, the CPR leaders stepped up the international pressure. In September the CPRs mobilized a dramatic march/caravan of more than 600 CPR members who journeyed to Guatemala City to protest the attacks and demand recognition as civilians. Though the CPRs have yet to be recognized by the government as a civilian population, they have received an outpouring of support from national and international sources.

Building a Church Committed to Justice

Only within the unique confines of the refugee camps in southern Mexico and the Communities of Population in Resistance has a vibrant expression of the church of the poor emerged. Not coincidentally, both areas lie largely outside of military control. Elsewhere--in the highlands, along the southern coast, in the marginalized communities of Guatemala City or even within the popular movement itself--liberating pastoral work has been undertaken cautiously and has been received even more cautiously. It is true that the church of the poor has not developed into the kind of mass movement for social justice that Catholic Action gave rise to in the late 1970s. However, there is a presence of liberating pastoral work that is growing gradually in the marginalized communities of Guatemala City and in certain indigenous communities in the highlands, evidence that the pastoral experience over the past thirty years has not been "liquidated" as some observers have suggested.[40]

The single most important factor which has inhibited the growth of the church of the poor and other groups seeking social change has been the collective fear of repression. One organization, CERJ (Council of Ethnic Communities "We Are All Equal") which works to end the illegal recruitment into the civil defense patrols (800,000 men under arms) has had 25 of its members assassinated. Despite the return to civilian rule in 1985, human rights abuses have continued unchecked. According to the Archdiocesan Human Rights Office, there were 248 extrajudicial executions in 1993 and overall documented human rights violations increased by 65% from 1992 to 1993. In 1994 the situation worsened still; more violations were committed during the month of August than any previous month since the Archdiocese established its human rights office. In Guatemala City, unidentified tortured cadavers are found on a daily basis. Church people who organize the poor to seek social justice or who support poor people's organizations are no less immune to the threats or actual use of repression.[41]

Proponents of the church of the poor have realized that because of the repression as well as changes occurring within Guatemala the church of the poor today cannot be a simple replication of the grassroots movement of Catholic Action in the 1970s. The movement needs to be much broader and to include theological institutions, progressive religious orders and denominations, faith-based development groups, as well as Christian base communities and church-based coalitions working for political change. The larger institutions help provide protection, training, personnel and funding which the grassroots groups lack. CIEDEG, the Conference of Evangelical Churches of Guatemala, is one such progressive group and in addition to its official functions has played an instrumental role in supporting the Christian-led Campaign for Peace and Life and also CPR communities. Vitalino Simolox, the head of CIEDEG, said recently, "It has been the blood of the people and the clarity of their struggle which has shown the Church how to follow a Christian path. The Church is not leading the people. The Church is learning and trying to follow the people."[42]

The Conference of Guatemala Bishops (CEG) too has undergone a significant shift since conservative Archbishop Mariano Rossell Arellano died; the Conference is now one of the most politically progressive Catholic hierarchies in Latin America. On a regular basis the Catholic Church has made strong calls for the Church's involvement in social justice. In a series of pastoral letters, "In Order to Build Peace" (1984), "Education: Challenge and Hope" (1987), "Communique from Coban" (1989) and particularly "The Clamor for the Land" (1988), the bishops proclaimed openly the preferential option for the poor and the rights to life of the poor, including enough land to farm, education, health care, etc. The bishops recognize that they have been conscienticized over the years by the church of the poor. They owe their prophetic insight to "the blood of our martyrs which has fertilized our soil."[43]In their 1988-1992 Comprehensive Plan, the bishops call the Church to[44]

> present the message of Christ in all its fidelity; to form Christian communities where all people, especially the poor, find welcome; to value sisterhood, brotherhood and solidarity; to denounce the injustices and make possible the construction of a society that is truly human and characterized by the values of the Gospel; to be a Church that through its acts and life serves the kingdom of God.

The prophetic vision comes not only from the Conference but also from individual dioceses.[45]

The Bishops' call for the Church's involvement in "liberation," as they said elsewhere in the Comprehensive Plan, has not been always carried out in practice. Despite their pastoral letters and other public denouncements of human rights abuses, the Catholic hierarchy has not always acted as a protagonist in defense of the poor as did so often, for example, the Salvadoran Catholic Church under the leadership of Monsignor Oscar Romero. According to some of the hierarchy's critics who have written in *Guatemala: retos a la iglesia católica,* [46]

> in their writing the Bishops identify with the option for a liberating pastoral plan. The Bishops emphasize their "preferential option for the poor," the formation of Christian communities, the vital link of faith and life, the need to analyze the social reality and the liberating objective of evangelization. Nonetheless, ... just as in their social discourse, the Bishops *avoid contextualizing their pastoral commitments.* [Emphasis added.]

The inaction by the bishops following the release of their politically controversial pastoral letter "The Clamor for Land" in February 1988 was one example of the Church's lack of contextualization. The introduction of their letter reads, "The clamor for land is undoubtedly the strongest, most dramatic and most desperate cry heard in Guatemala...Certainly the critical problem of land ownership is at the very heart of the propagation of injustice." The bishops go on to analyze in detail the "excessive inequality" of land ownership, and then echo the words of John Paul II to "put into effect daring and profoundly innovative transformations...to bring about, without further delay, urgent reforms." (2.2.1)

The bishops, however, conclude the letter saying, "Our pastoral service is limited to describing and situating the problem in the context of human dignity, common good and Christian love." (4.4) They go no further than identifying and describing poignantly the injustice and fail to commit the Church to concrete actions on behalf of justice. The

Bishops fail to offer a praxis to the pastoral letter, a *pastoral de la tierra* (pastoral of land).

Too harsh a criticism of the Catholic Church leadership is perhaps unfair. At great risk the bishops have supported the CPR communities. Bishops Julio Cabrera (Diocese of El Quiché) and Alvaro Ramazzini (Diocese of San Marcos) have visited the CPR communities on many occasions and have consistently and courageously acted in their behalf.[47] CONFREGUA (the confederation of men's and women's religious orders) as well has performed exceptional work in organizing and empowering the displaced population and for years has helped channel to the international community denunciations about human rights violations.

Observers see that the Church has tried to play more of a mediating role with the government rather than an advocacy role on behalf of the poor. The Church offered important leadership in pressing for peace negotiations between the government and the URNG insurgency with Monsignor Quezada Toruño (Bishop of Escuintla) serving as conciliator for much of that process and later moderator of the Assembly of Civil Sectors which offered consensus positions on the negotiation issues. Nonetheless, there are many, such as Auxiliary Bishop Juan Gerardi (former bishop of El Quiché) who recognize that actions such as these do not constitute a systematic commitment by the Church to empower the poor, yet as he says, the task of transforming society belongs to all social forces and not just to the leaders of the churches.[48]

The Church of the Poor at a Crossroads

At a grassroots level the church of the poor has not been able to summon up the amount of participants nor the spirit of social activism that it enjoyed in the 1960s and 1970s. The largest expression of a grassroots organization is the SINE program (Comprehensive Service of Evangelization) . Though SINE resembles base communities, the program is administered by the dioceses and run by the parish priests. Decision-making remains at the top and little lay participation is encouraged.

In the mid-1980s Guatemalan Christian Action (ACG) began quietly organizing a base of former catechists involved in Catholic Action who were living as displaced in the highlands, in the refugee camps and CPRs, along the coast and in the marginalized communities of Guatemala City. Their non-confrontational methods and their caution, for example preferring the words "theology of life" rather than "theology of liberation," were a response to the repression against the work of the church during the period of the church of the catacombs. Its initial leaders began meeting with former catechists and members of Catholic Action and the CUC from Quiché and Huehuetenango, almost all of whom had been uprooted by the repression. These people did not need to be conscienticized; they needed to be persuaded that if they organized again, repression would not strike as it had before.

After years of organizing clandestinely, Guatemalan Christian Action (ACG) had established a base of support in six departments and had over one hundred trained catechists. In 1989 Guatemalan Christian Action emerged publicly stating that their goal was to rebuild the network of Christian base communities that existed in the highlands through the 1970s and into the 1980s.

It has become increasingly evident that pastoral work in the refugee camps and CPRs has flourished while organizing in the other areas has lagged. Practically all of the pastoral work among Catholics in the refugee camps and the CPRs has been coordinated by ACG (an estimated more than 500 catechists have been trained by ACG in the camps and the CPRs) with formal or informal support of the corresponding Bishop. In the rest of Guatemala, ACG's work is seen by many lay people and clergy as too political or dangerous.

The church of the poor in Guatemala is still in search of a model, or models, which respond to the contemporary reality of the poor and indigenous of Guatemala. In all likelihood, it will not be a single organization which defines the movement as Catholic Action had from 1965 to 1980, though groups like the Campaign for Peace and Life and Guatemalan Christian Action may have a large influence. The greater the variety of expressions of the church of the poor (ecclesiastical and independent as well as Catholic, Protestant and ecumenical), the greater the impact of the church of the poor will be with the marginalized. One issue appears clear, however: Models that worked in the past are not necessarily valid for the current period. During the peak years of Catholic Action's influence, the popular movement was just in formation, and the Church offered the protection of a meeting place and forum for people to discuss problems, propose solutions and even voice dissent. Today that role for the Church is no longer needed as the poor and marginalized have found their own voice and way to express themselves through the popular organizations.

The church of the poor must continually test the waters and allow a new form of being Church evolve, as it has in the CPRs and refugee camps, and avoid the temptation to apply old models such as Catholic Action to a new historical experience. Attempts by the Catholic Church hierarchy through SINE or by any other group to jumpstart a Christian base community movement (which has never been strong in Guatemala) without taking into consideration historical changes--the introduction of televisions in every community, for example, or the inroads made by evangelicals--will be likely met by failure.

Experienced pastoral workers acknowledge that for the church of the poor to succeed it must stubbornly defend its autonomy both from the clergy who would dominate the structure, as has already been the case with at least one Christian group (*Encuentros Cristianos*) and from those who would utilize the pastoral message for solely political purposes. Clearly the church of the poor is a force for political change, just as Jesus and his disciples preached and acted for political change. However its spirituality and charism cannot be sacrificed for a political commitment to liberation. Only if the poor, which means primarily lay, indigenous and marginalized people, control the direction, character and structure of the church of the poor will the movement maintain its vitality.

The possibilities, however, for cooperation between the institutional church and the church of the poor is at a new stage. The Episcopal Conference of Guatemala (Catholic), with the appointment of a number of young Bishops, has shown an openness to work with popular organizations and faith-based groups such as the Campaign for Peace and Life and Guatemalan Christian Action. That relationship may deepen. Likewise, the prophetic actions of the Protestant churches through CIEDEG and their commitment to stand by and learn from the poor gives an opportunity for closing the distance between denominational structures and the church of the poor.

The new directions for the newly reborn church of the poor still are difficult to determine. Among many indigenous Christian activists there are tremendous hopes that the church of the poor can facilitate a process which happens within the indigenous communities and which leads to an indigenous-oriented theology and pastoral work. The Catholic Church hierarchy has already taken great strides in this area with the Pastoral Letter on the 500 Years and the establishment of a *Pastoral Indígena*, but perhaps the church of the poor is even better placed to bridge the gap between indigenous concerns and Catholicism. Particularly with the resurgence of indigenous pride and culture, particularly Mayan traditional religious beliefs, on one hand and with the theology of the liberation of the poor on the other, the church of the poor could help heal the decades-long animosities between Christians and *costumbristas*. There is a tremendous potential in what Guatemalans refer to as the *cuestion étnico*, the indigenous question, which if untapped could further the liberation of the indigenous people. An indigenization of a theology of liberation (or theology of life) offers one path for the future.

The challenge of the church of the poor is not just to offer consolation to growing numbers of people dispossessed, but it is also to ground the Gospel message of liberation in a social context. The clamor for the land presents itself as one such context. Already peasants are organizing around local and regional issues to reclaim the land which was stolen from their ancestors, but so far the efforts have lacked the cohesion, vision and unity to bring off a national movement. Earlier experiences have shown that if the Church backs those who are struggling to gain plots of land, it can help mobilize and consolidate a growing movement.

It is for Guatemalans to work out the course for the growing church of the poor, but whatever direction it takes, the experience will offer the rest of Latin America new models which express the faith of the people and demonstrate the Church's commitment to the poor in their desperate struggle for life.

FOOTNOTES:

[1] Documentation from "Caminos de Silencio, a 1989 film produced by Felix Zurita."

[2] Fernando Bermúdez, *Cristo Muere y Resucita en Guatemala.* Later published in English by Orbis. The reference to the "Church of the Catacombs" should not suggest that the people disassociated from the Catholic Church and that this expression of Church was outside of the Catholic faith. Rather, Army repression forced practice of Catholic religion into clandestinity.

[3] JIm Handy, *Gift of the Devil: A History of Guatemala* Boston: South End Press, 1984), p. 238.

[4] Luís Samandú, Hans Sieber and Oscar Sierra, eds., *Guatemala: retos de la iglesia católica en una sociedad en crisis* (San José: DEI, 1990), pp. 71, 75.

[5] Author's interview, May 1991.

[6] Priests and nuns active in Catholic Action have described their experiences in detail in an unpublished manuscript entitled *Quiché: su pueblo y su iglesia (Una Experiencia Pastoral 1960-1980) [Quiché: Its People and Church (Pastoral Experience from 1960-1980)]*

[7] EPICA interview.

[8] Cited in *De Indios y Cristianos en Guatemala*, Rafael Mondragón. Claves Latinamericanos (Mexico City: 1983).

[9] Ibid.

[10] Promoters of Catholic Action were constantly being accused of introducing "communist" ideas to the peasantry. In Santa Cruz, for example, residents who sympathized with the Army maligned the road building projects sponsored by Catholic Action. One catechist involved in the project remarked in an October 1991 interview with the author,

> [The Army sympathizers] denounced us for building the road and the bridge. They said Communists would be able to drive into our village and to steal our children and to close down our churches. They said Fidel [Castro] had paid for the roads. At first many people believed them. They thought Communism was a big baby-devouring monster.

[11] EPICA interview with Fr. Luís Gurriarán.

[12] Author's interview in May 1991 with Fidel Hernández, a Sacred Heart priest formerly working in El Quiché.

[13] *Guatemala: retos de la iglesia católica,* p. 81.

[14] At that time the newly founded Christian Democrat party did not have the reputation for corruption and elitism which it earned through the 1980s.

[15] Schools such as the Escuela Normal para Maestro de Santa Cruz, Instituto Básico Obispo Marroquín in Chichicastenango, Instituto Indígena Santiago in Guatemala City, Instituto Femenino Santa Cecília were either founded in the 1970s or graduated their first class of indigenous youth during that period.

[16] For documentation on the development of Catholic Action in Estancia, please see two sources: "This Is Our History," (a 14 page testimony by a catechist and CUC leader) in *Guatemalan Indians: Beyond the Myth,* Guatemalan Church in Exile (Managua: 1984); and "The Story of Santa Cruz Quiche," by Robert M. Carmack in *Harvest of Violence,* Robert M. Carmack, ed. (Oklahoma: Univ. of Oklahoma Press: 1988).

[17] *Guatemala: retos de la iglesia católica,* p. 83.

[18] *Guatemala: retos de la iglesia católica,* pp. 83-84.

[19] The Guatemalan Church in Exile, *Martirio y lucha en Guatemala.* Mimeograph. p. 61.

[20] *Quiché: su pueblo y su iglesia,* p. 40.

[21] Author's interview.

[22] F. Hernández refers explicitly here to a model of Church which benefits from close relations with the State and, in turn, which legitimates the State.

[23] *Educación: Desafío y Esperanza,* pastoral letter from the Guatemalan Conference of Bishops, April 19, 1987. Cited in *La Iglesia en Centroamérica,* (Mexico City: Centro de Estudios Ecuménicos, 1988).

[24] Communiqué from the Diocese of El Quiché, "Al pueblo católico de El Quiché." Cited in *Guatemala: retos de la iglesia católica,* p. 61.

[25] Author's interview, April 1991.

[26] For example, the testimony of a young catechist follows

> The soldiers come to our village and search all the houses. In a few homes they find Bibles. They tear the pages out, stamp on them, burn them on the ground in front of the owners of the houses and catechists and they tell us, "If you keep with this, the second time we'll kill you. You have to stop [with this stuff] of the Bible."

In *Cristo Muere y Resucita en Guatemala.* p. 28.

[27] Author's interview. November, 1991.

[28] The CEG denounced in May, 1982 for example: "Not even the lives of old people, pregnant women or innocent people were respected. Never in our history has it come to such grave extremes."

Mexican Bishop Samuel Ruiz of San Cristóbal de las Casas, Chiapas, was even more outspoken. "There is genocide [in Guatemala] I collected the testimony of refugees giving proof of it." He went on to describe the massacre of San Francisco, Huehuetenango which killed all but 12 of the village's 350 people.

[29] IGE, "*Ofensiva del Pueblo: Campesino contra Campesino,*" July 1989, p. 15. ·

[30] One international visitor who sat in on a math lesson in the CPRs in the Ixcán during September 1993 reported the following exchange. Teacher: "Students, why do we need to study division?" Students: "So we can learn how to divide things equally in the community."

[31] "El catequista a los hermanos refugiados en Chiapas," by Ricardo Falla, SJ in *Christus. 1986.* The Guatemalan Church in Exile (IGE by its Spanish acronym) was formed in 1980 following the closure of the Diocese of El Quiché and has served as a center for documentation on human rights issues in Guatemala.

[32] Author's interview with catechist from the communities in resistance of the Ixcán which took place in San Cristobal, Chiapas in Mexico. April 1991.

[33] "*Carta de un agente pastoral,*" Ixcán, January 11, 1988. Mimeograph.

[34] One catechist in the refugee camp spoke proudly of collecting 3000 nylon bags and $5,000 from the refugees in the camps to donate to the Communities in Resistance. Author's interview, October 1991.

[35] For example, in January 1991 the CPRs of the Ixcán issued "A Declaration to the Government and People of Guatemala and to the Governments and Peoples of the World" which read, in part,

> The different life in the jungle forced us to learn new things. We had to unite and develop systems of self-defense for the protection of our homes and farm plots. We had to learn to build refuges, to cook during the night, to warn all the communities when the Army approached and to flee in an organized form when it was necessary. We had to learn to work collectively on the plots and in raising fowl, to share the fruit of our work to feed the orphans, the widows, the old people and those who serve the community, just as the early Christian communities did in Acts 2:42-47. We learned to overcome fear!

[36] Author's interview. April 1991.

[37] Interview with Ricardo Falla, SJ, by Joe Nangle and Jeff Shriver for *Sojourners* on March 2, 1993.

[38] *"Pastoral de la resistencia,"* by Ricardo Falla, SJ in *Siglo XXI,* February 14, 1992.

[39] Ibid.

[40] *Guatemala: retos de la iglesia católica,* p. 110.

[41] Just days after the Bishop of El Quiché, Monsignor Julio Cabrera, had returned from his first visit to the refugee camps in southern Mexico where he pledged his support for the politically controversial refugee return, an agronomist working with the Social Secretariat of the Diocese of El Quiché was murdered. A U.S. nun, Diana Ortiz, who was part of a pastoral team in Huehuetenango working in the indigenous communities, was raped and tortured by Guatemalan security forces. In Guatemala City, the Church has acted cautiously in its work with marginalized and displaced persons yet still has exposed itself to reprisals. In November, 1991 the Dominican House in Guatemala City was broken into twice by assailants who left death threats against the Superior, Sr. Alba Méndez Cabrera, because of her work in assisting the displaced. One of the Dominican sisters has subsequently left the country because of the threats.

[42] Spoken at Guatemala Strategy Meeting in Washington, D.C. on July 31, 1993.

[43] *Plan Global de la Conferencia Episcopal de Guatemala,* cited in *Guatemala: retos de la iglesia católica,* p. 46.

[44] *Plan Global,* p. 29. Cited in *Guatemala: retos de la iglesia católica,* p. 158.

[45] Or for example, pastoral letters from individual bishops. For example, the Bishop of Escuintla wrote in his diocesan pastoral letter *Unidos en la Fé*

> No one feels secure and satisfied while there exists in the prelature of Escuintla a single family without housing, a farmer without land, a laborer without work, a child who does not attend school, and the sick and elderly without medical attention.

Cited in *La iglesia en Centro América* by Colectivo de Análisis de Iglesias en Centroamérica (CAICA), (Mexico: Centro de Estudios Ecuménicos, 1991), p. 41.

[46] *Guatemala: retos de la iglesia católica,* p. 158.

[47] On his first visit to the CPRs of the Sierra, Monsignor Cabrera called the communities "God's special people." Monsignor Ramazzinni is the CEG designated liaison with the CPRs after Defense Minister Mario Enriquez' statement calling the CPRs "an instrument of subversion," Ramazzini accompanied a delegation of CPR representatives to meet with President de León Carpio in September, 1993.

[48] Author's interview. July, 1989.

E̲L S̲ALVADOR

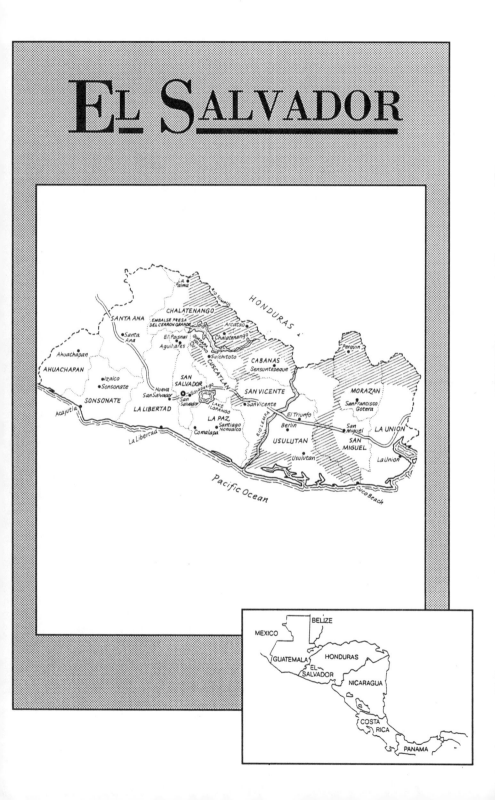

Older woman who lives in the repopulated communities in the Department of Chalatenango protests against the abuses of the Salvadoran Army.

Repopulated Communities in El Salvador

Martha Thompson

S an José de Las Flores is a small town in the Department of Chalatenango, one of the most heavily conflictive areas of El Salvador. In July 1981, the Salvadoran Air Force bombed and launched rockets against the community, and then the Army invaded, burning everything and killing everyone the troops could find. Most villagers escaped, grabbing their children and a few clothes, and hid in the ravines. The town was left deserted and in ruins. Only destroyed buildings and a few, scattered belongings remained.

Two years later in July 1983, the villagers began to gradually return to the community. Still, they lived in hiding, careful not to show any sign of habitation that could be detected from the air. With help from the FMLN, they began to democratically elect their leaders, form literacy groups, and establish communal work that permitted their survival.

In January 1986, the Army reappeared in San José de Las Flores and occupied the community. The residents attempted to hide in their bomb shelters but were starved or flushed out. The soldiers rounded up the people and turned them over to the International Red Cross who sent them to a church-sponsored refugee camp.

Six months later, one hundred people who had been forcibly displaced in January triumphantly returned to San José de Las Flores in a caravan of buses, accompanied by international delegations, press and solidarity groups. They repopulated the town claiming their rights as civilians who live in a conflict zone. They set up self-governing structures and communal enterprises. Within a few weeks, 300 others who had been hiding in the surrounding hills joined the repopulated community.

During the celebration of the fifth anniversary of San José de Las Flores in June 1991, the military once again entered the community, this time in the presence of international delegations, popular organizations from San Salvador and journalists who were attending the celebration. Community leaders demanded that the Army leave. One of the officers yelled back. A journalist approached, and the officer threatened to shoot him. The crowd began to jeer, and the officer fired a volley at the church wall right above their heads, another volley at their feet. Enraged, the people rushed the soldiers who retreated but not before releasing tear gas at the people.

More than Just Victims

In the early 1980s Army massacres and Air Force carpet bombings nearly destroyed El Salvador in an unsuccessful attempt to eliminate the guerrilla insurgency. The war took the lives of more than 100,000 people and deeply marked nearly every Salvadoran. This story is about the survivors, such as the residents of San José de Las Flores who fled the massacres and bombings, who lost family members, farms, possessions and crops, who lived like hunted animals hunted by the Army. They survived, but they saw friends and relatives killed, children hanged from the rafters, old people who could not flee hacked into pieces with machetes. They experienced things which most people can not even visualize, and they survived to give the history of what they lived. Their story, however, is more than survival.

In the midst of the conflict, the refugees and displaced returned to their deserted and bombed communities, rebuilt their homes and developed a new way of life in the midst of war. They planned reconstruction projects, they organized ways of governing themselves and sharing community responsibility, and they experimented with ways of working together. They insisted on their right as civilians living in zones of conflict and denounced the military's violations of their human rights. The returnees could not end the war, but they did build a new life within it.

When the war ended in January 1992, the repopulation movement continued to pose a challenge to the government. No government services existed in the conflict zone, so the repopulated communities formed their own local government and provided services based on grassroots participation. The former refugees and displaced people began to believe in their own worth and ability to think and act for themselves.

How did the changes in San José de Las Flores and other communities in conflictive zones happen? How did civilians, hounded by soldiers and forced from their homes, seven years later confront those soldiers and even defy the Army's attempts to capture community members? How did campesinos who had lived much of their lives treated by the government as if they were expendable, as if they did not deserve education, health care or respect for their human rights, begin to plan and develop communities based on grassroots participation, defense of human rights and collective responsibility?

Transformation took place, both at an individual level on the part of the returnees and at a social and structural level. Repopulation meant rebuilding destroyed communities in the war zones, but it also meant re-creating the sense of community among a people torn by war. The people in the repopulation movement not only wanted to return to their homes but they also wanted to re-create the communities in a new mold based on justice and participation rather than based on the old unjust system.

The refugees and displaced people who were involved in repopulation underwent an inner transformation. They changed their conception of themselves, their rights, their capabilities and their relationship to those who had power. They viewed what had happened to them in the war in a new way. They saw themselves no longer as helpless victims but as people who have rights and capabilities, as people who could respond collectively and not just as individual victims. The vision of the repopulation movement is necessarily a vision to transform Salvadoran society. Thus, repopulation is a transformation process at two levels: an inner transformation of the displaced as a response to the forces of war and oppression, and secondly, a social change movement formed as a response of the poor and oppressed to long-standing structural injustice.

DISPLACEMENT: A CATALYST FOR CHANGE

Repression to Maintain the Status Quo

Since colonial times, the legal and political structures in the country have been based on maintaining power through repression. For the powerful sectors of Salvadoran society, the lives of the poor and marginalized have little human value and, therefore, killing them poses no moral dilemma. On a deeper level, the wealthy elite fear the poor because they know their privilege rests on their ability to monopolize the majority of the resources in the country. The elite are afraid that education may help the poor majority to wake up and begin to challenge the status quo. Therefore, the elite have to enforce the status quo with repression, making the cost of protest too high for the poor. The wealthy in El Salvador have been convinced that if people are terrorized, they will remain docile. The Army and the security forces (the National Guard, Treasury Police and National Police) have kept order, repressed dissent and protected the wealthy while forcing peasants off their land and onto large plantations to work at starvation wages.

Social and political tensions over the economic, social and political injustice in El Salvador broke out in the 1970s as opposition to the military government spread into the middle classes. The presence of armed guerilla groups (which in 1980 united to form the Farabundo Martí National Liberation Front-FMLN) in parts of the countryside by the early 1970s brought increased military control. By 1977 the security forces and paramilitary squads such as ORDEN were apprehending people in daylight, torturing and killing them and leaving their mutilated bodies in the roads as warning. Community leaders, in particular, were targeted. Villagers were reluctant to go to neighboring towns where they risked being branded as supporters of the guerrillas. The following testimony by the widow of a Catholic catechist (known locally as a "delegate of the word") gives an idea of life in the countryside in the department of Morazán in 1979.[1]

> The last time I saw my husband he went to the market to buy some salt and rice. He never returned. At the convent the nuns told me that the military had captured my husband. The nuns were frightened for me and my eight year-old son. They told us to run home, pack and leave. They helped us through the back door into an alley so that they wouldn't see us. I began running with my son. It was getting dark and I couldn't keep running, but my little boy kept saying hurry, hurry. We were so scared, I was crying, and then at the highway, we saw a body, a shirtless man in blue pants who was missing one arm. I just wanted to give up, but my son pulled me on.

Not only peasant leaders, but anyone who opposed the military government–or was suspected of doing so–was in peril. An average of over 1,000 people a month were being killed or disappeared by the military regime. Priests, teachers, lawyers, reporters, union leaders, university students, health workers, and literacy workers were all death squad targets. Between 1979 and 1984, the most intense levels of death squad activity, over 36,000 civilians were killed.

"Scorched Earth:" A Deliberate Policy of Depopulation

The government's aim was to eliminate the FMLN. However, in the northern areas of the country where the FMLN was the strongest, the military waged war predominantly against the civilian population. "Scorched earth" tactics meant killing any person or animal left behind and burning houses and crops. Why did the military target civilians? The military wanted to eliminate the social base for the FMLN which provided information and logistical support. The policy of the Army was to destroy food and water sources, housing, ground cover, and other infrastructure--anything which the FMLN could use to survive, which also meant anything which supported the civilian population. Furthermore, the military wanted to make an example of what would happen to anyone suspected of supporting the guerrillas.

Depopulating areas where the FMLN operated was an essential part of military strategy. Beginning in early 1980, huge military operations moved into the Departments of Chalatenango, Morazán, Cabañas, Cuscatlán, and La Union, all areas where the guerrillas were active. At first people in the communities stayed in their homes hoping that the Army brutality would not reach them. But as more and more communities were eliminated, thousands of people fled. Those who have survived, including a Chalatenango woman who gave the following testimony, have agonizing stories to tell.[2]

> We were in the kitchen when we heard the helicopters coming up the valley. I grabbed my baby, my small children--one was fetching wood so he didn't come when I called. I didn't know what to do--I was crying, I didn't want to leave my chickens and a little calf--but a man called to me, "Forget the chickens. They'll kill you as well as the chickens. Run!" he said. I ran pulling the children, calling for Rutilio, the missing one. We found other people who took us to hide in a cave by the river. We hid there for four days and suffered horribly with so little food and water. We were close to the river but it was dangerous to go for water because if the soldiers saw anyone, they would kill them.

> We could smell the smoke of the fires set by the soldiers. We could hear them walking around, yelling, looking for people. They found an old man hiding and, with one slash of the machete, they cut off his head. We had to cover the mouths of the children with clothes so that the soldiers wouldn't hear them crying. After the Army left, we asked ourselves, what do we do? Go back to our houses? A man told us that everything was burnt, that there were so many bodies. He was crying. We started to walk into town... everything we saw was burnt, the animals dead...

> All of a sudden fighting was all around us, the bullets, the soldiers running after us. I thought I was going to die. My child was shot and he fell. I tried to stop, to call to the others, but they ran ahead. My son died in front of me. I was crying when a man pulled me on, telling me to run. I ran past two little children, both fallen and bleeding, but we couldn't stop--I had the baby in my arms, and he was pulling my hand. What happened to those little children? Later, we found the others. My other two children were there, and I had the baby in my arms but I was so sad--Rutilio lost, Enrique shot while running beside me.

> We started walking again, now we were a big group of people, walking at night. Walking and walking for two weeks. We took water off the leaves of the plants and chewed grass for food. What little we did find to eat made us sick. Some of the children died from either hunger or disease. After a long time we arrived to the Sumpul River and crossed into Honduras. After suffering so much, we finally made it to the refugee areas.

This testimony, like any one of thousands, reveals what people had learned from the war against them. Those who fled joined together in groups to survive; they hid in the mountains together; their lives depended on strict discipline, on obeying and trusting the leaders who emerged, on sharing food and water, on making decisions–often as agonizing as leaving behind wounded family members--based on the good of the group. This experience, like no other, welded people together. They realized that they could survive united, but that unity had to be based on cooperation and trust.

Counterinsurgency: Civilians as Military and Political Targets

By the end of 1983, the Salvadoran military was in serious danger of losing the war. The country was in chaos. Despite the massive displacement of the civil population, the FMLN was gaining military and political strength. The Army atrocities against the population did not deprive the FMLN of political support; it only provoked outrage and increased support for the FMLN. One campesino farmer who joined the FMLN in 1981 remarked, "Yes, we took up arms, of course, they were killing us like animals. They just kept on killing us. If we had not joined the FMLN, there would not even have been anyone left to bury the dead."

By 1983 the United States had given tens of millions of dollars of arms to the Salvadoran government to wage the war. U.S. military tacticians began to look for a different plan to prevent what looked like defeat for its ally. They designed and implemented an overall strategy of low intensity warfare. This meant far more than a purely military strategy. It was an effort on all fronts: social, political, diplomatic and military. The U.S. put forth a comprehensive social, economic and political model in order to have an alternative to the revolutionary plan advocated by the FMLN. The Christian Democratic Party, under President Napoleon Duarte, agreed to the plan of framing elections and democratic rule around a counterinsurgency effort. Elections were held, and a new Constitution was written. Mild economic reforms were introduced, and every effort was made to build the Christian Democrats as a safe alternative to the FMLN. El Salvador became characterized as a fledgling democracy.

At the same time, the military war intensified. Newly U.S.-trained Salvadoran officers alongside U.S. military advisors converted the large fighting battalions into small roving patrols and intensified the air war against rebel-held territories. This time, the military actions went hand in hand with a political objective. Not only was it necessary to deal with the military strength of the FMLN, it was necessary to confront their political strength and win over the population which supported the FMLN. The strategy for depopulation was modified. The goal was still to depopulate the war zones by ground operations and massive bombing. The difference was that the population would be brought under the control of the military and the government.

U.S. military advisors helped the Salvadoran military design a strategy based on removing the population from FMLN territory and into government control and on winning their hearts and minds. The strategy consisted of four steps. First of all, it was necessary to physically separate the civilian population from the guerilla forces by carrying massive air war into areas where the FMLN was active, thereby forcing the remaining civilians to flee. When the civilians persisted in remaining despite the massive bombing, the military frequently went in by helicopter, rounded them up *en masse*, and took them to centers for displaced people.

Secondly, it was necessary that the Army keep the displaced dependent on government and military administered assistance through civic-military programs. The Army also tried to prevent any projects that would help the displaced find an independent way to resolve their own problems.

Thirdly, when areas of the country had been regained by the military from the FMLN, the displaced would be resettled in these areas under the control of the military and the government who would provide the assistance in a comprehensive aid program.

And lastly, once resettled, the population would be compelled to aid the military with logistics and information about the guerrillas.

A TRANSFORMATION PROCESS

Of the hundreds of thousands of displaced persons, those who actually began the repopulation movement came from either the church-sponsored refugee camps in El Salvador, the U.N.-sponsored refugee camps in Honduras or from the civilian population who remained in the conflict zones and survived by constantly fleeing Army invasions. Each experience contributed to transform the displaced persons' own conception of themselves and their capabilities. Although these three situations were very different, they shared common elements, including: the brutality of the displacement that made people question what was happening to them, the mutual dependence people developed in order to survive, and access to outside influences, such as the non-governmental organizations (NGOs), the churches and the FMLN.

Learning to Use Testimony and Advocacy

> Monsignor Romero first said things that no one else was brave
> enough to say. We couldn't say those things. Who would believe us?
> Who would care? So he said those things and when he did, he said
> he was speaking for those without a voice. Now Monsignor is dead
> and can no longer raise his voice for us, but you see, we are changed.
> We have found our voice. --Former refugee, now a catechist

In the twenty-five church-sponsored camps which housed thou-sands of people, the displaced began to comprehend how to "fight back" against the violence. The San Salvador refugee camps were accessible to Church officials, humanitarian agencies, human rights workers, visiting delegations, and reporters who began to visit to gather informa-tion on what had happened in the countryside. The displaced began to understand the concept of human rights as an issue, and the word "testimony" entered their vocabulary. They began to know of organi-zations which documented and denounced violations of human rights.

Likewise in the refugee camps in Honduras, the refugees provided constant up-to-date information unavailable anywhere else on the situation in the war zone. They understood that human rights observers and others would use their testimony to denounce the violations. Seeing that they were important in the eyes of other people made the refugees begin to see themselves in a new light. Hearing each other's testimony, they learned that they were not alone and that what happened to them was happening on a massive scale.

The refugees began to see the direct link between bringing human rights violations to the attention of international human rights groups and gaining greater protection for themselves. By the mid-1980s, whenever there was an incident between the Honduran military and the refugees, the camp leaders would take the testimonies, send information out to international agencies and press the UNHCR to exert international pressure. They had begun to think in a new way; they could have some effect on what happened to them, and they could, in some measure, protect themselves.

Moving toward Self-governance

In the refugee camps in Honduras, the feared security forces and the traditional municipal authorities were gone, replaced by sympa-thetic representatives of NGOs and the UNHCR who encouraged the refugees to elect leadership. In all three Honduran camps--Mesa Grande, Colomoncagua, and San Antonio--the refugees chose leaders who could represent them *vis a vis* the NGOs and the UNHCR. When these leaders had to deal with authorities such as the Honduran army or Honduran government, the refugees found support from the international community. In the Church-sponsored camps in El Salvador, the refugees also elected representative leaders.

Moving towards self-government was a long process. Many displaced persons were uncertain of their ability and worried about criticism from the rest of the community. Some had experience as delegates of the word, health promoters or cooperative members, but in the camps, their role was different. Formerly, community leaders challenged the traditional authorities; now in the camps they were the authority. They had to set up the system. Being a leader meant learning to overcome shyness, speaking out in meetings, making agendas, resolving disagreements through discussion and opening a channel of communication between the community and the NGOs, the Church and the UNHCR. The leaders set up schools and health services, established community structures and organized life in the camps.

The absence of externally-imposed authority also meant that the leadership had to find a way to deal with anti-social behavior. In a refugee camp, the mechanisms of punishment were limited largely to community pressure. On the whole, the camps were very self-disciplined communities, but alcoholism, robbery and abuse did occur. In Mesa Grande, there was an experiment with a jail for problem cases. The women in Mesa Grande developed a system for alerting each other about men who were drunk and for undertaking a "citizen's arrest" to jail the offending party.

Learning to Discuss and Strategize

Historically in El Salvador, the security forces never distinguished between discussion and dissent. Members of ORDEN spied on community meetings for the military and "fingered" leaders for repression. Within the relatively protected environment of the camps, people could freely talk about their experiences, compare notes, reflect together and even speak out against the government without fear of reprisal.

In both the Honduran camps and the Church refugee centers, women formed mutual support groups to reflect on what had happened to them and to forge a community identity. In these groups, they shared experiences of the war, their flight, their anguish of losing their children, husbands or other family members, of losing their homes. Within the groups women could comfort each other; the groups also served to help them interpret what had happened to themselves. It was a place for women to understand themselves and their situation.

Group discussion and participatory decision making were the tools used to forge community and to resolve problems at all levels. Few problems were too small for group discussion. The camps were divided into sub-camps which in turn were divided into groups of tents. Discussions took place at each of those levels, and the conclusions were communicated through representatives. The following incident is an illustration of how community discussion and participation was used as a tool to resolve the issues of everyday life in the refugee camp of Colomoncagua. The refugees had received kettles to boil water and water jugs to store boiled water, but there were not enough for every family. The discussion focused on how to distribute what there was. "Do you agree to this plan, or do you want to change it?" asked the representative of a subgroup of houses, referring to a plan to share kettles to boil water for multi-family houses. Some women put up their hands and suggested that people will fight over who gets the kettle, shouldn't there be a rotation of the kettles? Everyone agreed. One woman said that she thinks people should be able to report back to the head of the subgroup if there were any problems. Others disagreed, afraid it would be a source of too much tension. Another woman suggested that they should pick someone in each house to be responsible for the use of the kettle. Some people thought that no one would want that job, "too much hassle." Others disagreed, and eventually, they took a vote, and the majority decided to try the rotating system and discuss it again in a month.

This kind of discussion was part of the patient, pebble-by-pebble approach to grassroots participation with which the refugees built their new structures. This process was time consuming, but the campesinos learned that each person had valid opinions about all aspects of life, that each had a right to express themselves and then the majority would make decisions. People could disagree with each other without reprisals, and, for them, this was a new experience. Each refugee was committed to the outcome because he or she had an active part in the decision. Whether kettles, water jugs or other issues, the refugees used the same painstaking process of discussion, participation and community decision-making for all issues that affected them.

Learning to Work Together

As displaced in the camps and the conflict zones, people were uprooted and placed in situations where the accustomed cycle of basic grain production and seasonal work on the plantations was gone. The challenge to survive was acute, and cooperation was essential for survival. In the church centers in San Salvador, in order for large groups of people to live in extremely crowded conditions for years, they needed to develop strict community organization to carry out the everyday tasks of feeding, sleeping, recreating, schooling, etc.

For civilians who remained in the conflict zones, life was completely reorganized around surviving Army invasions and, from 1983 on, the massive bombings which made El Salvador the most heavily bombed country in Latin America. The goal of the military was to make

Thousands of Salvadorans were born in the refugee camps in Honduras during the ten year period. Most of the refugee children had never experienced anything but the refugee camp before their return to El Salvador.

life in these areas impossible, and so civilians avoided the bombed-out shells of the former towns or villages. Any sign of life--a whole roof, clothing hung out to dry, freshly-planted corn--provoked air attacks. In order to survive under these conditions, the population had to be highly organized. Everyone had a task and understood that the individual survived only if the community survived.

Of all the groups, the refugees in the camps in Honduras had the best opportunity to develop a model for community work. They were not living in the war zone, and they had more room, freedom and resources than the displaced in the Church-sponsored camps in San Salvador. The refugees first developed a democratic, self-governing structure similar to the Church camps, with slight variations. The camps were divided into sub-camps of 1-2,000 people each. In turn, these were divided into groups of houses. Each group of houses elected their coordinator. These group coordinators formed a sub-camp council and elected two representatives to the overall camp council. The camp council ran the camp, conducted general "town meetings" to discuss issues and dealt with outside authorities.

The refugees also developed a participatory economic and social structure. They divided up community life into the areas of health, nutrition, workshop production, agriculture, animal husbandry, construction, sanitation, water, children, women, education, and goods distribution. In each sub-camp there was a coordinator for each work area or sector who responded to coordinators in that particular sub-camp. Teams were developed in each sub-camp to assume responsibility for each area. They received training from other refugees or from NGOs in their area of responsibility. Everyone received food clothing and supplies to meet their basic needs.

There were fewer men than women so there was a real need for women to participate in community affairs in a way they had not done before. Daycare centers and community kitchens run by refugee women freed other women to go into production, teaching, healthcare, goods distribution or coordination tasks.

The exceptional circumstances of their exile made communal work a pragmatic, not ideological, choice for the refugees. It was a learning process. They experimented, used what did work and jettisoned what did not. Community production was encouraged because it solidified the community and seemed to be a system which gave the majority the most equal access to resources. The community work process helped people see that they could work together more effectively than they could working alone. Community work was emphasized because it was useful, but it soon became the framework for looking at a new vision of society based on sharing of resources and providing for the needs of the community as a whole.

Learning New Skills: the Refuge as a School

Particularly in the refugee camps in Honduras, but also in the San Salvador camps and in the conflict areas, many of the displaced had access to education and training for the first time. When the refugees first arrived in Colomoncagua in 1981, they were estimated to be 80% illiterate; when they returned to El Salvador, 80% of the population was estimated to be literate. In Honduras the refugees had the chance to learn skills ranging from making their own tools to making their own clothes. Through the workshop programs they eventually learned how to make almost everything they used. Young people started to ask that they be put in different workshops to learn different skills. In one Colomoncagua sub-camp, twenty boys under fourteen made all the utensils for 2,000 people. Women began to learn carpentry and mechanics. People learned health care, literacy teaching, typing, warehouse administration. In later years, the refugees, who had been illiterate upon arrival six years earlier, requested training in planning, administration, accounting and computer use. One leader of the refugee camp at Mesa Grande said, "We were farmers. We didn't know that we could do all these things--mechanics, carpentry. It seems as if we have done a pretty good job, looking at this camp."[3]

As years went on, the refugees saw their skills as ones that would be necessary in a new society, to help them provide for their own needs and lessen their dependence on people from the outside. As a refugee in one of the workshops in Mesa Grande put it, "We want to use our time here to learn something, so that when we go back we can help rebuild our country."

Learning Advocacy

In the refugee camps in San Salvador and Honduras, the refugees became acquainted with the world of international humanitarian relief efforts through the agencies working in the camps. They learned how to negotiate for resources with the agencies and churches supporting them. In Honduras, the refugees had to deal with the UNHCR for their relief program and their security. When the refugees first arrived to Honduras, they were grateful for the assistance and protection of the UNHCR given all that they had suffered. Over the years, as collective discussion and reflection in the camps matured, and the refugees made their own plans about their work and experimented with self-government and grass roots participation, they began to question and disagree with the UNHCR over policies and work methods particularly around security and protection issues.

These conflicts led the refugees to develop a whole series of non-violent protest methods directed against the UNHCR: petitions, letter campaigns, marches carefully planned for the visits of high-level delegations, hunger strikes, and the composition of witty songs, poems and popular theater on the current controversies. For the refugees, the situation offered a protected environment in which they could develop methods to express their opposition, with less harsh retribution than expressing opposition would have brought them in El Salvador. It helped them demystify "authority."

In both Honduras and El Salvador, the refugees related to international agencies and solidarity networks. They learned about developing letter campaigns and giving their testimonies to delegations and visitors. This turned out to be an effective method of gaining financial support, material resources, and political advocacy from international groups. Both sides realized the importance of this relationship and worked on communication within their networks.

All of these experiences helped the displaced begin to recognize themselves as human beings with full rights and capabilities. The practices of reflection, discussion and community work helped them to grapple with new ideas, engender greater participation and make decisions agreed on by the majority in the community. The experiences with training gave them more faith in themselves and their abilities. They realized that they held in their hands the capacity to solve some of their basic needs. The experience in self government made them decide they could not return to the old type of life and power structures. The experiences with the agencies and the UNHCR showed them that there were resources available to which they could get access. They learned how to discuss and negotiate and how to use advocacy.

Other Displaced Persons: Dispersion and Government Camps

The majority of the displaced had a very different experience from those in UNHCR or Church-run camps in Honduras and San Salvador. They lived either as dispersed displaced or in government-run camps. What distinguished most dispersed displaced from the marginal communities they joined was that they were severely affected by the shock, loss and violence they had suffered and had no way to deal with the trauma. Unlike the refugees who had gone into the camps and experienced solidarity with other refugees, the dispersed tried to hide by blending into the population at large. Fear was the motivating factor. At that period in El Salvador, anyone from the conflict zones was identified by the authorities as a participant in the conflict. The displaced had to lie about where they were from, change their names, and train their children to repeat fictitious personal histories. The personal cost was high. As one campesina woman who was displaced in San Salvador commented,[4]

> Do you know what [the military] took from us? We lost our husbands and our sons, and we could not even say the truth about who killed them. We had to lie and say that the guerrillas killed them. We lost our husbands, and we could not talk about it.

In 1981 and 1982 hundreds of displaced persons every week were pouring into the larger towns and cities seeking security and a way to survive. The government as well as the churches set up feeding stations. As the war continued, the groups of people who received this emergency assistance grew into permanent concentrations of displaced often set up as camps. The camps bred distrust, trauma, apathy, division, and a state of paralysis. People could not speak openly for fear of the wrong person overhearing. The military was closely involved in the distribution of aid and selection of NGOs to work with the displaced.

THE RIGHT TO RETURN

Organizing among the Internally Displaced

Low intensity conflict, as the war strategy came to be known, was a war for "hearts and minds." For the Army and the government, this meant the need to control groups and institutions in civil society. Groups independent of the Army and government were suspect and seen as susceptible to infiltration and control by the FMLN and, therefore, illegitimate. Any groups opposing government policies regarding the war were illegal. Under these parameters, any displaced person who was not under a government program of assistance would be seen as a potential supporter of the FMLN. For example, the displaced civilians who opted to stay in the war zones were characterized by the government as guerrillas and treated as such. As well, the Catholic Church and some of the Protestant Churches came under suspicion and persecution by the government because they insisted on providing support to displaced persons in a way that was independent of government programs. This provided the displaced with an alternative to the civic-military programs.

Until 1984, the churches were the only institutions publicly raising their voices on behalf of the displaced. Church leaders were also becoming increasingly concerned about the dependency patterns developed by the refugees within the camps. The churches felt that the camps, once seen as temporary shelters, were becoming permanent. The churches' decision to relocate refugees was an impetus to greater organization among the displaced who wanted to return under their own, not the Army's and not the church's, conditions.

The Formation of CRIPDES

The first organization of the displaced and refugees inside El Salvador was the Christian Committee of Displaced Persons in El Salvador (CRIPDES, by its Spanish acronym). One of the founders of CRIPDES, who presently serves on its Coordinating Council, spoke at length in June 1992 about the organization's formation.

> In 1984 the Catholic Church in San Salvador operated fourteen refugee centers. There was still a lot of repression, but the Church wanted to close down the refuges and relocate people to the countryside because the Church thought the refuges were not a good way for the people to live. The refugees were worried, and there was a lot of communication between the people in the different refuges. On July 14, 1984 we held a forum involving four hundred families--all refugees--to talk about the Church's decision to relocate us and decide what to do. We decided to form an organization of displaced to talk about our problems, to find a way together to solve our problems and to see if we could return or look for other rural areas to live in. We formed CRIPDES.
>
> The alternatives we proposed were: join other communities, join cooperatives, or relocate to abandoned lands near conflict zones such as the department of Usulután. We elected a coordinating committee which had committees in the different church-sponsored refuges.

Over the next two years, the churches shut down all but one refuge and moved the people into cooperatives, communities in Usulután or new communities. CRIPDES committees worked in all these new communities. Their promoters from the refuges helped form the community councils, developed the community work plan, and helped people look for solutions for health problems. There were CRIPDES committees in all the new settlements. Soon, the CRIPDES promoters began to reach out to the dispersed displaced in different parishes and nearby communities.

As the displaced relocated, CRIPDES helped organize the displaced into local coordinating committees to petition and distribute food and medicine, facilitated health and literacy training and represented the displaced, seeking emergency assistance from churches and humanitarian institutions. They denounced human rights abuses against the displaced. They trained leaders in the communities, and the leaders promoted discussion within the communities about the search for solutions. Through its creation CRIPDES was a forum for the displaced and the refugees in the church camps to meet, discuss and analyze their problems. By 1986 CRIPDES coordinated work in 27 displaced communities in four departments. CRIPDES also began to work in urban communities and to assist displaced people move onto abandoned land in the eastern part of the country.

CRIPDES was a turning point for the internally displaced. The displaced moved from being victims of the war towards taking action about their situation. They responded to the proposal to shut down the refuges with their initiative of organizing themselves for resettlement. CRIPDES broke the silence about the government policy of forced displacement in conflictive zones with marches, religious services and denouncements published as paid advertisements in the newspapers. In the midst of the counterinsurgency war, CRIPDES insisted on the right to protest the government policy of forced displacement and to pressure the government for a solution.

Grassroots Organization Vs. Low Intensity Conflict

The work of CRIPDES was directly opposed to the military strategy of low intensity conflict. Low intensity conflict is based on maintaining geographic, political and psychological control and on keeping the population dependent on the government and the military for protection and subsistence. Col. Wagelstein of the U.S. Southern Command in Panama succinctly described the strategy saying, "The most important territory to hold in a guerilla war is the six inches between a peasant's ears." In counterinsurgency war, civilians are seen as either under the control of one side of the conflict or under the control of the other. At the most fundamental level, low intensity conflict strategy negates the concept that civilians can ever be neutral or that civilians have rights. The military aspects of the war become political, and the political aspects, such as assistance to displaced, are militarized.

As part of counterinsurgency, the government had its own plan for repopulation, called United to Reconstruct. It involved forcibly removing the civilian population from contested areas, securing those areas militarily, then bringing in displaced people under civic-military assistance programs and forming a civilian defense patrol against the FMLN. Not surprisingly, the government saw CRIPDES as an organization in direct opposition to its own agenda. CRIPDES was labeled as an FMLN organization by the government and military, and its leadership and members were subjected to constant harassment, intimidation, capture and torture. On more than one occasion their office was searched and ransacked by the military. Despite the vast obstacles, CRIPDES continued to grow and to gain strength as a voice for the organized displaced.

The work of CRIPDES, however, did not halt the Army's campaign to displace civilians in the conflict zones. Mass bombing and a number of large-scale military operations in the northern part of the country characterized the last months of 1985 and the first months of 1986. By January 1986, the number of displaced had risen to an unprecedented level of half a million. On January 10, 1986 the government launched the most concentrated displacement campaign of all, Operation Phoenix, in the departments of San Vicente, Cabañas, Usulután and Chalatenango. In one area alone (the Guazapa volcano located only 39 kilometers from El Salvador) over 1,500 civilians were forcibly removed.

The Search for Permanent Alternatives to Displacement

The first permanent solution for the displaced was the repopulation of the town of Tenancingo, a project sponsored by the Church and FUNDASAL.[5] The repopulation occurred after Church negotiation with both the FMLN and the government. The initiative came from the Church and agencies, not from the displaced themselves, but it nonetheless demonstrated that repopulation was a legitimate solution, and that civilians had an internationally recognized right to return to their homes even in the war zones. It also demonstrated that financial resources existed for repopulation, and that the Church was willing and able to pressure in favor of the displaced.

In May 1986, CRIPDES called a national conference to discuss the overall situation of the displaced. CRIPDES members decided that the only durable solution for the displaced was to return to their homes in the conflict zones. El Salvador had signed the Second Protocol of the Geneva Convention which guaranteed civilians the right to live in zones of conflict and bound the government and military to respect that right. Repopulation was seen as a legitimate right and adopted as a political position and policy of CRIPDES. As a result CRIPDES formed the National Coordination for Repopulation (CNR) to promote and facilitate future repopulations.

The First Community Repopulations

Although the military did not foresee it, the Operation Phoenix in 1986 took on a connotation reminiscent of its classical meaning, a bird rising out of the ashes. Civilians who repopulated their homes in the conflict zones were the same people whose homes had been burnt to the ground and bombed during Operation Phoenix. The people had been forcibly displaced by the operation and placed in the Church refugee camps together with the refugees who had already learned about human rights abuses, agency resources, and the potential of church support with the displaced. They both had experiences in types of self-governance, community work and discussion as a means to community participation. The people from the conflict zones did not want to wait in a refugee camp for the war to end, they wanted to return to their homes. They started mobilizing immediately. A member of the

CNR executive council, tells the story of the San José de Las Flores repopulation.[6]

> If the people were to return alone or in secret, the military could capture or kill them since it was a zone of conflict. The people wanted to return publicly, to request safety, to have the right to plant their cornfield. That's why they took over the Cathedral in San Salvador, to make their demands public.
>
> We in the CNR, took on the public advocacy role, and the churches provided the quiet support. I don't think that the military wanted the repopulation to happen. We got funding to rent buses and organize a big caravan. That first day they put up so many checkpoints. At each they stopped and searched us, but they couldn't send us back. We had too many people with us, too many press, too many internationals. Here was President Duarte talking about democracy, liberty and human rights, and here we were making a big public return. The people also had a lot of confidence they would succeed. How could they stop us?

The first community repopulation to San José de las Flores opened a door into the conflict areas closed off by the war. The audacity of the repopulators and their wide national and international support caught the military off guard. In a few weeks, the hundred or so repopulators were joined by several hundred civilians who had remained in the zones, and they began the process of rebuilding the community. The military set up roadblocks to limit access to the area, to delay assistance and in other ways harass the community, but the return had been too highly publicized for the government to deny there were civilians returning to the zones.

A similar repopulation to El Barillo from the Calle Real refugee camp in August 1986 was also successful. When a third attempt was made to repopulate San Carlos Lempa in the Department of Usulután, the military resisted and detained the people. In that case, the repopulators had underestimated how important the logistics and international support were to overcome military opposition. It was too late, however, to stop the repopulation movement. The two successful efforts showed that community repopulation in the midst of war was, in part, a solution.

Filter-up Repopulation in Morazán

On the other side of the country from Chalatenango, in the northeastern department of Morazán, another kind of repopulation was taking place. The Torola river formed a natural boundary separating the northern part of Morazán which lay under the control of the FMLN from the southern part under the control of the Army. The infamous 1981 Mozote massacre, where over 1,000 people in the area were taken out of their houses by the military, shot and clubbed to death, was illustrative of the campaign of fear and terror that caused most civilians to flee this area. Nonetheless, some people stayed, hiding out from the military operations, planting corn in forgotten hollows, and receiving food and medical aid during the occasional Red Cross visits.

Throughout the early years of the war, other groups of displaced people would quietly return north across the river to cut coffee around the Perquin area or check their homes. In 1984, family by family, a small number of people began to return, filtering north gradually, joining those who had stayed, eking out a living that was marginal but better than life as displaced. There was an internal self-selection process as only people who had not had problems with the FMLN made the decision to return to areas controlled by the FMLN.

By 1984, the military in the area began to realize that small groups were returning to an area they had taken great pains to depopulate. By this time, the Army's options were more limited. Widespread use of scorched earth tactics in conflict zones was no longer politically viable because it would threaten the flow of international aid, particularly from the U.S. The military altered tactics and began to stringently enforce an economic blockade of the area. When the people would come south with fruit or wood to sell, the military would often confiscate their goods at the checkpoints or threaten them. When people passed the checkpoint on their return to northern Morazán, the military would limit their quantities of basic goods or confiscate them. The Army also continued to bomb the area, burn crops, capture and kill people in isolated areas.

The newly returned population learned survival techniques from the few who had hung on during the war. To avoid the bombing raids, people farmed in even more remote areas and dug trenches for shelter. The more that the Army moved to displace the people, the more the communities turned against the military and began to regard the FMLN more favorably.

A major concern, besides survival, was education for their children. In most of the repopulations in northern Morazán, community organization formed first with the schools. Most communities formed Parent Councils for the schools, built rustic classrooms and contributed small amounts to pay a literate community member to teach their children to read.

The turning point came in late 1985 when the military tried to displace the community of Nahuaterique, an isolated town near the Honduran border which had never been depopulated throughout the whole war. The community's resistance to displacement was due in large part to its social organization, primarily its strong Parent Council for the school. The military was not able to cow the villagers into leaving in 1985, and this news quickly spread to other towns. More communities decided to form community or school councils. Those councils often took the step of representing the community in confrontations with the military. The community school councils found support from the FMLN which gave political orientation to the groups and from two Catholic priests who worked in the area. The priests worked with the community councils and also helped form parish councils and train delegates of the word.

The First Mesa Grande Repopulation

While people were filtering back to northern Morazán and the community repopulations were taking place in Chalatenango, the refugees across the mountains in Honduras waited. Penned up on the windy dusty plain that was the Mesa Grande refugee camp, 11,000 refugees were waiting for the war to end before returning, but the repopulations in Chalatenango and Cabañas made a tremendous impact on them. Like striking a match to a bonfire, the idea of returning home spread through the tents and wood houses of Mesa Grande. The refugees began assembling a strategy to return which formed the basis of all subsequent repopulations. The principal elements were:

Returning to their places of origin. Anything else would mean returning to become displaced within their own country. They selected five main sites to which they could return: Las Vueltas, Los Ranchos and Guarjila in Chalatenango, Santa Marta in Cabañas and Copapayo in Cuscatlán.

Community repopulation. Repatriation in large groups would improve their protection which was a grave concern of theirs, particularly since the government considered them FMLN supporters or subversives.

Rights as civilians in conflict zones. The refugees claimed their rights as civilians based on international human rights and humanitarian law.

International Support. The refugees strategized that one of their guarantees of safety lay with their ability to convince the government of sustained international support for the return.

The national and international churches and the NGOs initially expressed reservations about the refugees' decision. The two community repopulations that did exist were still fragile enterprises and the conflict zones were still largely cut off from the rest of the country. Nonetheless, the churches and the NGOs made the decision to support the refugees' proposal acknowledging the refugees' right to propose their own solution. The UNHCR, too, supported the refugees' insistence on returning to their places of origin and on returning in community knowing that the refugees were determined to return, with or without UNHCR participation.

The Intransigence of the Salvadoran Government

By September 1987, nine months after their first request, the refugees were losing patience with the process and the delays from the Salvadoran government. They announced to the UNHCR, the government and the Church in El Salvador that four thousand refugees had taken the decision to return to El Salvador to their chosen sites, on October 10 with or without government approval or the support of the UNCHR. If they were not let into El Salvador to go to their places of origin, they would camp out on the border until their demands were met. They carried out their preparations and packed as if everything were settled. From all sides–foreign governments, agencies, human rights groups, churches and solidarity organizations, the Salvadoran government was pressured to allow the repatriation.

At 10:00 pm on October 9, the Salvadoran government capitulated and agreed to let the refugees cross the border. At 5 a.m. the following day, a hundred buses pulled out of Mesa Grande carrying 4,000 people, and bus by bus, the refugees arrived to the border. After heated negotiations over the route, documentation, and accompaniment, the refugees completed immigration forms and crossed over into El Salvador. The joy and achievement of their return was a sharp contrast to the helplessness and anguish of their forced departure nine years earlier.

The October 1987 repatriation from Mesa Grande was followed by the following community repatriations: 2000 people repatriated from Mesa Grande in August 1988; 2000 people repatriated from Mesa Grande in October 1988; 1,500 repatriated from Mesa Grande in October 1989; 8,000 people, the entire camp of Colomoncagua, repatriated during November 1989 and the first three months of 1990; 1,400 people, the entire camp of San Antonio repatriated in March 1990; 500 people from Mesa Grande repatriated in April 1990; 500 people from Mesa Grande repatriated in April 1992.

Each community repatriation, especially those in 1988, 1989 and 1990 was negotiated with difficulty and tension between the government, the UNHCR and the refugees. Each followed the same general pattern established by the first Mesa Grande community repatriation. They used the skills in negotiating they had learned in the refugee camps, and that process helped to strengthen the community organization they had built in the camps. They had left El Salvador fleeing as hunted animals, hiding at night, eating what they could find, seeking refuge as victims of the war. When they returned however, it was on their own terms. They were no longer victims.

Relationship with the FMLN

All of the first repopulations were in conflict zones which were more or less controlled by the FMLN (some of the later repopulations were in areas through which the FMLN passed but which they did not completely control). This deeply influenced the repopulations. The FMLN would not permit people to repopulate who were hostile to them or whom they considered security risks. The FMLN enforced a type of frontier justice in the area which included the prohibition of alcohol and the right to evict people if they saw necessary.

Most of the people who returned supported the political platform of the FMLN; they believed in the need for political, economic and social structural changes to improve their situation. The FMLN encouraged the types of community leadership and participation which was taking place in the repopulations. The repopulated communities saw the FMLN as a force sympathetic to and protective of them. The people in the communities were convinced that the presence of the FMLN in the conflict zones kept the military from wholesale attack against their communities. The presence of the communities also benefitted the FMLN. The communities broke the isolation that the FMLN had experienced during the mid-1980's. But the priorities for survival for the communities were not always identical to those of the FMLN. This generated a great deal of discussion between the FMLN leadership and the community leadership.

AN ALTERNATIVE MODEL

By 1987 the presence of high numbers of organized civilians living in conflictive zones with international support had made massive depopulation untenable as a military strategy. The repopulations, organized on the basis of political participation, local control of resources and a recognition of their members' humanity, abilities and rights, were a threat to the established status quo. Their new social, political and economic structures challenged the historical relationships of unequal power among the different classes in El Salvador and increased the military's need to develop tactics to de-legitimize and harass the repopulations. The military wanted to prevent more repopulations from taking place and to isolate the communities which existed, but they also wanted to prevent the success of the new collective model.

Conditions of the Repopulated Communities

The sites of the first repopulations were abandoned and over-grown. There were no health or education services, no transport communication, no utility services, in fact, no presence of the state at all. The zones were under the political and military control of the FMLN. There were also no landowners, wealthy elite, "*coyotes*," mayors, state security or paramilitary forces. One of the refugees who repopulated his home in San Antonio Los Ranchos recalled the day they arrived.

> Snakes in the houses…I remember when we came back there were just snakes and trees growing in the houses. We had to begin from nothing. Just what we brought and our determination. We had to send teams of men to clear the road with machetes. We've repaired the roof of the school so the children can learn something. The government would never send us a teacher or a doctor, and even if they did the military wouldn't let them through. We have our own teachers from the community. We have our own healthworkers. The mayor, he's in San Salvador and afraid to come back here. Now we have the community council. Some of the houses have been bombed and are destroyed, but others still have a roof. We agreed on who would take which house. Some are the houses belonged to rich people. We weren't allowed in those houses before. Now we live in them.

The repopulations had to provide their own health and education services, produce their own food, and rebuild the community infra-structure including the houses, school and water system. They needed transportation and a basic system of commerce and they desperately needed financial resources. Moreover, the returnees had to deal with the war itself, and the military's additional efforts to prevent the repopulation movement from taking root.

They had, though, certain advantages: newly-developed self-confidence, the absence of the former oppressive authorities, a commonly shared commitment to work together, and the strong encourage-ment of the FMLN to create new organizational structures. The majority of the people who returned were very poor--which eased the class differences that communities had experienced previously. The isola-tion of the communities in the war zone both made life difficult, but also provided space for people to develop political, economic and social structures to replace what had disappeared.

Political Organization

"The former mayor was only here to steal and fill his pockets," remarked a community leader from northern Morazán in March 1992. Before the war, the rural towns in El Salvador were almost always dominated by the mayors, its few wealthy residents and landlords, and the security forces. By 1982, the war forced most of the mayors to abandon the towns located in conflict zones.

In contrast to the former model of organization, the repopulated communities built a governing system involving grassroots participation based on the models experimented with in the refugee camps or in the conflict zones. An education worker in Teocinte, a repopulated village in Chalatenango, described in April 1992 how their local government worked.

> Our community, has a *directiva* (council) elected by the general assembly (town meeting). We have a President and a Vice President. Representatives are elected for the areas of health, education, discipline and projects. The *directiva* meets every week and makes decisions. When there are problems, we have an open meeting and everyone votes. We began with a combination of communal work and individual work, four days a week on the communal land and three days a week for their family plots. The widows and old people got food from the communal land.
>
> There is an education team that organized the school. The health team works with the regional health association and provides health care for other communities. When we first came, the community teams worked together to build the houses and the community buildings. We established a community store, and the profits go for community expenses. Agency and solidarity money finances the health and education work and community projects like cattle raising. When we have community projects like road repair or work on the water system, everybody works together. When there are discipline problems, it's discussed in meetings.

Experimenting with New Economic Models

> We all have our own cornfield, but we work together to get the credit for the fertilizer. Every family works on the community-owned coffee harvest. We use that money to pay for the literacy work.   --Perquín community leader in January 1991

From the beginning, communities operated on the basis that all members of the community had equal right to land, credit and other resources needed for production. Generally, access to land--a central cause of the war--was not a major issue in most of the repopulated areas. Since the population was still much smaller than the pre-war population and the large landlords were all gone, abandoned land was available for the community members in the conflictive zones.

Credit for production was the next priority. Traditional sources of credit--the "coyote" lenders and the banks--had been either chased out or were too scared to enter the repopulations. The communities needed access to an alternative credit source and alternative commercialization methods. They looked to sympathetic international NGOs for grants, credit, agricultural inputs and technical assistance.

In the departments of Cabañas, Cuscatlán and Chalatenango the initial repopulations involved thousands of people. The communities organized collective methods of production, dividing the work week into four days on the collective fields and two days on the family plots. Goods from the collective work were sold, people were paid for their labor, and the profits invested back into the community and the productive enterprises. A percentage of the profits and the produced goods was allotted to the widows, the old and other vulnerable members of the community.

Particularly in the area of basic grains production, there was not enough surplus to make this system viable, and as time passed, people began to invest more effort into their individual plots and less into the communal. Fewer days in the week were dedicated to communal production and more days dedicated to individual production.[7] Presently, the trend in repopulations seems headed towards satisfying basic family subsistence needs through individual production and community needs through community production. In addition to basic grains, most of the repopulated communities have developed workshops which produce clothing, tin products (pots, pans, cisterns and grain bins) and animal husbandry projects (pig, poultry and dairy cows). Generally the projects have been funded by international agencies, and the community has provided all the labor. The products are distributed according to community consensus with products such as milk, for example, going to the vulnerable population or to school children. This system makes it difficult for any one or two families to gain economic dominance by providing goods that require capital investment which other people cannot afford. So far these projects have not proven to be self-sustaining and remain dependant on outside funding.

The model posed by each repopulated community differs to a degree; Segundo Montes[8] in the department of Morazán, for example, looks more to semi-industrial development (trade workshops, small factories) because of the high concentration of the population and the poor quality of the land, while the Chalatenango repopulations are much more agriculturally oriented. Broadly speaking however, the communities are similar in that they challenge traditional economic structures and economic assumptions. For example, the community assumes a responsibility to donate labor to provide for the vulnerable members of the community. In Morazán, the communities donated labor to communal coffee production and logging enterprises in order to earn greater profits to be used for literacy programs in the communities. The community council provides a democratic decision making structure for both economic and political power. The person in charge of production or projects is part of the community council so the issues are discussed by the community in general assembly. Community control of resources, land, labor, inputs and distribution are decided by the community. This reinforces the relationship of the individual to the community and makes it difficult for individuals to control any one of these aspects in order to gain disproportionate economic power.

The repopulation model combines communal areas of work, namely production, commercialization and purchasing, with individual work which makes people less vulnerable to economic exploitation from the outside. Developed in the absence of the traditional power structures and outside of the economic mainstream, people have been allowed to put their new skills, learned as refugees, to use. A commonly accepted assumption that the specific production skills of an individual should be shared to benefit the community prevails. Access to outside funding remains a key ingredient to this model of an economic alternative.

Social Services

> These people are *chusma* (rabble), its no good giving them anything. They live in filth and wouldn't know how to care for anything you gave to them. They wouldn't know what to do with education. --A wealthy woman in San Miguel[9]

> Campesino, lift your head up! / You are also a human being / Don't humble yourself!　--Song used in literacy courses in the refugee camps in Honduras

In El Salvador where 48% of the population is illiterate, there exists no demonstrable commitment on the part of the central government to educate its poorer citizens.[10] Health services in the countryside are scarce; health centers in the bigger towns cost a few *colones* but it is often more than a campesino could pay. The earnings from seasonal labor could get swallowed up by buying medicine for one child.

The repopulated communities understand that human rights include the right to education, healthcare and daycare, and they have attempted to provide these services in their communities with some success. This has been achieved because of three factors: community leaders have made providing services a priority, the community leaders have had training as literacy teachers and health promoters in the Church refugee camps, and they have had access to resources to pay for providing services. The experience in the refugee camps has provided a backbone of trained health, literacy and daycare workers to the repopulated communities. Many repopulated communities have made education and health care one of the ways to reach out to the surrounding communities which were cautious of contact with the repatriations and the repopulations. The neighboring communities saw that the health and education work was being carried out by campesinos just like them, and not by doctors and nurses and teachers from the government ministries. The majority of the funding came from agencies and solidarity groups, but some support comes from the profits of the community projects. The dependency on outside funding for social services continues to be a problem. However, the fact that people feel that they have a right to such services reflects a marked change.

Regional Community Organizations

> Three things united us: the repression, the need to work together to survive and the need to bring order out of the destruction caused by the war. At first we returned in small groups with each community on its own, but this didn't work because of the repression. The military could just isolate and pick off each community. We had to be united to survive the repression. --Council President of San Fernando, department of Morazán[11]

The repopulated communities quickly learned that their survival was linked to their unity. The communities in different regions began to work together and share problems held in common. Dealing with the military was a catalyst towards building regional organizations. One of the community leaders in northern Morazán explained how they began to coordinate.[12]

> In 1986 after the military had captured some of our people, we had to talk with the Colonel about their release. We were scared to go alone. So leaders from five other communities joined us. Then all the community councils started to plan work together. We began to clear a road together, then repair the water system and so on.

In Morazán, the original five communities learned that together they could press a common agenda with much more strength than as an individual community. The community councils in the area began to meet to discuss strategies about how to respond to the military campaign to displace them, how to deal with the economic blockade and how to improve life in the area. In 1987 the community councils in the repopulated communities in the Departments of Morazán and San Miguel formed a regional organization, PADECOMSM, composed of representatives from different communities. The PADECOMSM council began to go to the military to negotiate when people were captured or when the military would not permit lumber trucks into the area to purchase lumber harvested by the communities. Not only did PADECOMSM get permission for the lumber trucks to pass through military checkpoints, they also won the right to tax the lumber in order to pay salaries of the community literacy teachers. By 1988 there were 62 communities in PADECOMSM.

A similar experience of regional coordination was happening in the other repopulated areas of Chalatenango (with the *Coordinación de Comunidades de Repoblados*-CCR), Cuscatlán and Cabañas (with the *Comunidades Repoblados de Cabañas y Cuscatlán*-CRCC). The regional organizations were a framework for representative self government and a structure within which to articulate and address their common needs. The coordinated groups defended the rights of the people in their communities, formed a body to negotiate with the military, and provided a forum of discussion for regional policy, services and economic initiatives. They quickly began to seek assistance for their communities, linking with NGOs working in those areas. In some areas they organized services, in others they provided the organizational framework. From their initial role as spokespersons for the communities in the conflict zones, they evolved into vehicles through which economic and political life, protection and social services were organized.[13]

The regional community organizations were all based on community representation on a regional council such as the CCR in Chalatenango. Each community council in Chalatenango elected a president and all the presidents of each community met at the regional level once a month. This meeting of the community presidents elected the regional leadership, the executive committee of the CCR. On the CCR executive committee, there was a president, vice president, secretary, treasurer and a coordinator for each area of community work, health, education, production. Each community council also had a coordinator for each work area. This provided a dense network of inter-relating structures that provided input and discussion at a series of levels for planning and implementing projects. Each community's representative to the CCR linked the community concerns into the regional agenda and brought the regional level discussions to the community. Most of the regional community organizations combined regional and work area representation, integrating political accountability and popular participation in service provision.

The repopulation movement was built on community strength, but it was not centered solely on the community level. A regional network made economic planning more feasible and offered the sharing and coordinating of resources. It provided a much bigger scope to plan from at all levels and a greater possibility to organize self-sufficiency. It was much more effective in terms of defending their rights than each community would have been on its own. It also helped people understand the difference between improving one part of their life in one community and the need for transforming society.

The Dangers of a Good Example

> The people in communities which haven't been repopulated look at us now. Before the war started we were the same. We didn't have anything, and they didn't either. They saw us hunted, they saw us flee into the mountains.

> Now we have come back, and they see that we have a clinic, we
> have our own school, we have the cooperative, and people are
> learning to sew and make shoes. There is the daycare center, we have
> the community car. They don't have anything. And they ask "Why
> is it that you people who were running to the mountains to hide,
> now you are back and you have done all this? --Member of the
> Community Council in Las Vueltas[14]

The success of the CCR, the CRCC and PADECOMSM was not lost
on the surrounding communities. The regional organizations sent health
and education workers to offer services to other communities. In
Arcatao, Chalatenango and Torola, Morazán, campesinos came from
Honduran communities for health services. The Santa Marta repopulation
in Cabañas shared their tractor with other communities in the area. The
regional organizations invited other communities to form community
councils and integrate them into the regional meetings. The CCR has
been particularly successful at bringing new communities into the
regional overall structure and sharing self-governing skills learned in the
zones and the refugee camps. Although the military worked to defame
the regional community organizations, the work with new communities grew slowly, sharing problems and benefits and building on
common ground.

When the repopulation movement began to develop, they not only
became dangerous to the completion of counterinsurgency war, they
became a danger to the historic myths that rationalize the structure of
Salvadoran society. The fact that the repopulation communities are
hammering out a vision out of practice, experience and experiments for
a new society makes them dangerous to anyone seeking to maintain the
status quo. Campesinos from one valley demonstrate to other campesinos
in the next valley over that they can successfully reorganize economic
and political structures, rebuild a community, govern themselves, adopt
new work projects and even confront the military. The example
explodes the prejudices that justify the injustice.

The Military Response to Repopulation

The repopulation movement made the military's practice of forced
depopulation of the conflict zones no longer viable. It removed the
displaced from the dependency on the civic-military assistance programs that were a central element for the success of counterinsurgency
to a situation of greater independence. Not surprisingly the military
employed a whole series of tactics aimed at weakening and destroying
the repopulation movement. The military patrolled the repopulations,
established checkpoints, requested documents and searched people.
They tried to limit the access of outsiders to the area. Without any legal
basis, the military required that the communities apply for written

permission to bring every shipment of food, building materials, fertilizer, medicine, tools, etcetera, into the conflict zones. They delayed vital supplies for days or weeks which set back planting or construction.[15]

The military also frequently threatened or captured community members and leaders. Within two years of the formation of PADECOMSM, every member of its Coordinating Committee had been captured by the military, some beaten and tortured, all subjected to food and sleep deprivation and psychological pressure.[16]   The military frequently attempted to isolate the repopulations by characterizing them as terrorist or subversive and warning other communities not to have contact with the repopulations. Moreover, the civilian communities were treated as military targets. Bombing, mortaring, grenade launching, and rocketing occurred frequently in the vicinity of the communities and sometimes in the middle of them. According to the military, if the FMLN was present in or near the communities, attacking the communities themselves was legitimate.

The Community Response to Military Control

The military harassment pushed the communities to develop strategies of survival to defend their rights. More than any other factor, the development of these strategies served to weld a collective strength in the repopulated communities as they saw that they gained ground bit by bit against the military. The first community repatriations confronted these difficulties using their knowledge of human rights and non-violent resistance which they gained in the camps. The repatriations were, therefore, initially more assertive with the military than the other repopulations, but their example soon spread. Their strategy was simple but effective: confront the military when their rights had been violated, call public attention to the incident and mount collective action in the defense of individuals. They refused to be silent in order to survive. When the military entered Segundo Montes in August of 1991 and killed 500 chickens, Army officers certainly didn't expect the people of Segundo Montes to react as they did. The community threw the 500 dead chickens in a truck, drove down to San Francisco Gotera and dumped them all in front of the 4th Detachment.[17]

Demanding Their Rights as Civilians

Throughout the war a steady but subtle media censorship existed in El Salvador. Bombings, mortaring and the daily effects of the war in El Salvador were not covered in the news unless the military was claiming a victory or denouncing an attack by the FMLN. Beginning in 1987, the popular organizations placed paid announcements in the newspaper to publish protests against the government. In a few cases, some radio stations allowed community members to speak on the air protesting bombings or captures. This brought the direct experience of the war to the attention of the urban population as well as to the diplomatic corps and the press. It also publicized the existence of organized groups of civilians in the conflict zones, refuting the military's claim that there were only guerrillas in the conflict zones. Once the press and other groups in the city began to know people who lived in the conflict zones, they reacted quickly when incidents happened.

The organizations in the repopulations worked with lawyers in providing grass roots training on human rights issues in the communities. Campesinos learned how to gather all the necessary evidence and to make formal denouncements with the human rights offices. By 1988 people were smuggling testimonies about bombing, killing or torture, down to the capital. By 1990 some groups were using computers and faxes to send information to the capital and around the world.

Compared to 1980 when one thousand Salvadorans a month were being killed by the security forces and death squads largely without the knowledge of the international community, a decade later a barrage of international protest would be directed at the military when it captured a community leader in the repopulations. A key link between reporting and protection was provided by the rapid-response networks utilized by the press, members of the diplomatic corps and the church networks in the U.S., Canada and Europe. The following incident is representative.[18]

> After I was in my cell for two days they took me to see the Colonel. He was very angry. He was throwing some papers at me. "Who do you know in the U.S.?" he shouted. "How is it that all these people know you are captured? They are sending these telegrams here." He was very angry, but after four days he let me go. He said that too many people were making a fuss.

The human rights reporting and rapid response networks did not eliminate the repression or human rights violations, but they raised the political cost for the military. People continued to be captured or beaten, but there was less chance the person would be killed or disappeared and more chance that he or she would be released.

Direct Confrontations with the Military

> "You have no right to treat me like that!" -- A Community Council member from Segundo Montes to a soldier at the Army garrison in April 1990

From the beginning, the community organizations sent delegations to negotiate with the local Colonel, either to permit goods to come or to make protests over captures. Every time they went to talk to the military, they gained more confidence, and the concept of military power became a little more demystified. An important factor in this process was the presence of the UNHCR in the repopulated areas. The UNHCR accompanied community representatives to meet with the military. Many of these same military officers had participated in the massacres and scorched earth tactics. Now they had to sit down to talk with the communities and the UNHCR.

When a nine month-old girl was killed in a military attack near one of the communities in Chalatenango in January 1992, thousands of people from the repopulated communities marched on the provincial capital, in the first public demonstration against the military that town had seen for ten years. The townspeople, who literally live in the shadow of the barracks, were amazed to see that the campesinos had the courage to protest against the military. Said one townsperson,

> There hasn't been a mass demonstration here for almost ten years. People have been too frightened. And now, this. All these people marching in the streets, right in front of the barracks. We thought they would fire, but they didn't.

Townspeople also saw that the protesters were sometimes beaten or captured but that they continued to struggle over these issues. This was dangerous for the military. Fear was a traditional means of social control. When people lost their fear, the use of fear lost its power.

None of these tactics could have succeeded without the courage of the people involved. It was not the courage of a night or a day, but an enduring courage to face the fact that one might have to pay with his life, his health, or the life or health of a family member at any time. This courage was grounded in a deep understanding that the goal was greater than the individual, and that no one's individual action would achieve the goal. But if everyone would struggle despite the risk, they would bring the goal closer. After the entire PADECOMSM leadership had been captured, many having been beaten or tortured, one of leaders commented,

> We were targeted because they thought they could stop [the movement] like that. And what did they find out? The people went right on organizing. Now they know that they can't stop the people by capturing the leaders.

PROBLEMS OF THE ALTERNATIVE MODEL

Working in Community

Working in community is not an easy option. Problems arise when people expect benefits from the community, like food rations, without being willing to work for the community. The community model also restricts the individual. Participation in decisions means that everyone has to abide by those decisions. Individual initiatives have to be checked out with the community first. Outside visitors and offers of assistance are channeled through the community council. The challenge is finding the best balance between the restriction of personal freedom and the survival/improvement of the community. The repopulated communities are still experimenting and learning.

The struggle to form communities demands a great deal of effort and investment. For collective models to succeed, members of the community need to clearly see that the advantages outweigh the disadvantages. The need for demonstrability of success applies to economic systems as well as social systems where social problems are addressed in a collective way, altering anti-social behavior because it clearly affects the well-being of the community. A woman community leader from Arcatao gave this example.[19]

> Many men have five or six children with their wife, and then they want to be with a new woman, and they leave the first woman and their children. Before the war, if a man wanted to go with a new woman, he would throw the wife out of their house. Now in the communities, if he wants to go with a new woman, he must leave his first wife in the house, he can't throw her out. But he leaves her and doesn't take care of the children who become the responsibility of the community. The man decided to do what he wants but the community pays.
>
> When one man did this, we women talked and we said to the council they would have to put this case in front of the general assembly. I spoke up and said, "If a man wants to go and live with another woman, shouldn't he take responsibility for the children, or does the community have to support them?" The older men said, "We've worked all our lives, and now we are providing for the children of those men who take it into their heads to go off with another woman. We have to stop this." So the community took a vote, we decided that if a man left his woman and children to go off with another, he had to continue to support his children or leave the community.

Economic Dependency

The repopulations have been able to develop extensive community infrastructure (schools, housing, latrines, roads, bridges and daycare centers), and economic enterprises (basic grains, livestock and light industry workshops) but it has been dependent on considerable external funding. This offered relative independence from the Salvadoran government but not economic self-sufficiency.

Deep questions revolve around the sustainability of the economic initiatives developed in the repopulations. At this point they are very dependent on outside funding. Obviously, the heavy subsidizing of the production model is not economically feasible even in the mid-term. Developed outside of the existing credit and banking systems in the country, the economic model of the repopulated communities still needs to integrate more comprehensively within the national market if the model is to be viable. The communities purchase agricultural inputs from and sell their goods in the national market, but to a large extent the local repopulated economies are still economic islands. What are the indications that the government will grant these communities access to credit, technology, and resources? What can these communities produce and market that will bring them into the national market system as real players? Are their enterprises profitable? The true viability of the repopulated community model is still to be seen.

Unless access to resources for the campesinos is addressed at a national level, there is a danger that the repopulated communities, if they do achieve self-sufficiency, will remain economic islands in El Salvador and not reproducible models of economic justice.[20] One of the CCR leaders touches on that point:[21] "Our struggle cannot be only for the repopulations, the structural injustices in the economy must change. We are not just talking about making life better for us, it has to be better for all of the poor." The problem is that the kind of resources that were available to the repopulations are not available to the majority of the campesinos in the present economic structure in El Salvador. The economic mode of most campesinos is bare subsistence, not consumption or surplus production. Production of basic grains is at best marginally viable, and without access to low interest loans, cheap fertilizers, good land, technical training and markets there is little chance that small farmers will prosper in or outside of the repopulated communities.

Social Services: Who Pays?

In one meeting in Las Vueltas, the health promoters were discussing how much they work: 2-3 days full time service in the clinic, plus a night of duty every week, 4-5 hour walks to visit patients, meetings every two weeks with the other health promoters in the regions, monthly training sessions on weekends and trips down to the capital with hospital-bound patients. They provided free health care to the community, but they were not paid and had almost no time to earn a living. How were they supposed to survive?

The community didn't have the resources to pay the social service providers, nor did community members have sufficient cash to pay for services to sustain the healthworkers. But the community needed and demanded healthcare as a right, regardless of income. In the end, the community opted to solicit outside funding for stipends for the promoters. This does not completely solve the problem, however. Other community members work almost full time for the community and are not paid. The community needs their work but cannot support them financially.

This illuminates a structural problem in El Salvador. If everyone agrees that the poor have a right to basic services, how are they paid for? The repopulations took a big step forward in asserting that they had rights to these services, and they took another step forward in discovering their own ability to provide many of these services. The unanswered question is what responsibility society has for providing those services or guaranteeing an economic level that enables people to purchase them. If people cannot earn a living wage, they cannot pay for health care, child care, social security or education. If people cannot pay for services, their only chance of getting access to them is if the state or other entities provide them free of charge. If the state provides resources for those services, will they agree to do it through the grassroots structures? Where will the popular health worker or the popular literacy worker be in all this?

The Role of Women

Poor women in El Salvador have been traditionally an oppressed sector within an oppressed class. This is deeply embedded in culture and politics, economics as well as social relations. Displacement and repopulation created certain conditions which forced women to take on different roles. Many more women were heads of families and had to assume economic responsibility when their husbands went to war, were killed or disappeared, or left the country. In the refuges, women outnumbered men, and the scarcity of adult labor necessitated that they take on new work. In the refuges women were trained as seamstresses and pottery makers and also as carpenters, shoemakers and mechanics. They became camp leaders and spokespersons.

The communities found that the women were extremely effective in confrontations with the military. When the military came to capture people, the women in the community dispersed, surrounded them, remonstrated against them. From 1988 on, 90% of the leadership of the CNR were young women. The women leaders in the communities learned to negotiate and confront the military, providing new leadership role models for the second generation. The women also shared the resultant capture, torture and beatings.

The repopulations brought certain positive changes for women, especially opening access to leadership roles and to learning new skills. However, women continue to bear some of the heaviest burdens of work. The number of single mothers continues to be high, and their ability to earn a decent living with basic grain cultivation is limited. They usually have to pay a laborer to work the family plot and share the harvest with him. Women have less education than the men and are often completely economically dependent on their husbands. Some daycare for women working outside the home has been provided by the community through outside subsidies, but it still has not solved the problem for all of the single mothers. Women in the repopulations have been able to articulate their problem, but until now, there are still too few solutions in the form of policy being put forward in the regional community organizations.

"During the war, we put up with everything because we had to survive and because we believed that things would change. We haven't seen that much has changed for us," said a woman in Las Vueltas community in Chalatenango in June 1992 addressing the issue of women. A fair policy towards women which takes into account their exceptional circumstances and special needs, both gender specific and caused by the war, will be essential if the repopulations want to build on the advances that were made for and by women during the repopulations.

Power and Authority

The traditional concept of power in El Salvador seems to be that power exists to be abused. There is almost no historical tradition of using power for the benefit of the powerless. In the past, the "patron" or the boss had absolute rule over the conditions of the lives of the poor. When that concept is enforced by violence with no recourse for the people and no one to support their rights, there is little hope for change. The repopulations sought to form new ways of structuring power, consensus, justice and accountability. It takes a long time, though, to change how people think. Sometimes community members had a hard time accepting other campesinos as their leaders simply because campesinos were not associated with roles of authority. A continuing challenge for the people is to see power as something everyone is responsible for.

Among the leaders, there was a strong temptation for them to take advantage of their role to make their life marginally better. Traditional models of power show that the person with authority uses some of that power to make his own life better. Structures such as the Community Council and General Assembly in which the leadership is accountable to the community serves as a check in this system. However, the success of this check depends on the community's willingness to speak out.

The interplay between the potential for abuse of authority and the community's control over it depends on the community's confidence that protest will not bring reprisals. If someone on the community council has hit his wife or if his child does not work, the community members have to feel they can bring it up in the General Assembly, that they can criticize and question the leadership without retribution. Likewise, the leaders have to learn that freedom to question and to criticize paves the road towards cohesion. Since societal control in El Salvador has been historically built on controlling protest through reprisal, this is a long and difficult process. Campesinos, like the rest of humanity, are not free from the temptations which power brings. Structures have to change, but also people have to change their concepts of power and authority figures.

Repopulated Communities in Peacetime

As of the signing of the peace accords between the FMLN and the government on January 16, 1992, much of the area depopulated by the war had been repopulated. The regional organizations (the CCR, CRCC and PADECOMSM) had become semi-governmental organizations with functions of building social and physical infrastructure and governing the communities. The populations of these areas had spent five years developing and working on grass roots participatory processes. They had developed nonviolent methods of resistance towards the military and the government civic action programs. They had gained experience in managing their own resources. They had experimented with different types of economic structures. This was all done with no governmental involvement except for five or six government-paid teachers in repopulated areas.

When the peace accords were signed, one of the government priorities was to bring in the 44 exiled mayors of towns in the conflictive zones in order to re-establish political and administrative control over formerly guerrilla-held territory.[22] The government found that they had to negotiate with the regional community organizations. The government representatives realized that the regional community organizations were made of people who would not accept leadership imposed on them. They had a wealth of experience in negotiation and a proven capacity in meeting their own basic needs better than the government had. They were a group of people whose concept of government, social services, and participation had fundamentally changed. The president of PADECOMSM said[23]

> The rich people want to come back and be the leaders. These are the same people who paid the poor people a miserable wage before the war, now want to come back as if nothing has changed.

> But things have changed. Now any poor campesino will ask
> questions and insist that the rich coordinate with the community.

Members of the repopulation movement have been involved in a
process of internal transformation and then in a process of building new
economic, political and social alternative structures. They want to set
their own terms for development. As a repopulation leader stated in
May 1992,[24]

> These agencies that want to come in, they are from the
> government or AID. They want to organize their own community
> councils. They ignore our community councils. They say that they
> have to work with their own councils. They try to go to the poor
> people around the community councils to divide us. They say they
> will bring in their own technicians. We don't trust them. Why don't
> they give us the money and we can contract technicians who will
> give us real help, not these people who just come in and earn money
> and do nothing. We need people who can give us the kind of training
> we need. We can hire them.

The regional community organizations in the conflict zones have
proposed that the mayors and the regional community organizations
form municipal councils be composed of equal representation from
both the mayors and the communities, and that special committees
manage resources such as reconstruction funds.[25] They are negotiating
with the mayors and the National Municipal Institute, a difficult but
educational process for all involved.

The economic models of the repopulations were experiments in
communal working, and communal management of resources funded
from the outside, but they are not sustainable as part of the present
economic structure of El Salvador. The conditions of the war precluded
economic development. In peace the repopulations raise the essential
question of where the poor and marginalized fit into the economic
system in El Salvador if they are not subsidized by outside funding.

It is a question not just of credit and land distribution, but of markets,
commercialization, products, agricultural inputs, economic planning
and access to resources. If the municipal system manages to limit the
repopulations' access to resources, the communities will not be able to
move forward. Their development will be cut short unless the land
distribution called for in the accords is carried out, unless commercialization and credit are available and until their economic concerns are
taken into the wider national picture. They no longer exist in isolation,
and the fundamental structure of Salvadoran society has not changed
as radically as their perceptions of themselves have changed.

Conclusion

The repopulation movement grew as a response to the scorched earth tactics and the counterinsurgency war. The displaced and refugees–created by the war–changed from being victims to becoming protagonists. They began to analyze their situation. Their reflection led to a search for the solution to their problems. Once they found a solution, repopulation, they pursued it against almost overwhelming odds. From a few initial repopulated communities, repopulation became a movement; it was the vehicle home for eighteen thousand refugees living in Mesa Grande Colomoncagua and San Antonio in Honduras. The repopulation movement changed how the war was fought militarily. In rebuilding their communities, the participants in the repopulation movement created new economic, political and social systems that changed traditional power relationships. They realized the potential existed for outside support of their initiatives. They also discovered their ability to stand up to the military and to defend themselves.

The initial people involved in the repopulation movement had been changed by the experience of displacement in terms of how they saw themselves and their world. They now set the terms. As more and more people became part of the repopulation movement, they became changed by their participation in the movement. The process of defining the movement itself helped the repopulated communities project an alternative system that challenged the inequalities in the country itself and exploded the myths that the poor were incompetent and uneducable. The constant challenges–getting supplies past the military checkpoints, negotiating with the military to free a captured community member, getting funding for a project–were in part overcome giving the movement a series of victories and momentum.

Peacetime presents the repopulation movement with a dual set of challenges, one internal to the movement and the other external. The first is the question of how a movement that was a creative response to war now defines its role in peacetime. The approach of the repopulated communities to the return of the traditional authorities suggests that the repopulation movement has much to offer El Salvador in a time of peace.

The second challenge facing the repopulated communities comes from the deep economic, social and political inequalities in El Salvador which were the root causes of the war. The Peace Accords do not substantially address that problem. Their fundamental reform of the Accords is to prevent military influence in the political sphere and to guarantee that the conflicts in Salvadoran society can be played out and resolved in political, not military, forums. This does not provide solutions to the problems that caused the war, rather it sets new terms for finding political solutions to the tensions in society.

For the repopulated communities, the first challenge is the most immediate. The war zones, with all their uncertainty, were a very structured environment; people knew the rules, ways to survive, and how to avoid what was dangerous. Peace changes the rules and the significance of many things. During the war, planning was inevitably focused on the immediate. People were interested in survival. Even short term behavior, which was acknowledged to be unhealthy, such as dependency of the repopulated communities on outside funding, was not to be dealt with until after the war. The war precluded any real solution. The war caused a degree of isolation, which in *some* ways offered the communities space to test their development model. But that no longer is true. One of the pressing issues is that the repopulations have to define their relationship with the FMLN in peacetime. They have to find ways to reintegrate ex-combatants into communities when the lands are redistributed under the peace accords. In short they must readjust to a very complex new set of circumstances that peace has brought.

The second challenge, however, may be even greater. The repopulations were able to build more just economic and political structures because they had changed the way they saw themselves, they had access to outside resources, and the old political and economic powers in the zones were gone. Now that the war has ended the old forces are returning to the repopulated areas, and the overall economic structures in the country have not changed significantly. The old economic powers in the areas are returning: the man who had the transport monopoly, the owner of the coffee plantation. How do these people fit into the new economic structure? The land distribution provided for under the Accords is still not implemented for all of the ex-combatants or for the civilians it is supposed to benefit. In all the talk of the Accords, there was never any mention that the government provide restitution for the houses and possessions destroyed in the scorched earth warfare practiced against the civilian population.

Perhaps of more concern is that there have been no real changes that give greater opportunity for the poor and displaced in El Salvador. Everyone agrees that the repopulated communities should not be dependant on outside funding, but the reality is that there is no credit plan within the national banking system that would permit campesinos to develop profitable and sustainable small-scale agriculture. The government's health and education services are not as extensive as those developed in the regional community organizations. The government still does not provide social security for the elderly and the infirm. The repopulated communities all took that on as part of community responsibility.

Participants in the repopulation movement have always been very clear about what peace means. From the years in the refugee camps, they have refused to welcome peace at any price. "Peace is land and fertilizer and schools and healthcare," said a community council member from Torola.[26] The terms of the Peace Accords make it clear that the new repopulated communities will have to work to build peace with justice.

In the past few years they have been an inspiring illustration of what campesinos are capable of creating and of the dignity of the human spirit under subhuman conditions. Members of repopulated communities have made a historic break with how the poor and the marginalized saw themselves before in El Salvador. Their process of transformation has been, at its best, a victory at a personal and community level. Now they face the challenges of re-defining the repopulation movement in peacetime and, as a movement, seeking creative ways to change the fundamental inequalities of El Salvador.

FOOTNOTES:

[1] Interview by the author with a refugee living in the Colomoncagua refugee camp in Honduras. The interview took place in 1984.

[2] Interview by author with woman from Chalatenango in Mesa Grande refugee camp in Honduras during April 1993.

[3] Interview by author in April 1987.

[4] Interview by author with campesina woman in San Salvador in 1989.

[5] FUNDASAL (in English, the Salvadoran Foundation for Minimal Housing) is a Salvadoran NGO which specializes in housing. As a response to displacement, they drew up a plan to repopulate the bombed-out town of Tenancingo located 29 kilometers from San Salvador.

[6] Interview by author in June 1992.

[7] The exception to this was El Barillo, repopulated in August 1986. El Barillo had been a cooperative before the war with established patterns of collective production, and they had excellent land. They have maintained a higher priority for collective production.

[8] Upon returning to their homes, the repopulators named their community "Segundo Montes" to honor the Jesuit priest of the same name who was assassinated on November 16, 1989 along with five other Jesuits, their housekeeper and her daughter.

[9] Interview by author.

[10] In the countryside the illiteracy rate is even higher, as much as 80% according to informed estimates. There are more illiterate people in El Salvador today than there were one hundred years ago.

[11] Interview by author.

[12] Interview by the author in June 1992.

[13] A good example of the advantages of regional coordination is how PADECOMSM organized their revolving loan fund during the war. In each of the sixty communities, the community council took a count of the families who wanted to take loans for purchasing agricultural inputs. They tallied the count in each region and reported back to the directorate. The person on the directorate in charge of projects wrote about the project and sent it to the city office to be sent out for funding to the international agencies. When the money was approved, the PADECOMSM directorate chose a small group to go down to the capital or to the docks and negotiate a bulk purchase of several thousand pounds of

fertilizer, seeds and insecticide according to the totals ordered by the community. At this point each community had to send their council and community members to do the negotiation with the military to get their particular part of the shipment to their community. This gave each community experience with the frustrations of dealing firsthand with the economic blockade, but it also gave them the essential experience of successfully negotiating permission from the military.

[14] Interview by author in 1988.

[15] In the spring of 1990 the military colonel in Cabañas refused to let the trucks of fertilizer through the checkpoint although the planting season was well under way. Since the fertilizer was badly needed by the community, three hundred residents from Santa Marta hiked several kilometers into town and stood outside the barracks demonstrating until, three days later, the colonel agreed to let the trucks through.

[16] In some cases, the military would capture people and then go to the community and tell them that different people had talked under torture and incriminated other community members of helping the FMLN.

[17] Another example occurred in 1987 when a bomb hit a small community in the closed off conflict zone of northern San Miguel, and a young man and his daughter were killed. Like so many other anonymous deaths during the war, it was not reported in the newspapers, nor was it mentioned outside of the human rights circles. In contrast, in January 1990, in a fire fight between the FMLN and the military in the Ignacio Ellacuria community in Chalatenango, one of the repatriated communities, a rocket hit a house and killed a father and four children. A US congressman visited the site, it was reported in the newspapers, there was international pressure from Europe and the US. In the intervening four years between the two incidents mentioned above, the repopulated communities had organized, reported human rights abuses and created so much pressure that they had made the real cost of the war visible and therefore ultimately morally indefensible for the Salvadoran military.

[18] Interview by author with representative of PADECOMSM in June 1989.

[19] Interview by author in June 1992.

[20] In most of El Salvador, a campesino has very little access to credit through the banking system, he is subject to exploitative arrangements with a "coyote" for loans, usually trapping him into debt, he has limited access to land, is at the mercy of a distribution system controlled by a small sector and can only have access to those services for which he can pay.

[21] Interview by author.

[22] Since the war had as its goal the political control of "hearts and minds" as well as military control, the government of El Salvador consistently refused to admit that there were areas of the country independent of their control during the war. To emphasize this, during elections, the displaced in the provincial capitals would vote for the townships from which they had fled, and elect a mayor. These mayors would then set up small offices in the provincial capitals. Many of whom were elected with less than one hundred votes, but the government recognized them rather than the community regional organizations such as the CCR, CRCC and PADECOMSM. The mayors' initial tactics met with strong opposition from the regional community organizations.

[23] Interview by author in June 1992.

[24] Interview by author.

[25] One of the CCR leaders explained the situation in an interview by the author in May 1992. "We are not opposed to the government coming in," she said. "We are insisting that they recognize the structures that exist. Otherwise, the government will not worry about benefiting these communities; they will just do some things, make a show and then go away. We will be living in the same conditions."

[26] Interview by the author in June 1992.

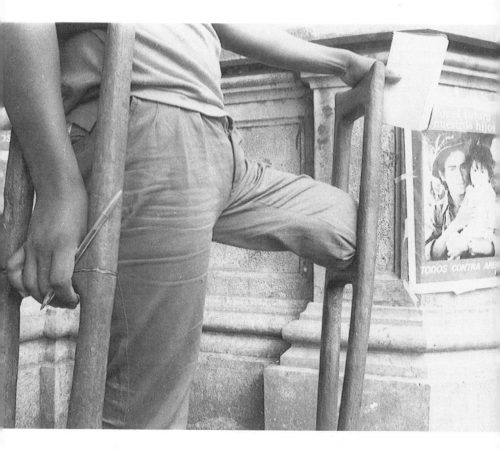

"For the future of our children, all against Arena" reads the poster as
an amputee combatant looks on.

BUILDING AN ALTERNATIVE: THE FORMATION OF A POPULAR PROJECT

MARIO LUNGO UCLÉS

I n this article we will trace the development of the popular movement in El Salvador over the past fifteen years and look at its role within civil society and its relationship with political organizations and parties. We will discuss the relationship of the popular movement with the guerrilla insurgency, the points in common and differences in the history of the two movements, their visions and methods of struggle. Finally, we will look at the evolving role of the popular movement in building an alternative popular project.

The concepts of "popular movement" and "popular project" are commonly used in El Salvador and just as commonly understood to mean many different things. The terms, as we use them here, warrant some explanation. *Popular* in its sense in Spanish is not just an economic or social class distinction. Rather *popular* is characterized by an identification with social transformation in economic, political, cultural, and social terms that benefits the marginalized. Those who act for social justice identify with and make up the popular movement. It is the political option, not their economic status, which defines the participants in the popular movement, although participants are as often motivated by Christian values, moral indignation, personal and class interests as by political orientation.

Popular organizations are the organized representation of the interests of the poor and working classes. Some, such as labor unions and student groups, have long histories of struggles. Others, notably women's organizations, refugee organizations, marginalized community associations and even environmental groups, are more recent expressions.

The popular project is the collection of goals of the popular movement. While not a final blueprint for a "new society," the popular project is based on relations among people which promote social justice and the common good. During the war, the popular project was more easily recognized in terms of what it was against rather than what it was for: against repression, against the feudal-like economy maintained by the fourteen families, against the extreme concentration of wealth. This was more readily seen in local and immediate struggles, for fair wages in the workplace or for decent living conditions for farmhands on a plantation. Throughout most of the war, the popular project was seen as revolutionary (this changed somewhat over the course of the war), and the FMLN insurgency was closely identified with the popular project. Within the popular classes, though, the popular project was seldom a precise idea.

The analysis presented here is based on two principal elements. First, the popular movement's impact on political life takes place at all levels of society, from the *barrios* to the meeting rooms of the elite. Secondly, the development of a popular project is an open process which continues to develop and change. It takes shape through struggle and through winning political spaces. The popular movement and the popular project, their evolution and their interaction, are the foundation for this article.

A Movement of the Masses (1977-1980)

In the late 1970s El Salvador was the staging ground for the confrontation between one of the most dynamic popular movements in Latin America and one of the most repressive governments in Latin America. The Salvadoran mass organizations (*frentes de masas* in Spanish) had united campesino groups, trade unions and students and could consistently put 100,000 to 200,000 people on the streets in demonstrations. They were becoming increasingly radicalized. In combination with land takeovers in the countryside and occupations of Embassy and government offices in the cities, the mass movements threatened to destabilize the government. Only when the two large marches of January and March 1980 ended in massacres was the movement halted and forced underground.

The roots of the mass movements lay in the conscientization of the campesinos in the late 1960s and through the 1970s who formed agricultural workers unions such as FECCAS and UTC in northern El Salvador. Their initial demands, that landowners rent them land at reasonable prices, went unheard. Facing the prospect of literal starvation, FECCAS appealed to the Ministry of Agriculture for a solution.

When the Minister was silent in the face of their petitions for land, FECCAS began to forcibly occupy fallow land and plantations.

These occupations were significant for two reasons: the takeovers allowed large numbers of campesinos to survive who otherwise would not have. Secondly, the dramatic actions, illegal according to the laws written to protect large landowners, broke the fear–for many, the terror–which the campesinos had felt since the massacre of 1932 when the government put down a small campesino uprising and in reprisal arbitrarily killed up to 30,000 campesinos. As a result of the land takeovers, the Salvadoran countryside was changed forever.

By 1977 the campesino made up most of the rank-and-file and much of the leadership of the mass organizations. This was an extraordinary achievement given that agricultural workers unions (farmworkers unions, for example) had been illegal in El Salvador for more than a hundred years.

From 1977 through 1980, large popular fronts or mass organizations were formed. The three largest coalitions, the *Bloque Popular Revolucionario* (BPR), the *Frente de Accion Popular Unificado* (FAPU) and the *Ligas Populares 28 de Febrero* (LP-28), acted on the social and economic demands of their members but were also seen, with some justification, as political fronts for the insurgent groups. Though each coalition related closely to one of the political-military organizations of the guerrillas (the BPR with the *Fuerzas Populares de Liberación*, the FAPU with the *Resistencia Nacional* and the LP-28 with the *Ejército Revolucionario del Pueblo*), it would be an error to see the popular fronts solely as appendages of the guerrilla groups; rather, the fronts were the broad-based political expression of the revolution. This close relationship between the mass movements and the guerrilla groups, forged through the adoption of a common political project in spite of differences in methods of struggle (which would result in confrontations between the different political tendencies at times), was necessary in order to confront such a powerful foe, the Salvadoran elite backed by a repressive Army.

The configuration of the mass organizations changed in 1980 when the five guerrilla groups joined to form the Farabundo Martí National Liberation Front (FMLN). Subsequently, the mass organizations and a coalition of left-leaning political parties created the *Frente Democrático Revolucionario (FDR)* which together with the FMLN was seen as the real opposition to the regime. The role of most of the popular fronts and mass organizations of the 1970s was not a long-lived one as the widespread repression beginning in 1980 forced almost the entire popular movement into clandestinity, exile or the guerrilla organizations.

Historically, the labor movement in Central America has never been large, principally because small industries and manufacturing are only a small part of the predominantly agricultural economies in the region. Since their formation, trade unions have been badly divided along political lines. Many unions were founded or heavily influenced by conservative U.S. and international federations such as the AFL-CIO, the CLAT and the ORIT. Other smaller unions have been controlled by right-wing political interests or parties. Still other unions were supported and influenced heavily by the communist parties in the region. An analysis of the labor movement would show a politically divisive movement that could not overcome internal political differences; the idea of cooperation or joint acts was unimaginable.

Beginning in 1974 with the formation of revolutionary organizations, the Salvadoran labor unions were subject to new political influences. The revolutionary groups had a high impact on labor and led to new methods of organization, coordination and struggle. By 1979 labor's growing links with the guerrilla groups helped to overcome the divisions within the labor movement. Those links also brought labor closer with other sectors of the popular movement in spite of the heterogeneity of the movement.[1]

Between June 1980 and January 1981 as political tensions heightened in the capital, three general strikes were called. The strikes were crucial for the labor movement because they included unions from the manufacturing sector, a powerful force in El Salvador's small labor movement. The first strike (June 1980) enjoyed limited success, but the later two strikes in August 1980 and January 1981 had limited participation and negative consequences. The strikes revealed fundamental limitations, namely that the strikes were planned to coincide with calls to insurrection and guerrilla attacks both in urban and rural areas. The January 10th offensive, in particular, was seen as a "final offensive" and the strikes were to be part of a popular insurrection. The strikes were an integral part of an overall political/revolutionary strategy. At that time, however, the member organizations of the FMLN could not call on as much military strength as they could political strength, and their military actions were not strong enough. The general strikes as well as the intended insurrection did not succeed.

The demonstration of nearly 200,000 people in San Salvador on January 22, 1980 marked the peak of non-violent popular struggle (yet even that demonstration had self-defense militias) and the beginning of the end of open political struggle. The demonstration ended in a massacre. The March 1980 demonstration during the funeral of Archbishop Romero was also fired on by government troops killing more than one hundred people. The avenues for this form of struggle were closed. State-sponsored repression increased throughout the countryside and on a widespread scale. Following the January 1981 offensive, open political work was no longer viable and most of the leaders of the mass organizations and many of its grassroots base were "transferred" to the recently created "rural war fronts" in FMLN territory.

For the next two years the popular movement practically ceased to function. The FMLN was the only expression of opposition and dissent in the country, and the war between the guerrillas and the Salvadoran Army was the only arena of struggle. For the popular movement, this period marked a transition towards new and increasingly diverse forms of popular struggle and organization which responded to a new set of political conditions.

Rebuilding the Popular Movement (1983-1989)

By mid-1983, with the realization that the war would be a prolonged one, leaders in the popular movement began slowly to re-build their social base. They debated how to organize and incorporate new people into their movement within a radically different context. The political situation in El Salvador had changed–although not necessarily improved–dramatically.

With the U.S. government seeking to justify its extraordinary levels of funding for the Salvadoran military, the issue of "democracy" began to play a more important role. The U.S. pressured for elections that would create a constitutional framework, including an elected civilian as president, to legitimize an internationally discredited regime. José Napoleon Duarte, a Christian Democrat with both reformist credentials and a proven ability to work with the Salvadoran military (he served on the civilian-military junta from 1981-1983, the most repressive years in El Salvador), established himself internationally as an acceptable figure to lead the country and the counterinsurgency war.

With strong U.S. backing, Duarte won the presidency in 1984 by promising to end the war and by offering a series of reforms to create a new social base of support for the Christian Democrats.

Many Christian Democrats had a genuine interest in addressing the historic problems of El Salvador's poor, but the reforms (land reform, nationalization of banking and nationalization of exports including coffee) were designed principally as counterinsurgency measures. The reforms would partially ameliorate the pressing demands of the popular classes (thereby weakening the position of the FMLN as an alternative) but would not alter substantially the balance of power between the dominant and subjugated classes.

For the new government even the concept of "democracy," which was seen in its traditional sense of respect for certain liberties, respect for the rule of law and protection of the constitution, was used as a counterinsurgency measure. Elections served the purpose of legitimizing the party in power and delegitimizing the FMLN, particularly during the period when the FMLN was boycotting the elections. This kind of "democracy" in El Salvador, in addition to its counterinsurgency purposes, however, also played the positive role of opening up political space for organizing and for expression of dissent.

For the first time public employees began to play a leading role in the Salvadoran political scene. Throughout El Salvador's history, union organizing within the public sector had been outlawed, and attempts at unionizing had been met with repression. For decades public employees had been utilized--through coercion if necessary--as the political and electoral base of support for each successive ruling party. The Duarte government was no different. During the 1984 elections Duarte promised public employees their right to organize while the American Institute for Free Labor Development (AIFLD) pledged millions of dollars to the new unions--as well as to many other conservative unions--in an effort to create strong pro-government unions. Duarte won the elections with the support of an important sector of labor, including public employees, and many believed that the recent reactivation of organized labor would be easily co-opted and controlled by the new government.

The political spaces opened up by the elections, however, were quickly taken advantage of by the popular movement. In late 1983 labor unionists formed the Salvadoran United Labor and Association Movement (MUSYGES) and began to take their struggles back to the streets. MUSYGES, a coalition of trade unions, was significant because it linked economic demands with a national political platform including the search for a political solution to the war. The public employees realized that their true interests did not lie with their "bosses" (the government) and began to play an extremely important role, with 50,000 of their members going on strike during November 1985.

The Christian Democrats' greatest hope for broad-based support lay with the campesinos. Before 1980 none of the campesino organizations had supported the Christian Democrats or the military-led governments. The campesino movement arose out of the Christian base community movement and had been practically absorbed by the FMLN. The land reforms of 1980 (designed by U.S. advisers and implemented by the Christian Democrats in the junta) were intended to create a social base of agricultural cooperatives which would be loyal to the government. In this sense, the land reforms were part of a larger counterinsurgency effort. In the early 1980s land reform cooperatives were almost completely financed by the U.S. government. However, as time passed the beneficiaries of the 1980 land reform decree found themselves in increasing conflict with the government both over implementation of the land reform (especially over access to credit and government manipulation of the cooperatives' managers) and over broader issues such as the demand for peace. The independence and even belligerency of the cooperativists rose. Most of these groups allied themselves with other popular and labor sectors after a March, 1986 march of 22,000 of their members and became, together with the public employees, one of the most dynamic sectors of the popular struggle in the 1980s.

The popular movement also demonstrated growing autonomy with respect to the FMLN and its priorities. This raised contradictions in regard to traditional leftist political ideas–such as the role of a vanguard–which will be dealt with in a later section. These different conceptions led to an ongoing dialogue between the political-military organizations of the guerrillas and the popular organizations.

Another development, and an extremely important one, was the enormous diversity and flexibility of the popular movement. The elections, the war and the economy were taking the country in new directions, and each turn provided new opportunities for organizing among those disaffected by the regime. Rapidly, the movement created new organizations to incorporate new sectors or to face changing conditions. By one estimate more than four hundred popular organizations existed in El Salvador by 1989. In response to the military's policy of massacres and forced displacement, the victims formed an organization of displaced people (the Christian Committee for the Displaced of El Salvador - CRIPDES) and then a movement of repopulation back to their abandoned homes (the National Coordination of Repopulation - CNR). After the calamity of the October 1986 earthquake left 200,000 people homeless, the affected communities organized the National Union of Earthquake Victims (UNADES) to coordinate relief efforts and then to press for adequate land and housing.

Likewise the Committee of Unemployed and Fired Workers (CODYDES) formed in July 1986 after industry and government laid off workers as the war-time economy deteriorated. The marginalized communities which represented one of the fastest growing demographic groups in El Salvador were not left behind; they formed community councils and then national associations.[2] During 1986 members of marginalized communities took over land to spawn new shantytowns. These actions, sometimes spontaneous and sometimes coordinated with other efforts, were the first urban land takeovers since 160 families took over lands adjacent to Metro Centro on August 4, 1970.[3]

Not only were new sectors of the population becoming organized, but the structures of organization were becoming more sophisticated. MUSYGES, which originally incorporated trade unions and labor associations, reached out to include non-traditional organizations which by 1985 led to the formation of the Worker's Solidarity Coordination (CST) including both unionists and formerly pro-government cooperativists. This presented a strong labor-peasant coalition which was a new development in El Salvador. Likewise national and municipal workers formed the Coordinating Council of State and Municipal Workers (CCTEM), the first organization of its kind.

On February 8, 1986, the process reached another peak with the formation of the National Union of Salvadoran Workers (UNTS), the broadest progressive coalition so far. The UNTS united the most important associations of urban and rural workers from the productive and as well as the service and public sectors. That month the UNTS led one of the largest opposition demonstrations of the mid-1980s putting approximately 60,000 people on the street.

The coalition, ironically, was led by the public employees unions and the cooperativists which the Christian Democrats had seen as their social base since their rise to power. Later the UNTS would become the organizational structure for other social groups which organized around non-work related concerns, such as displacement from the war or reconstruction after the earthquake. In March of the same year the UNTS model was applied regionally with the organization of the Eastern Workers Coordination (CTO) in the eastern departments.

But the counterrevolutionary project was not to be left behind. On March 6th, the Christian Democratic government fostered the creation of the National Worker and Peasant Union (UNOC), a pro-government labor coalition which was structured along the same lines as the UNTS. The difference, however, was that the UNOC included groups created out of the counterinsurgency project including, among others, the Democratic Workers Central formed by the AFL-CIO in 1984.

From 1986 on the UNTS-led popular movement was tending towards greater belligerency. Some actions of UNTS members generated debate over the choices of methods of struggle. Violent actions such as burning vehicles, painting graffiti and puncturing tires to block traffic were seen by some as an erroneous throwback to obsolete methods of struggle, and the actions provoked internal tensions within the movement. The failure of several strikes was attributed to the fact that violent actions scared off many potential supporters. This led eventually to a tactical re-evaluation of the use of violence in demonstrating popular discontent, but not before the debate had become even more heated with renewed FMLN calls for insurrection towards the end of the year.

Demanding a Just Peace (1989-1991)

Two events of transcendental importance made 1989 a key year for the revolutionary project and for the popular movement. First of all, in May, Alfredo Cristiani who owns the largest coffee finca in San Vicente, won the presidential elections for the ARENA party. For the first time since the 1920s, the dominant economic classes began to exercise direct political power (previous regimes were led by military officers or ex-military officers who had been installed by the oligarchy), and they systematically dismantled the structural reforms initiated by the Christian Democratic government. ARENA eliminated the nationalization of banking and export, privatized state enterprises, devalued the currency, slashed state subsidies for the poor and cut drastically other social expenditures. This set of policies was part of the neoliberal model for economic growth.

The second critical event occurred on November 16, 1989 as the FMLN launched its largest sustained offensive of the year changing the course of the war. After controlling large parts of the country and San Salvador for more than a week, the FMLN retreated but only after the Salvadoran Army had displayed to the world its barbarity by bombing poor neighborhoods and executing dozens of innocent people, including six Jesuit priests, their caretaker and her daughter at the University of Central America campus.

For the popular movement, the consequences of ARENA being in power were dramatic. Many of the popular groups, for example the land reform cooperatives and the public employees' unions, had been openly critical of the Christian Democrats, but they also received support from the Christian Democrats. ARENA was seen as an openly hostile government to the popular movement. The threat of reversing the agrarian reform and eliminating thousands of public sector jobs hovered over their heads. For the rest of the popular movement, which had maintained its opposition to the Christian Democratic counterinsurgency policy and whose position coincided considerably with the FMLN, the new government represented the threat of a new wave of repression. These threats soon became real. Weeks after ARENA took power, the Army forcibly broke an important strike at the INSINCA factory on the outskirts of San Salvador. On October 31, 1989 the brutal bombing of the FENASTRAS headquarters killed eight labor leaders and provided the justification for the subsequent FMLN offensive. For everyone in the popular movement, ARENA represented a future of greater poverty and denial of basic rights.

For most of 1989 the FMLN was preparing for a major offensive in the capital and throughout the country. When the negotiations stalled and after the FENASTRAS bombing, the FMLN launched its largest military operation of the war seizing the northern third of San Salvador and controlling large areas of the countryside. Though the move did not spark a popular insurrection as many within the FMLN had hoped, the November offensive accomplished two important things. It proved to the Salvadoran Army that the FMLN could not be defeated militarily, and to the international community it unmasked the continuing brutality of the Salvadoran Army which for years had been undergoing training in "professionalization." More than any other single event, the FMLN offensive set the framework for a negotiated peace between the two sides, neither of whom had the military capability of defeating the other.

While the offensive may ultimately have helped push along the peace process, it had negative repercussions for the popular movement. Many activists within popular organizations were involved in preparing logistics for the offensive, blurring further the line between military and non-military struggle. Many of the rank and file of the popular movement were not able to remain on the sidelines of the fighting and were incorporated into the armed struggle. After the Army was successful in forcing the guerrillas to withdraw, the security forces attempted to round up popular movement leaders. Emergency decrees prohibited any organizing activity, and for the next five months the popular movement went underground. A dramatic march on March 24, 1990 commemorating the tenth anniversary of Msgr. Romero's assassination helped open again the space for public demonstrations. Altogether, the offensive marked a historical rupture and set off a new period for the popular movement and its struggles.

AN ANALYSIS OF THE POPULAR MOVEMENT

Tracing the development of the popular movement from the 1970s to the present shows a remarkable history of growth and diversity and a search for new forms of struggle. Other processes which are fundamental for any struggle of social transformation emerged as well. The popular organizations demonstrated a gradual but growing independence from the political-military organizations, i.e., the member groups of the FMLN, and from the political parties (the Christian Democrats, the social democratic parties and the Communist parties). The demands of the popular movement, too, evolved as activists more and more articulated a demand for democratization with all of the potential, ambiguity and contradictions which that implied.

The rebuilding of the popular movement since 1983 was not an attempt to reconstruct the mass organizations from the earlier period. Different forms of struggle are appropriate for different moments in history.[4] Public demonstrations such as the 100,000 people who protested on January 22, 1980, cannot be repeated at will, which is not to say that in the future similar large-scale actions will not be carried out.[5]

In effect, 15 years of war have radically changed Salvadoran society and economy. The structure of employment today includes activities that were not as significant a decade earlier: land reform cooperatives, high levels of organized public employees and a greatly expanded informal sector in the larger cities, a phenomenon exacerbated by the large numbers of internally displaced people. Since 1983 the popular movement has expanded by incorporating new social groups of the disenfranchised into an increasing number of new organizations and has reached a point where the range of popular organizations covers almost all sectors. The structural heterogeneity of the Salvadoran movement had become more complex daily. This dynamic inevitably has limits, however, and by the end of 1989 even a decrease in the expansion among organizations and sectors took place.

The following table points out the wide range of social sectors which make up the popular movement, without detailing the name and number of organizations within each sector.

TABLE 1: A TYPOLOGY OF ORGANIZATIONS

Sector	Types and levels of organization
1. rural workers	associations and unions
2. agriculture cooperative	associations, cooperative federations and confederations (sectorial and regionally based)
3. manufacturing industry/ private service workers	unions and federations (sectorial)
4. public employees	unions and associations (sectorial and institutional)
5. teachers	associations
6. students	associations
7. community	councils, development and community improvement groups (regional and sectorial)
8. repopulated and war displaced persons	association (regional)
9. others (human rights, political prisoners, women, Christian base communities, etc.	associations

A number of groups such as the Permanent Committee of the National Debate (CPDN) or the UNTS are coalitions and hence work in all sectors. This table does not reflect the important role which numerous non-governmental organizations have played in the current period as the needs for technical assistance, training and financial management for community-based projects have grown enormously.

TABLE 2: CHARACTERISTICS OF THE MOVEMENT

Characterics	1968-1980	1983-1989	1990-1991
GROWTH	Incorporation of new sectors	Continuing the same tendency	Continuing the same tendency with less growth
COMPOSITION	Tendency towards diversity	Increasing diversity	Continuing the same tendency with less growth
FORMS OF STRUGGLE	Fundamentally illegal forms of struggle, massive participation	Development of legal forms with occasional use of illegal ones, decrease in participation	Continuing early tendency but with resurgence of illegal forms of struggle but with greater social legitimacy
NATURE OF DEMANDS	Sector-related demands within an adherence to programs or overall projects of political parties or the revolutionary organizations	Sector-related demands and incorporation of overall revolutionary platform (e.g, negotiated solution to the war) in relation with the changing political programs, especially of the FMLN	Sector-related demands and overall platform reflecting a new vision of participation in the process of the construction of programs of social transformation
RELATION WITH POLITICAL PARTIES OR REVOLUTIONARY ORGANIZATIONS	High dependence, though not absolute	Vacillating relationship of dependence and autonomy within a mutually shared political option	Growing autonomy

Since the re-emergence of the popular movement in 1983, we can identify two distinct periods in its recent development. The first, between 1983 and 1989, was characterized by irregular growth and a constant experimentation with new forms of organization and struggle. The November 1989 FMLN offensive marks the break between the first and second period. In the second period, from late 1989 on, there have been major events such as the FMLN offensive in November 1989, the peace accords and the 1994 election which has greatly altered the landscape and made characterization more difficult.

The next challenge for the popular movement is to continue its development and expansion, particularly at the base. The growing heterogeneity and complexity of the popular movement is not a temporary phase. A number of factors-the privatization and economic restructuring implemented by the ARENA government, the changes in the world economy, the negotiated end to the war and the initiation of reconstruction--have all brought more changes and must be taken into account when analyzing the role of the popular movement in developing an alternative model for El Salvador.

New Ways of Struggle: The Use of Legality

One of the marked differences between the popular movement in the 1970s and the movement in the 1980s was that its actions and indeed the movement itself were primarily illegal during the 1970s, while in the 1980s they would acquire, for the most part, a legal status. In El Salvador, defining "legality" in a strictly juridical sense is inadequate, since throughout this century organizations and their activities have largely been, juridically speaking, illegal. For example, it was not until the 1980s that public employees could form unions; it is still illegal for agricultural workers to strike during a harvest. A more appropriate definition of what is "legal" would describe the degree of social legitimacy an organization or its actions has attained. If the regime cannot deny the organization a certain degree of political space (or the cost of such denial would be prohibitively high), then the organization or its actions can be considered as belonging to the realm of legality even if it is not legally recognized. This process of opening political space in which to operate has been used creatively by the popular movement in recent years. In some cases organizations have even gained official recognition or legal standing.

The gradual but significant changes in the political system during the 1980s played a decisive role in altering the FMLN's and the popular movement's attitudes towards legality. After two rounds of largely non-fraudulent elections, political space opened gradually but surely. For opposition political parties and other groups, a broader conception of what was considered legal came to exist. The political arena had shifted from the clandestine to the open, and not only was the popular movement permitted (with serious limitations), it was even obliged to enter into the arena of "legal" struggle. On one hand this restricted certain options for the popular movement–puncturing tires or throwing molotov cocktails were no longer effective in winning demands or garnering popular support–but on the other hand it opened other alternatives, such as pressing claims through the court system, as in the case of the National Association of Salvadoran Indigenous who had

During a May 1989 UNTS march, demonstrators protested the illegal capture of labor leaders. A young boy glues a poster demanding the freedom of Margarita Navarro and Alfredo Lemus.

been fraudulently stripped of their cooperative by the government and won their case before the Supreme Court.

The boundary between that which was legal and that which was illegal was never clear during the war and now as a result of the peace accords is even less clear. The legality issue changed during the establishment of electoral democracy in 1983, and again as the FMLN modified their goals significantly. In the 1970s the FMLN fought to overthrow what they saw as an illegitimate and oppressive regime; fifteen years later their struggle was defined in terms of reforming the liberal, bourgeois model of democracy so as to permit revolutionary changes through a democratic process. Through the negotiations and the peace process, the FMLN opted for scenarios of legal struggle.[6] Even formulations such as a quasi-legislative body which represented both the FMLN and the government, which throughout the war would have been illegal, became institutionalized as the Commission for Peace (COPAZ), a change which required changing the law and amending the Constitution.

The Use of Negotiation and Democracy

Creativity, expansion of the popular movement and use of legality were not the only areas of change; the movement also developed an increasingly sophisticated conception of political demands. Now the struggle for democracy occupies a central place. Up until 1980, the demands of the mass organizations were revolutionary. With the rebuilding of the popular movement in 1983, demands were inherently social and economic, and specific to each organization (wages, working conditions, labor rights, etc). Political demands, if they existed at all, were generally limited in scope (for example, demanding the release of a captured labor leader, or the withdrawal of the military from factories which were on strike). Rarely did these political demands transcend the necessity of the moment or a particular sector. Gradually the popular movement began to articulate, albeit in general terms, a political platform. Its central demand was that the war must be resolved through a process of dialogue and negotiation and not through military confrontation.

The politicization of the popular movement, or more properly said, the sophistication of its politicization, constitutes a qualitative leap which continued to expand over the following years. Little by little, first dialogue, then negotiation became seen as the process which would put an end to the war. The military resisted strongly at each step of the way, yet the process was driven by the impossibility of a military solution to the conflict and an overriding desire for peace on the part of the majority of Salvadorans. The popular movement insisted on an active role in pressing for negotiations and with the collaboration of the

Catholic Church organized the Permanent Committee for National
Debate (CPDN) which involved practically every organization within
the popular movement in demonstrations to support the negotiations.[7]
Though the popular movement did not gain a formal role in the
negotiations between the FMLN and the government, it played a vital
role in expressing the demand for peace and in articulating key
elements needed in the negotiations. Popular mobilizations by the
CPDN were key in pressuring the government to move ahead with the
negotiations at critical junctures. When the peace accords were formally
signed on January 15, 1992 the FMLN and the popular movement
participated in the largest demonstration held in El Salvador since the
Romero killing twelve years before. This time the people celebrated
instead of protested.

Alongside the demand for a negotiated end to the war, the popular
movement as a whole articulated the demand for democracy. Their
vision was not limited to demanding a negotiated solution to the war,
but rather, overcoming one of the principal root causes of the war, the
anti-democratic nature of the ruling regimes. For the popular movement
the use of legality and the calls for democratization were closely related.
With a more democratic system in place and guarantees of liberties
enforced, the popular movement had greater incentive to resort to legal
methods of struggle. Leaders within the popular movement made
proposals on how to democratize the negotiations process and how to
bring about a democratic system which would respond to grassroots
needs. One of the most comprehensive proposals was formulated
during the First Congress of the Coordinating Council of Private
Institutions for Human Development of El Salvador (CIPHES), in April
1991.[8]

Democracy also begins at home as the popular movement and the
FMLN painfully realized. Particularly in the post war period, the popular
movement's calls for democratization of society raised questions in
regard to the internal processes within the popular movement and to
the relationship between the popular organizations and the FMLN. This
caused considerable tensions both in the popular organizations and in
the relationship between the popular movement and the FMLN. We
discuss that relationship in the next section.

Throughout the decade of the 1980s and into the 1990s there has
been a marked transition of the popular movement, one of moving
from playing a supportive role to the programs of the political parties
(Christian Democrats and progressive parties) and of the revolutionary
organizations to one of taking on a protagonist role in asserting and
constructing an alternative model of social development. Increasingly
this new role has included activities to promote community development and to help people address their own problems and not just

protests or making demands. The organizations have begun participating more actively in transforming the structures of Salvadoran society through what Salvadorans call programs of *auto-gestión,* which can be broadly defined as self-help. Inherently this shows an assertive, pro-active orientation on the part of popular organizations, rather than just protest politics. This is a radical change in the role of the popular movement in this process of social transformation, and it raises numerous questions and challenges which will be explored in the final section.

It should also be noted that the change in the role of the popular movement in formulating its demands has altered the dichotomy between reformism vs. revolution (where any reforms less than full-scale revolutions have been seen as palliative measures which erode some of the support for a revolution. The land reforms of 1980 would be a case in point). That dichotomy has produced negative consequences throughout this century in the popular movement struggles around the world. As the popular movement has sought to address the daily problems affecting its members, that dichotomy has become less significant.

The diversity and the multiplicity of organizations and causes, however, have brought new dangers. If the movement becomes too atomized, it could lose its cohesiveness and the unity which gave it real political power. Alongside its diversity, the movement nonetheless has needed to maintain sufficient cohesion that would hold all of the actors to a central vision. Certainly the danger of atomization has existed and the discussion of this problem leads us to the complex point of the relationship between the popular movement organizations, the political parties and the FMLN.

The Popular Movement and the FMLN

Throughout the 1970s the growing popular movement and the increasingly more consolidated political-military organizations forged a close relationship. They shared a common vision of the social and political transformations which were needed in the country as well as a common history of oppression and resistance. Almost all the early leaders and cadres of the guerrilla groups came out of the popular movement struggle before undertaking an armed insurgency. In 1980 much of the membership of popular organizations such as the campesino groups FECCAS and UTC incorporated into the guerrilla movement after repression closed any space for open organizing. It is important to remember, too, that the guerrilla groups were political organizations as well as military ones. Much of their work coincided with popular organizations: organizing, conscientizing and non-violent resistance. Many of the guerrilla cadre were non-combatants whose

Salvadoran troops search the office of CRIPDES after capturing fifty of their members in April 1989.

principal function was political. The principal difference between the popular organizations and the guerrilla ones, and it was a significant one, was how they chose to wage the struggle.

Opponents of the revolution and the popular groups, notably the Army, the government, and the right-wing press regularly categorized the popular fronts as appendages of the guerrilla groups rather than as the broad-based political expressions of the revolution which they were. Without a doubt there were organic linkages between the FMLN and the popular movement, but it would be a mistake to characterize one as dependent on the other. More accurately, one would see the two groups as mutually dependent or influencing one other.

With the rebuilding of the popular movement in 1983 and the political changes in the country in 1984 analyzed above (the reforms and the beginning of the establishment of bourgeoisie democracy) the FMLN and popular movement leaders recognized the need to structure a different relationship between the FMLN, the progressive political parties and the popular movement. While the revolutionaries had not given up hope of taking power, they also had realized the need to create an alternative, popular and democratic development model. The revolutionaries had to respond on the political front as well on the military front. Throughout most of the 1980s progressive political parties were outlawed which meant that the popular movement had to play a strong political role. The return of the political parties which had formed the FDR, namely the *Movimiento Popular Social y Cristiano* (MPSC) and the *Movimiento Nacional Revolucionario* (MNR), to El Salvador after years of exile allowed greater differentiation in roles between political parties and the popular movement.

The FMLN's military strength and the non-military struggle of the popular movement organizations posed a double challenge to the highly repressive system of political domination historically maintained by the rich and powerful. The resurgence of the popular movement from 1983 onward and particularly from 1986 onward challenged the dominant classes in a way that the guerrilla insurgency never could. Through open, direct political challenges to a system that exploited the vast majority for the benefit of a few the popular movement confronted the dominant classes. Likewise, the guerrillas confronted the key institution, the military, which held the system of domination in place. This was the strategy of *doble cara* (literally "double-sided") which was outlined in a FMLN document analyzing the dual aspect of the political and military challenge to an anti-democratic regime.

Two factors contributed to a growing autonomy of the popular movement from the FMLN in the latter half of the 1980s. The first reason stemmed purely from a change in FMLN military tactics in 1984. As the FMLN attempted to expand its military influence from its traditionally held "zones of control" in northern El Salvador to "zones of expansion" throughout the country, it loosened the reins on social organizations in the controlled zones and looked for support from organizations in expansion zones. The second factor was that autonomy served the popular organizations well. The popular organizations which had more independence responded more directly to the needs of their members, exhibited greater degrees of democracy, and grew. Organizations which unduly looked to the FMLN for direction and even to assign them leadership stagnated. The independence of the popular movement in the latter half of the 1980s became an indispensable requirement for it to play its specific role. This is not to deny that mutual influences, support and protection existed between the FMLN and the popular organizations. Without the military threat represented by the FMLN it is likely that the popular organizations would have been destroyed by the repression as they had been in past decades. The popular movement would not have been able to force open political spaces which the

FMLN, as a guerrilla fighting force, was able to do. Similarly, the FMLN could not have resisted and developed without the logistical and popular support of the popular organizations.

The relationship between the FMLN, which the government regularly characterized as "terrorist subversives," and the popular movement which was seeking to assert its legality and broaden its base, undoubtedly generated internal contradictions since often the short term goals were seen differently by the FMLN and the popular organizations. Even popular movement support for the FMLN's political agenda (even if that agenda originally came from the popular movement; for example, the demand for peace negotiations originated with the popular movement, and when the FMLN gave voice to that demand the government accused the popular movement of serving as a front group) brought government accusations that the popular movement was a *fachada* or front for the guerrillas. In the mid 1980s popular movement leaders realized that they could not give wholesale logistical support to the FMLN, much less have their members serve in militia or urban guerrilla cells for the FMLN, without jeopardizing the legitimate work of the popular organizations. This was not always met with understanding by the FMLN. Despite the convergence of interests, it would be a grave error to categorize the popular movement organizations as front groups for the FMLN.

An autonomous relationship does not mean complete separation, however, and it is this mutually influencing relationship between the popular movement and the FMLN which impedes atomization and fragmentation of the popular movement's demands. Broadly, they continue to share a common struggle and a vision of constructing a genuinely democratic alternative development model for El Salvador. Presently, the problems arising out of a vertical decision-making structure within the popular movement are more frequently due to leadership styles of popular movement leaders from the old school, (specifically within the labor movement of the UNTS, who will not permit internal democracy within their member organizations) than it is due to the FMLN influence.

The discussion between the FMLN and the popular organizations continues, and there is a spectrum of opinion as to how the relationship should function. In principle almost no one believes that the FMLN should "*bajar la linea*" (send down orders), but almost no one believes either that there should not be a relation between the two. As the FMLN develops its new role as a political party (or parties), the relationship between the popular organizations and the party will need to be addressed. Particularly in the post war period, as civil society develops and NGOs take on greater roles in planning, training, developing, funding, and implementing social and community projects, it will not be political parties which direct popular organizations.[9]

Building an Alternative Popular Project

During the war years one of the greatest contributions of the popular movement was to engender hope in El Salvador's disenfranchised classes. Community and organization leaders could not promise their base that the future would be brighter, only that life was worth the struggle, and people responded with herculean efforts and incredible sacrifice. The popular movement inspired in its supporters a vision for El Salvador where there was work with just wages, arable land for campesinos, decent schools and health care, and where there was neither the very rich nor the very poor. There was always the implicit assumption that society would function more justly under a Marxist-oriented centralized state and economy, but the vision of the popular movement was always more nebulous than concrete on how to accomplish that.

One of the exceptions was the work of the National Debate for Peace (CPDN) which in 1988 gathered input from popular organizations, churches, universities and small businesses in order to assert the agenda of civil society for the negotiations process between the FMLN and the government. The CPDN proposal in its essence, however, expressed what ordinary people wanted in society rather than how it should be structured to provide those needs. The FMLN, too, in consultation with popular movement leaders, regularly offered proposals on how the government should respond to the social needs of the people,[10] but those proposals generally fell short of describing how that could be accomplished.

Nonetheless, during the years of war for the participants in the popular movement, whether community activists or union organizers, there was a clear conception of what the "*proyecto popular*" was. The popular project, at a community level or in the workplace, was the struggle for justice for oneself, for neighbors, for all the poor. It was a struggle against the dominant classes and the security forces. For most, the orientation came more from Christian faith or moral principles than from purely political beliefs. The popular movement was the political, non-military organizing and mobilizing component of the revolutionary struggle. Though many popular movement activists were members of the FMLN and joined the military struggle, the role of the popular movement was to assert its own agenda and not to recruit for the FMLN or be subservient to the FMLN.

In the latter years of the war as political space opened and international funding for projects became more available, the popular movement took on a new role of building alternative social and economic models in the communities and in the workplace. The repopulated communities and the urban land takeovers were seen as communitarian models with a degree of collectivity in production, social services and decision-making. Other projects as well--literacy and health promoter training in the communities, democracy in the workplace through the unions and even organizing in the prisons--were seen as building the new society here and now, not waiting for the taking of power. The popular movement's focus on *auto-gestión* attempted to give people the skills and the resources to solve their problems in a direct way and at a local level. The vision, then, within the rank and file of the popular movement was to extend these local-based communitarian models to a national level.

In recent years since the signing of the peace accords (December 31, 1990), the vision of the popular movement--its popular project--has broken down. There are a number of reasons for this. The expectations of the organized sector for a new society were unrealistically high. The terms of the peace accords largely did not address economic issues and except for those living in conflictive zones and for ex-combatants and their families who received land, the living conditions for El Salvador's poor did not improve and in fact have deteriorated. This has been disillusioning for many.

Secondly, it has been increasingly obvious that the conditions of the war helped maintain a unified vision within the popular movement and the FMLN. The struggle was against the repressive military or the imperial Yankees or the puppet government of the Christian Democrats or the fascist ARENA government. In the aftermath of the war, the "common enemy" syndrome no longer functions to hold the opposition together and, in fact, many of the popular organizations have looked to U.S. AID or government structures for resources and technical assistance. Through its participation in COPAZ, the FMLN has even participated in what some have called a co-governing arrangement.

The peace settlement also occurs at a time when at an international level the capitalist, neoliberal agenda appears increasingly consolidated, and socialism is in crisis. ARENA's goals are clear and unified and have found high levels of support internationally. In drastically reducing the state apparatus and social services, deregulating the economy, privatizing state-run enterprises and promoting an export-driven production model, ARENA has embraced the course thrust on other Third World countries by international lending agencies. For the producers and for foreign investors, the neoliberal model works. Foreign dollars are being invested in El Salvador, international lending agencies are granting more loans, and the growth rate is growing cautiously.

But for El Salvador's poor, the majority of the country, the model does not work. The domestic market, where most Salvadorans sell their goods and labor, is lagging. El Salvador's poor are largely excluded from participation as either producers or consumers, and the benefits of the neoliberal model accrue to others. Still, proposing viable alternatives is difficult. The popular organizations' focus on *auto-gestión* has exposed the flaws of a strategy which worked in war-time but proves lacking in peacetime; with *auto-gestión* the popular movement leadership becomes too involved in hundreds of small community-based projects, and no one focuses on the bigger picture of an overall alternative model. The failure of the FMLN and the popular organizations to propose a popular alternative to the government's National Reconstruction Plan was just one more demonstration of the lack of coherence and vision within the popular movement at this point.

Perhaps the most promising sign is that people within the popular movement are asking the right questions: "What kind of society do we want?" and "What should we organize for?" and "What is the alternative to privatization and structural adjustment?" These issues are not academic but rise from the daily survival concerns of the poor. It is becoming increasingly obvious that there is no single alternative popular project. People are recognizing that the project has to be built out of the efforts of many and that its construction is a process and not a formula.

In this essay there will not be an attempt to define the alternative popular project; still, there are key components for the alternative which for our purposes would be helpful to define here. Any national project, including ARENA's, will have to address at least the following four elements: a) economic growth and patterns of accumulation; b) social distribution of the wealth; c)the system of political power and the degree of participation by the citizenry; and finally, d) issues of culture and values. In building a popular project the popular movement must have a vision of what it wants in each of these four areas, be able to elaborate coherent proposals and then be prepared to struggle for them. The movement needs to understand the interrelation of each of these areas. Revolutionaries in particular should recall that without economic growth as well as political power it is impossible to promote social development that will benefit the popular majority.

In this examination of the most intensely-lived periods in El Salvador's history, we have found an evolution, at times abrupt and contradictory, that stretches from open war (1977-1991) to a negotiated political solution (1991-1992) and now to what surely will be a period of profound crisis. With the advantage of hindsight, we can identify the processes which, whether they were intended to or not, have trans-formed the economy, the government and the society. These will be the economic and social foundations for the building of the popular project of the future:

a. the 1980 reforms were unable to bring about economic democratization or generate pro-government constituencies, and many of the "beneficiaries" of the intended reforms, such as the cooperativists, later opposed the government;

b. high levels of U.S. economic and military aid kept the economy and the Armed Forces solvent, but also accelerated corruption and personal aggrandizement and converted the military into a central economic power;[11]

c. the forced displacement of hundreds of thousands of Salvadorans which has transformed the demography; the remittances sent home from emigrants to their families in El Salvador exceeds the value of the country's exports and has introduced distortion in the function of the national economy, in consumer patterns and in the habits and work expectations of the beneficiary families.

In political terms, the most important developments have not been the non-fraudulent elections but rather three other factors:

d. the constitution of a new political system, still in its embryonic stages, the characteristics and democratic content of which depend on future political struggles;

e. the evolution and development of the FMLN as a revolutionary organization and as a political alternative; and,

f. the formation and development of a broad-based popular movement, which is increasingly autonomous and which has an enormous creative potential unsurpassed in the history of the country.

These are the key historical factors which will define the possibilities for the construction and implementation of an alternative and democratic popular project which could replace the exclusionary neoliberal model currently being implemented. The fundamental trait of an alternative economic development model is its democratic nature. If, as we have suggested, any development model must address the four areas outlined above, how does this apply to the alternative economic model?

In terms of production, how can those processes which produce the national wealth be democratized? The concentration of private ownership of the land has long been seen as a crucial issue and has long brought calls for state-owned collectivization of property. History has shown that neither concentration of land in private hands nor collectivization of land in state hands is desirable. The issue is not whether property is private or collective but rather whether there exists democratization of production. Implementing the peace agreements regarding the transfer of lands from the large landowners to the ex-combatants and their families will be a positive step and will advance the democratization of production of the land. But the issue is not just access to land, but rather popular participation in the mechanisms and key decisions which govern the process of economic reproduction. The key issue for the 1990s is not so much the concentration of ownership of land as it is concentrated control of the financing sector. Just as fourteen families owned most of the land in El Salvador, five families now control the banks and finance sector. Without financing, developing a "popular economy" is impossible. This highlights the need for democratization of capital as well as democratization of production.

Given the vast inequalities among different social groups in El Salvador, it is valid to question how effectively the State has performed in terms of distribution of the production of the wealth. Questioning the State, however, does not automatically mean that the market is a viable mechanism to achieve a more equitable distribution of the wealth or that the private sector should assume the responsibility of distribution of wealth. The State itself has been dominated by the wealthy. A democratization of the distribution of national production implies the democratization of production itself, and both of these issues lead us to the problem of democratization of the political system and of power.

In recent years the issues of the rights of citizens and the rights of individuals have predominated in the political and human rights debate in El Salvador. These discussions are undeniably legitimate; however, the fundamental question of social justice has often been overlooked. The current political debate in El Salvador has concentrated on the question of political representation; it has ignored broader questions of political participation in other areas and failed to deal with the relationship between political representation and political participation throughout society. Within the political arena, democracy and the democratization process (which should be understood in El Salvador as a process of constructing a democracy heretofore nonexistent and not as recovering something that was temporarily mismanaged) cannot be limited to representation and the holding of fair elections (the traditional liberal vision which limits democracy to political-institutional representation), but must be extended to include meaningful participation of the popular sectors at all levels of the decision-making process. This is an issue of the democratization of power and relationships of power.

A truly democratic political culture must apply the rigors of democracy not only to politics but also to the private enterprise. Restricting the application of democracy only to the sphere of electoral politics and not dealing with the issue of lack of democracy within the market system only contributes to social fragmentation (which is very much in vogue within neoliberal circles).

The construction of a popular project, of an alternative, democratic development model should raise up the truly democratic values of justice and fairness. It should be conceived of as a dynamic process which continues to create "spaces" in which to transform relations of power; this includes political spaces (such as free elections and negotiations) as well as in areas of production, the economy, social organization, education and culture. It means, in synthesis, building a new form of organization and distribution of political power in the country, a form in which the popular movement has direct participation.

By now it is becoming increasingly clear to most Salvadorans that after fifteen years of bitter conflict, it is necessary to construct a national project which involves both the wealthy and the poor in a process of consensus-building. The war has proven that the organized poor are capable of resisting the project of the dominant classes; yet, the war has also proven that the popular project cannot be successfully imposed by force. By building a national project, neither the "project of capital" nor the popular project would dominate. In a sense, for El Salvador to survive as an intact society, both sides need each other. Without capital, technological and managerial experience, El Salvador would be destined to generations of extreme misery. However, without democratization of production, of the political system and of culture, El Salvador would be headed for a renewed and perhaps more prolonged civil war.

For the popular movement, the idea of looking to build a national project, and not a revolutionary or popular project, presents many dangers. Its leaders will be subjected to co-optation. In the economic arena, the developing communities and labor unions can be out-maneuvered, overwhelmed or strangled financially. For the popular movement to opt for a national project, it does not mean that the popular movement has abandoned the struggle. Defending the political, economic and social interests of the poor within the context of civil society is infinitely more complex than defending the poor in the context of guerrilla struggle. It is a struggle, however, that the popular movement must take on by gathering the diverse demands and human potential of the great majority and be prepared to wage.

FOOTNOTES:

[1] See Mario Lungo, "*Movimiento popular y movimiento sindical en El Salvador en los años ochenta,*" in *El Sindicalismo y la crisis centroamericana, ed. F. Ebert (San José: CEPAS, 1989).*

[2] Carlos Briones, "*Informalidad urbana y mercados laborales: características básicas de la economía informal del gran San Salvador,*" in *Informalidad urbana en Centroamérica,* eds. J.P. Pérez and R. Menjivar L. (Caracas: FLACSO/NUEVA SOCIEDAD, 1991).

[3] Ana M. Echeverría and Mario Lungo, "*El desarrollo del trabajo de concientización política en los asentamientos populares urbanos de San Salvador a partir de 1960*," San Salvador, 1979. Mimeograph.

[4] Mario Lungo, *La lucha de las masas en El Salvador,* (San Salvador: UCA Editores, 1984).

[5] Demonstrations on January 15, 1992 and February 1, 1992 to celebrate the peace accords put more than 100,000 people in the central plaza each day and showed that the era of mass demonstrations was not over.

[6] The May 1993 discovery of the FMLN arms cache in Managua was more for the FMLN a case of a reasonable hedging of their bets than it was a reflection of their commitment to armed struggle.

[7] "*Primer Foro Nacional por la Paz: Una Memoria,*" February 1988, San Salvador, and "*Documento Final,*" September 1988, San Salvador, both by the *Comité Permanente por la Debate Nacional.*

[8] Mario Lungo, "*Los modelos alternativos de desarrollo y el papel de las ONG's,*" Document presented to the Congress of CIPHES, April 1991, San Salvador.

[9] In the last five years in El Salvador there has been tremendous growth of non-governmental organizations providing a variety of technical services for development projects. Many of the progressive NGOs have been founded by the popular organizations or by the FMLN or by the communities whom the NGOs serve.

[10] Such as proposals including the *Gobierno de Amplia Participación Popular.*--

[11] This refers to the new economic wealth of retired and active-duty officers as well as to the investment power of military funds, such as the officers pension fund.

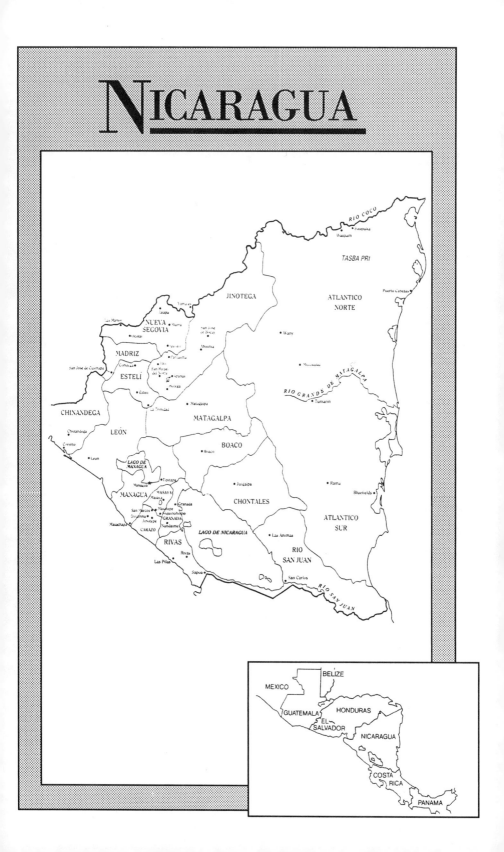

NICARAGUA

NEW AUTONOMY, NEW STRUGGLE: LABOR UNIONS IN NICARAGUA

TRISH O'KANE

In July 1990, the Sandinista unions, which had not held even one general strike during the 10 years of the revolution, nearly brought down the newly-elected government of Violeta Chamorro. For three days with the support of FSLN militants, they lifted barricades across Nicaragua, took over radio and television stations, completely paralyzed transport and commerce, cut off international communications, closed down the airport, and demonstrated a force that would be the envy of any guerilla army.

Just a few years later, the unions would not be able to muster enough support for a general strike, and would have trouble even carrying out successful partial strikes. The unions greatest enemy–the government's neoliberal structural adjustment program–had succeeded in seriously weakening the labor movement through massive unemployment. According to the Sandinista unions between 1990-1992, nearly 50,000 union members lost their jobs, and the unemployment rate hit over 50%.[1]

The Sandinista unions have not escaped the onslaught of neoliberalism that is debilitating labor organizations across the continent. However, the ease with which the Chamorro government pulled the plug on one of the strongest labor movements in Central American history, is also due to its origins, in particular, its complex relationship with the Sandinista National Liberation Front (FSLN).

From the beginning this labor movement was a corporative movement closely aligned with the Sandinista state which began to gain autonomy only following the Sandinistas' electoral defeat. The Sandinista party made a pact with the Chamorro government, basically supporting its economic program with disastrous consequences for the working class. During the first year of the new government, the union leadership went along with this pact despite increasing opposition from the base membership which pushed for a more autonomous relationship with the party and the rejection of the economic program. Partial autonomy was eventually gained and by 1991, the unions opposed the economic program. But it was too little, too late, as the movement had already been considerably weakened and was unprepared to fight structural adjustment.

Union History Until 1990

"Now we can communicate and defend ourselves. Before the revolution I was terrified of ever speaking in public. Not anymore," explains Berta Derring, a Sandinista factory worker.[2]

Before 1979, only 11% of the workers in Nicaragua were unionized. This was due primarily to a lack of industry and the repression of unions under the Somoza regime. When the triumph occurred there were four trade union federations in Nicaragua--the Federation of Trade Union Action and Unity (CAUS) affiliated to the Communist Party, the General Confederation of Labor-Independent (CGT-i) affiliated to the Socialist party, the Workers' Federation of Nicaragua (CTN) affiliated to the Social Christian Party, and the Council of Trade Union Unification (CUS).[3]

By the end of the 1980s, the percentage of unionized workers had climbed to 86%, according to the Sandinista Worker's Confederation (CST). However, while the FSLN and its organizations did have tremendous popular support in the early years of the revolution, the Sandinista unions often grew at the expense of opposition unions. Although some of the right-wing unions did have links to the CIA and specialized in being more "anti-Sandinista" than "pro-labor," the new government repressed unions on both the left and right, eliminating any possible competition. In the early 80s some companies and factories were closed down or taken over by the Sandinista army in order to eliminate the opposition unions, and their leaders were jailed. The government also approved legislation allowing only one majority union in any workplace to have legal status. The Sandinista government changed this law to allow multiple unions on April 19, 1990, just six days before Chamorro's inauguration.

However, in many factories and work centers with a Sandinista union, the workers do not hesitate to list the benefits gained in the first years of the revolution: the cafeterias, nurseries, food provisions, and medical attention. By the late 1980s, most of these benefits had disappeared because of the economic crisis, and workers had experienced a dramatic 90% drop in their buying power in 10 years.[4] It also must be emphasized, as CST leaders themselves point out in retrospect, that these benefits were the fruits of government policy and a paternalistic relationship between the unions and the state.

"We never needed to struggle for social benefits such as workers' cafeterias, clothes, medicine and transport. These were gifts from the Sandinista Front. Now we have to change our conscientiousness. The workers can only win something that they have fought for," said Luciano Torres, a CST leader.[5]

This relationship was not without cost. In exchange for these benefits the unions supported government policies by organizing workers brigades to harvest coffee, participate in the literacy crusade, and fulfill military service. According to Torres many times the union acted as a representative of the factory's administration, convincing workers to accept low wages and even firings.

"This is why in many cases the CST was considered by workers as a 'company union' and not as an instrument to defend their interests. From now on we must create a new image through a daily struggle. Everyone should see that we are a union that defends the workers. This is the only way that we will have the necessary backing to take our political demands to the negotiating table." Torres concluded.

In 1988, the Sandinista government imposed a dramatic austerity program that even Daniel Ortega admitted was "an IMF program without the IMF." The program hit workers and peasants the hardest with a dramatic devaluation of 9,900% leaving many without a penny in their pocket.[6] It was at this point the Sandinista unions began to realize that they needed to be more belligerent in terms of defending the workers' interests or they ran the risk of losing their base membership. At the same time the government began reorganizing state enterprises, which also forced the unions to assume a more aggressive role.

"Before 1988, for example, state agricultural companies were directed by a party official from the Agrarian Reform Ministry. This meant that in each company, the union's and the party's actions were considered one and the same given that the director was a party official. After 1988, the company directors were no longer party officials. This created new labor relations because the unions could not simply appeal to a political leader to resolve a problem," explained Luís Carrion, a member of the National Directorate of the FSLN.[7]

However, the "independence" did not go much beyond discussion. After some grumbling the union leaders gave their blessing to the austerity package although it severely hurt workers who were "compactados" (fired or "compacted") by the thousands. Between 1988 and 1989, nearly 30,000 were fired in the public sector, many swelling the ranks of the exploding informal economy.[8] Many union leaders at the base level, however, did not support this policy, and the education and health sectors went on strike in protest, forcing the government to reduce the cuts.

Baptism by Fire

"It was not easy to react to the electoral defeat. We did not have a strike fund or any communication channel with other sectors hit by the economic crisis. The first moments of struggle were due to the workers' natural resistance," explained CST leader Damaso Vargas following the electoral loss.[9]

In the aftermath of the elections, the Sandinista unions, like the other mass organizations linked to the FSLN, entered a period of profound change and crisis. After 11 years of a paternalistic relationship with the state, from one day to the next the labor movement had to modify and redefine its role and confront a new government with economic policies that were clearly anti-labor. At the same time the unions faced a membership crisis.

The unions had made the fatal mistake of believing that the party would always be in power. Consequently, they did not secure their financial future. Many Sandinista unions were not even legally registered in the Ministry of Labor. The collapse of the socialist block in Eastern Europe exacerbated the situation, given that these countries were a primary source of income for the unions.

From one day to the next, the entire structure upon which the unions relied vanished into thin air. The Finance Ministry under the former government had always guaranteed the payment of a "quota" to the unions, subtracting it automatically from workers' paychecks. One of the first actions of the Chamorro government was to prohibit the retention of this quota. With the deepening of the economic crisis in 1990, many workers could not afford to contribute even though the quota only amounted to one percent of their salary. An advisor of the CST estimated that in 1990 only 50% of the affiliates were paying their quota, and of this percentage only 20% were paying the full quota.[10]

The unions had to immediately begin to finance themselves. At the same time many union leaders decided to "return to the factories" not only because they were no longer on party payrolls but also to try and close the gap that had opened and widened during the 1980s between the union leadership and its base.

The Sandinista union leadership has since recognized that their close relationship to the Sandinista state and their support for the 1988 economic program was very costly in the long term. They also admit it was an error not to have made public their protests against corruption in the state sector. One long term cost of these policies was a wave of disaffiliations from the Sandinista unions in the sugar refineries, some industries, and the service sector. CST leader Damaso Vargas estimated that at least 10,000 workers left the Sandinista unions and joined other "opposition" unions after the 1990 elections.

¡Ni Un Paso Atrás! Not One Step Back!

Not withstanding the devastating situation in which they found themselves however, the unions did not waste much time crying over the electoral defeat. The seven Sandinista federations began a period of feverish organizing and on May 8, 1990, joined together to form the umbrella organization, the National Workers Front (FNT). Former CST leader Lucio Jiménez was chosen as the leader of the new umbrella organization.

Within three days of the organization's birth, a national strike was declared to demand a salary raise after the Labor Minister refused to meet with one of the FNT's most important federations, the Union of Public Employees (UNE). Government ministries were completely paralyzed as workers took over offices and denied access to ministers. Within a week the protests had snowballed into a general strike, with public transport paralyzed and international communications cut off. As the tension grew tremendously throughout the country with confrontations between riot police and workers, and between UNO supporters and Sandinistas, the government agreed to negotiate.

The agreements reached postponed the issue of raising salaries. The government promised to give a "complement" to the wage earned for the month of May and that a rapid revision and reclassification of salaries would take place the following month. This strike was basically a flexing of muscles by both sides and a postponement of conflict.

During May and June, 1990, the new government began to consolidate its power. The president signed several decrees, affecting property rights and calling for the revision of properties confiscated during the revolution. These measures were seen practically as declarations of war by the FSLN. Some of the legislation included changes in the structure of the State (Supreme Court, National Assembly and Supreme Electoral Council), and was declared "unconstitutional" by Sandinista jurists. While Chamorro and her son-in-law Antonio Lacayo had signed agreements promising strikers in May that no one would be fired in retaliation for the previous strike, some of Chamorro's ministers began firing Sandinista workers.

In the meantime, inflation hit hyperinflation levels of 86% monthly in May, and devaluations were occurring weekly, making any salary raises practically worthless before the ink had dried on the May agreements.[11] This combination of events led to growing political instability and tension. When the government refused to meet with the FNT on June 26, the FNT called for a general strike.

Early on the Monday morning of July 9, 1990, Managua residents awoke to an eery silence. No public transport busses rattling by. No taxis honking at the odd oxen or herd of wild goats that were blocking a major causeway. No screeching of newspaper vendors disturbing the stillness.

It did not take long to figure out what had happened. Strikers and FNT supporters in barrios across the country had spent most of the night prying up cement blocks from the roads and erecting brick barricades two to three feet thick. These barricades were an important symbol of resistance for the general population which had used them in the late 1970s to protect itself from Somoza's National Guard. Nearly every single intersection in the city and all major roads were totally blocked. The only way to travel was on foot.

Sandinista high school students took over a right-wing radio station. A group of college students demanding to read a communiqué suddenly appeared on the TV screen behind a minister much to his surprise on a government program called "Democracy on the March." The program promptly went off the air and did not return as the students took over the state TV station for three days.

Water and electricity services were halted. The country was entirely cut off from the outside world as telecommunications workers joined the strike and aviation workers closed down the international airport. On the second day, shooting began at some of Managua's barricades between Sandinistas, UNO supporters, and Contras who had supposedly demobilized. On the same day Vice President Virgilio Godoy brought together all Chamorro's political enemies on the right and held a press conference calling for the "salvation of democracy," and practically declaring a parallel government. The strike which had begun somewhat sluggishly the week before in the factories, banks, and government ministries, had suddenly assumed the proportions of a civil war.

On the third day, Chamorro held a press conference flanked by Defense Minister Humberto Ortega on one side, and Sandinista Police Chief Rene Vivas on the other. While her cabinet sat behind the trio in stony silence, she praised both the police and army for their support throughout the crisis, and announced that negotiations had begun with the unions. The vying of power between the government and the FSLN had quickly come to an end as both sides realized that the country was sliding into a civil war which no one would win.

The "real" negotiations however, had begun some time before between members of the FSLN leadership and Presidential Minister Antonio Lacayo. The unions were completely left out of these secret negotiations and the FNT leadership's only participation was to sign the official accords after the terms had already been determined.

The Concertation Trap

"The FNT was strong in a street confrontation. They knew how to fight with bombs, pistols, and molotov cocktails, but they did not know how to fight against the boss which for ten years had been the FSLN. This daily lesson was never learned," an FNT advisor commented.[12] The July strike was a turning point in the relationship between the FSLN and the government. The FSLN realized it could not afford to push the Chamorro government to the brink or it would have to deal with a much more extreme right-wing Virgilio Godoy. At the same time Chamorro realized that she needed the backing of the Sandinistas and in particular, the Sandinista army, because she could trust neither Godoy nor the Contras. From this time on the alliance was consolidated, and both sides agreed to begin a process of "concertación" or concertation–tripartite negotiations between the unions, business sector, and the government, in order to negotiate important issues that could be sources of future conflict, such as the minimum wage, property rights, etc. At the same time, there would be a continuous "unofficial" concertation between Lacayo and the FSLN leadership which would be used particularly during moments of crisis.

The strike was also a turning point, however, in the relation between the party and the FNT. FNT leaders were not happy at all with the role played by the FSLN leadership during the strike and the secret negotiations. Many union members at the base wanted to continue the strike. The union membership did not want to participate in the concertation process, and the FSLN had to pressure the FNT considerably to show up. The argument given by the Sandinista leadership was that if this concertation did not take place, the government would be unable to convince international creditors and lending institutions to provide aid to Nicaragua. If the aid did not arrive, there would be no funds to modernize national industry or raise salaries, etc. Some members of the FSLN leadership were particularly concerned with the party's public image and that the FSLN would be accused in the future of sabotaging economic recovery.

From October, 1990 to April, 1991, during the first six-month round of concertation, the government signed several agreements with the unions. The most important points that were agreed upon immediately affecting workers were job security, the creation of new jobs, wage increases, workers' participation in privatization, and respect for collective-bargaining agreements. The government did not honor one single accord signed during this time period. While the government agreed to "create new sources of employment," instead, its economic policies produced massive unemployment as national industry went bankrupt, and the state sector was reduced. The Nicaraguan Research Center,

ITZTANI, estimates that 70,000 workers lost their jobs during the first round of concertation.[13]

As regards salary increases, the government agreed to establish a minimum wage based on the price of the *canasta básica*, 53 basic products for a family's consumption. As of July 1991, a minimum wage had still not been established, and in fact, the government's economic program in March 1991, had actually reduced salaries dramatically. According to ITZTANI, the measures meant a 35% reduction for farmworkers, 40% for healthworkers, 50% for food and beverage workers, and 30% for public employees.[14]

Collective bargaining agreements were not honored in general, and in particular were broken by the state. The strikes in the first half of 1991 in the public sector were due precisely to these violations, particularly in the health sector, education, the customs houses, sugar refineries, banks, and port system.

With this record, why then did the FNT continue to participate in the concertation process? First of all, the unions' options were very limited by the real possibility of a civil war if a negotiation forum was not created. This was obviously not in anybody's interest. Secondly, the unions were pressured by the FSLN to participate, and given their economic and political dependence on the party, they could not afford to disagree.

The Marriage of Convenience

Old habits die hard. During the first two years of the Chamorro government, the FSLN-FNT relationship went through tremendous changes and became increasingly complex, as the formerly obedient "wife"–the FNT--began to fight for its own interests rather than depend entirely on her "husband"--the FSLN--to support her. Since the night of February 25, 1990, the FSLN's policy has been to support the Las Palmas group led by Antonio Lacayo within the Chamorro government, and forge a strong alliance in order to prevent or at least slow down the complete dismantling of the revolutionary state by an eager right- wing led by Godoy. This alliance, became official in the March 27, 1990 agreement known as the "transition protocol," which assured the FSLN that the constitution and laws written by the former Sandinista government would be respected in return for a peaceful transition of power. The institutionality of the Sandinista army was also respected, and Humberto Ortega was retained as Defense Minister.

As time passed, and after repeated attempts by the right to get rid of Lacayo and Ortega, the importance of this alliance to the party became paramount as it was practically a "co-government." The July strike almost brought down the Chamorro government, which would have meant the end of this "pacto" and plunging the country into a bloody civil war. This explains the party leadership's direct intervention in the July strike and their pressure on union leaders to participate in the concertation process that followed.

For the FSLN, the unions are like a bat with which the party can beat the government now and again and pressure for certain concessions. The government is interested in political stability and proving to international creditors that it has the situation under control. The FSLN can pressure the unions not to go on strike or mobilize in the street. And this is where the party's interests enter into direct conflict with the union's autonomy: in order to have this bargaining chip with the government, the party must be able to insure control of the union or at least be able to convince union leaders that instability is not in their political or economic interests either.

While the FSLN's interest in controlling the unions after the election remained basically the same as it had while in power, the unions' interest in "being controlled" did not. Union leaders could no longer assume that a government would take care of their interests. Workers who had sacrificed their basic economic needs for a decade and accepted the argument that this sacrifice was necessary to support a "revolutionary" government under attack, were not willing to make the same sacrifice for Violeta Chamorro. Thus the FSLN's support of the Chamorro government made the situation much more complex for the union leadership.

It was not long, however, before the unions found themselves once again seeking party support. The FNT's tremendous financial and organizational crisis following the election was to turn into a long-term crisis. The unions could no longer afford a staff of full-time "professionals." Union leaders had to face one blow after another and were continually "putting out little fires" as one union leader explained, rather than devoting themselves to elaborating a long-term strategy to combat the government's economic plan.[15]

Since the unions did not oppose the Sandinista government's austerity package in 1988 or prepare an alternative to it, they were not prepared to fight the new government's economic plan either. The FSLN's tacit support for the Chamorro government's plan created a dilemma for the unions. They found themselves virtually defenseless, as the vast majority of Sandinista economists who had formerly provided counsel to the unions had little criticism of the plan.

"What do we tell our base? We didn't prepare ourselves with economic arguments during the last ten years because the party was always 'right,'" one union leader declared in exasperation at an emergency meeting held on the first day of the economic shock plan.[16]

Autonomy: Two Steps Forward, One Step Back

The issue of the unions' autonomy from the party was tested in July, 1991, during the FSLN's first national congress. One of the most hotly debated issues leading up to the national congress was the right to elect the FSLN leadership secretly and individually. The seven-member governing body known as the National Directorate (D.N.), pushed forward a proposal to be elected by slate--meaning all or nothing, and leaving party militants without the right to replace any individual member. Since the electoral defeat and particularly following the July strike, severe criticism of certain members of the D.N. could be heard in the hallways of the CST among union members. The criticisms ranged from complaints over the D.N.'s lack of contact with the union base and its problems, for financial corruption, and for the intervening in negotiations between the government and unions. The D.N. had also pressured union leadership on various occasions to cancel planned mobilizations to comply with prior agreements made with the government.

Despite this criticism among the base, however, shortly before the national congress the FNT leadership announced that it fully supported the ratification of the existing National Directorate. FNT leaders admitted that the decision was not discussed with the base. While union leaders stated that the decision had been made to support the entire D.N. given the need for party unity, the unions' economic interests were also at stake. The FNT's goal was to secure shares in at least 82 of the over 400 enterprises that were to be privatized, and thus partially insure its financial future. The unions did not have the resources to acquire these shares and needed the D.N.'s backing to pressure the government into turning over enterprises to the workers.

The FNT's support for the D.N. contradicted its struggle for autonomy. Once again, however, the extreme complexity of this marriage of convenience came into play. During the congress, the union leadership also won several seats in the FSLN's second most influential governing body, the Sandinista Assembly. This means some lobbying power in determining future party policy.

By 1991, the FNT had also begun to take a very belligerent stance against the structural adjustment program while party leadership basically continued to support it. In March, 1992, FNT leader Lucio Jiménez for the first time publicly criticized the D.N. for its support of the government, calling them "collaborationists," and questioning their commitment to the poor.[17]

While some of the party leadership continued to support the government's program, the pressure from the FNT and other popular organizations in 1992 forced leaders such as Daniel Ortega to take a clear stand against it. In other words, the "husband" in this marriage, was finally beginning to listen to the "wife."

The Sandinista unions must continue to fight for autonomy and use the influence that they have won in their complex "marriage of convenience" with the party. Autonomy, however, does not mean that the unions should simply fight for economic benefits, while distancing themselves from any global political program. This would be an extremely short-sighted policy given the long-term implications of structural adjustment policies for labor movements throughout Latin America.

If the FSLN does manage to overcome the divisions that wracked the party in 1992 and develops an alternative to structural adjustment, it would be completely in the unions' interest to support such a project. In the meantime the Sandinista unions must continue their struggle alone, or face eventual extinction.

THE "OTHER" UNIONS

Although as of 1992, the FNT was still the strongest labor force in the country, another block of right wing and centrist unions grouped in the Confederation of Workers (CPT) also played an important role, particularly since the electoral defeat. The CPT was considered an "opposition" organization throughout the years of the Sandinista government. The unions in this confederation are: the Federation of Trade Union Action and Unity (CAUS) affiliated to the Communist Party, the General Confederation of Labor-Independent (CGT-i) affiliated to the Socialist party, the Autonomous Workers' Federation of Nicaragua (CTNa) affiliated to the Social Christian Party, and the Council of Trade Union Unification (CUS). The CTN(a) is a split-off from the CTN led by Carlos Huembes. All of these unions are affiliated to political parties in the UNO. The CTN is the only right-wing union that does not belong to the CPT, although it agrees with many of its principles and supports the UNO.

Following the elections, these unions divided along the same lines as the political coalition UNO, between those supporting the national reconciliation line of President Chamorro, and those who supported Vice President Godoy's "revanchista" line, meaning "revenge." Given this division, the unions closest to the President such as the CGTi, CUS, and CTN (a) went along with the social pact between the Presidency and the FSLN, and the retention of Humberto Ortega as Defense Minister. The CAUS and CTN took the Godoy position.

In comparison with the Sandinista bloc, these unions have historically had little following for several reasons. First, they did not have the resources to compete with the former state support for the Sandinista unions. As previously mentioned, the opposition unions were also repressed during the Sandinista government, although the situation cannot be compared to other countries in the region, such as El Salvador, where union leaders have been killed and tortured.

Another important factor was the extreme political polarization in Nicaragua during the war. Some of these unions were immediately identified as "anti-sandinista" for their CIA financial ties. In this sense they committed the same mistake as the Sandinista unions: responding solely to political interests rather than addressing some of the needs of their affiliates.

However, immediately following the elections these unions experienced a spurt in growth nationwide, due both to many workers' disgust with the behavior of the Sandinista unions in the previous years, and to the new government's promotion of these unions. It is very difficult to determine actually how many new right-wing unions formed since many already existing unions became legal for the first time. In many workplaces, secret-ballot elections were held for the first time, and the new leaders chosen were not Sandinistas, but from the right-wing unions.

One example of this trend was the election in the powerful dockworkers union in Corinto, Nicaragua's most important port. This union was founded in 1941 during the Somoza dictatorship and was affiliated to the CST during the 11 years of the revolution. On July 26, 1990, new union leadership affiliated to the CUS was chosen by secret ballot.

"The Sandinista union was a company union that took orders from the port authority. We lost many of our benefits. The former director always used the pretext that he couldn't increase our salaries because of the war and because we port workers had to subsidize other state enterprises such as the railroads and other ports. Today we do not have to subsidize a war or any other enterprise. But we're always ready to return to struggle with the new government or whatever comes after it--because governments are not permanent, but the unions are," explained Saul Cisnes Trujillo, a member of the new leadership. In 1991 the union went on strike to demand a salary raise from the Chamorro government.[18]

Another reason for the CPT's growth was the clear interest of UNO leaders and the Bush administration to promote the right-wing unions as an alternative to the Sandinista organizations. Although the UNO won the elections, the coalition did not have an organized social base that it could call out into the street as did the FSLN. The organization and strengthening of this base was simply the continuation of the U.S.'s policy of eliminating "sandinismo" in Nicaragua. During the Nicaraguan electoral campaign this strategy translated into financing for several right-wing organizations in Nicaragua, including the UNO. One of the unions in the CPT, the CUS, has been receiving funds from the AFL-CIO for years and is the strongest union within the CPT.

The other most important right-wing union is the CTN, which does not belong to the CPT. The CTN, led by Carlos Huembes, always maintained the most hard-line opposition position during the former government (during the 1984 elections the CTN was part of the opposition coalition--the *Coordinadora*), and is now the most support- ive of Virgilio Godoy. During the July 1990 strikes, the CTN supported the formation of the Committees of National Salvation promoted by Godoy, which were denounced as the predecessors of death squads by the Sandinista daily *Barricada*. The CTN is also very close to Cardinal Obando y Bravo.

"We are critical of the government's deviations and abuses. The people voted for a presidential formula, and one member was never assigned any functions or even given an office. A minister takes the liberty of threatening and laughing at the Vice President. We think this is a serious deviation which could create a series of disagreeable situations in the long term," Sergio Roa, a CTN national leader warned in an interview in 1990.[19]

Of the right-wing unions, the CTN experienced the most growth since the elections and particularly in sectors considered traditional Sandinista strongholds, such as health and education.

The Rebellion at the Base

Another phenomenon apparent since the 1990 elections is the growth of independent unions and the growing autonomy of unions that are affiliated to both the CPT and the FNT. There are two types of independent unions: unions which existed previously and were either affiliated with the CST or the CPT and have disaffiliated, and new unions which have not affiliated with any major organization. According to the Labor Ministry, this new tendency is due to many workers' disgust with the traditional union leadership of both the right and left, who have responded solely to their own personal and political interests.

"The CST responded fundamentally to the political interests of a party and the FNT continues to take orders from the FSLN. At times the FNT does try to attend to the demands of its base, but then it turns around and signs agreements that respond to party interests. This duality of positions could weaken the FNT in the future. These errors in the past led us to the decision to form an independent federation so we would not be linked to any political party as are the centrals," explained Marcial Cabrera Sandoval, Secretary General of FETRAHORESTUC, an independent federation representing approximately 1,500 workers in the hotel and restaurant sector.[20]

Cabrera, a Sandinista, was severely criticized by the CST when he left the organization in the late 1980s and founded the federation. He also sought and secured independent funding for the federation through the UITA, leaving the federation in a better financial state than many Sandinista unions which did not consider independent funding until after the electoral defeat.

The increasing autonomy of unions on both the right and left became apparent in 1991 during a series of strikes in the health sector, customs houses, education sector, and hotels. These strikes demonstrated the growing independence of the unions of both left and right from the political parties and of growing autonomy of the base of workers from the traditional union leadership. A slow rebellion was occurring in the ranks of the FNT and CPT as the base of both organizations began to act in unity to confront the government's policies.

The 1991 strikes contrasted with the two general strikes in 1990 since they were not immediately led by the FNT. They also differed from the past in that they were organized democratically, and because demands were more economic in nature than political. A wide range of workers participated from both Sandinista unions, the CPT, as well as non-union workers.

The Health Strike: The Rock in the Pond

The health strike which began in mid-January of 1991 and lasted two months completely paralyzed the majority of the hospitals and clinics in the country. The strike began with a group of 15 doctors who were not politically involved and basically conservative in ideology. Their demand was simple: higher wages, but this banner was taken up by health workers from janitors and security guards, to specialists across the country. "It was like throwing a rock into a pond," explained Dr. Efraín Fajardo, an orthopedist at one of Managua's major hospitals and member of the strike committee.[21]

The leadership of the strongest union in the health sector, the Sandinista FETSALUD, did not support the strike in the very beginning, although neither did it take a public stance against the strike. The union was following the instructions of the FNT leadership which had signed the concertation agreements with the government in October 1990, agreeing to a six-month truce on strikes in return for the halting of massive firings in the public sector. The leadership of the other unions in the health sector belonging to the Federation of Health Workers (FITS), affiliated to Carlos Huembes' CTN, came out publicly against the strike.

"Once we realized that the most important unions did not support the movement, the workers selected their own leaders and created their own organs. This is what makes this strike particularly important. Even though it was not backed by the unions, a very vigorous, independent, and aggressive movement in the hospital sector formed, with the capacity to coordinate a politically pluralistic strike nationwide," Fajardo said.

Although the Sandinista union leadership did not back the strike from the beginning, in health centers and hospitals across the country individual Sandinista union members were already joining the strike and participating in the strike committees elected in every workplace. Within a few days, the leadership followed the base's example, and supported the effort.

According to Fajardo, the strike was also unusual for its democratic organization. The strike committees in each work center based their decisions on the conditions in the surrounding neighborhood. This meant that tactics and strategy were decided by vote according to the specific needs of each workplace rather than by a national committee. This was particularly important for gaining public support given a campaign by the right-wing condemning the strikers and accusing them of being "murderers" for denying health care to the population. The decision whether or not to completely close down a health center or hospital was made by the workers in an election, after previously consulting the population in the surrounding neighborhoods. Most workers continued to go to work every day and in some centers, health attention was given depending upon the needs of the population and emergencies.

Political ideologies among the strikers ranged from Marxist-Leninists to Liberals, and some workers had no previous political affiliation. While the CTN leadership did not support the strike, many of its members did participate actively in direct defiance of their leadership. "Well, that's democracy," Huembes said somewhat ironically as he admitted that of the FITS' 25 unions in the health sector, at least 10 joined the strike.[22]

The strikers' demands were the following: job security, improved working conditions, the stocking of hospitals and centers with medicines (in many hospitals patients even had to bring their own cotton and rubbing alcohol at this time), and a salary increase. In the end, most of the demands were not met, and the government did not comply with the negotiation terms. However, according to Dr. Fajardo, the gains of this strike and others like it will be seen in the long-term, given the organizational experience gained by workers during the strike and the unity of the various unions at the base level.

"It was neither a victory, nor a defeat. This strike convinced us that the government is not really interested in dialogue or bettering working conditions. Any improvements will have to be the fruits of a struggle. The future is not very promising. It is one of struggle and sacrifice," Dr. Fajardo concluded.

The experiences during the education strike in April and May of 1991 were very similar to the health strike. This time however, the Sandinista leadership did not hesitate in supporting the strike demanded by the base from the very beginning. Once again the unions affiliated to the CTN did not support the strike, but their base did, and in the end CTN union leaders had to go along. On May 25, CTN leaders completely changed their position and criticized Education Minister Humberto Belli for walking out of negotiations.

Unity at the Base

One of the most hopeful examples of unity of action between Sandinista and CPT unions at the base was the strike at one of Nicaragua's most luxurious hotels, the Intercontinental, in which the state is the major shareholder. In March, 1991, nearly the entire staff went on strike and gained a higher wage raise that in any other public sector. This success was wholly due to the unification of the two existing unions, one Sandinista, and the other belonging to the CUS, which both dissolved forming a new completely independent union.

"The CUS used to be an opposition union, but now we realized that the CUS leadership is very close to the government. It's not in our interest for the union leadership to be saying 'si, señor' to all the government's policies. Because we united we had more force, and the administration was not able to take advantage of the former political division between the two unions. Now the administration has more respect for the union and must think twice about denying our demands. They know that if they ignore us, we can make life impossible," explained Juan José Jarquín, a waiter and the former leader of the CUS union.[23]

In October 1990, the two secretary generals of the unions began discussing possible unification. They first consulted with their membership and then held a general assembly in which the majority voted to form one union under the condition that it would never affiliate to any of the major centrals. The union can accept technical advice from any of the centrals, however, and Fernando Malespin of the Frente Obrero played an instrumental role in promoting the unity of these two unions.[24] A new committee was elected with four members from the former CUS union, and four from the former Sandinista union. A secretary general was also elected by majority.

"We believe that our experience can serve as an example so that workers in other centers can see that in reality we all belong to the same social sector and that we have to be united as a class to confront the attack from the rich," Carlos Ortega, secretary general of the new union emphasized.[25]

The unity at the base is also spreading to other sectors. According to Fernando Malespin, unity of action was observed at the state electrical and telecommunications plants, and particularly during the March strike in the customs sector when workers from both the FNT and CUS joined together to fight off riot police with tear gas and batons. The CUS leadership had told its base not to participate in the strike, but according to Juan Ramón Carvajal Matus, CUS leader at the Sandino airport customs: "even though our workers did not agree with all the actions of the Sandinista workers during the strike, when the tear gas canisters began to fly, we all became 'compañeros.'"[26]

There is long way to go before there will be any massive unity of action between workers affiliated to the FNT and CPT. A tremendous potential for conflict still exists in some workplaces between workers who support the UNO and Sandinistas. During the July 1990 strike, one worker died in the violence that erupted in the textile factories between workers affiliated to the Communist Union and Sandinistas.

However, several precedents for future unity have been set. By 1992, the union leadership of both the left and right began to follow their base and started to cooperate. In the sugar sector right and left wing unions went on strike together for the first time in late 1991 and early 1992 and won major salary raises (25%), as well as shares in several of the sugar refineries.[27]

The leadership from both ends of the spectrum also became much more belligerent in its dealings with the government. In March, 1992, the CPT leadership issued a communiqué for the first time publicly denouncing the "dehumanized monetarist policies applied by the president and her cabinet."[28] During the same month the FNT declared an end to its concertation "truce" on strikes.

During the first two years of the Chamorro government, the labor movement in general had few real victories in terms of salary increases and benefits. The gains that were achieved in terms of unity of action and increasing autonomy from political parties, however, laid the foundation for a future democratic labor movement with much wider political support. This movement, of which the Sandinista unions continue to be the backbone, if able to consolidate, grow, and acquire bargaining power, will be the only hope to confront the government's campaign to destroy the unions through structural adjustment.

FUTURE CHALLENGES

The greatest future challenge facing the Nicaraguan labor movement is the same for unions throughout Latin America–neoliberalism and economic structural adjustment programs. These programs, which are sweeping across the continent from Argentina to Mexico, threaten unions with complete disarticulation by creating massive unemployment and an exploding informal sector through privatization policies and economic liberalization.

The widespread implementation of these programs is the result of a new era swept in with the tremendous changes occurring in the beginning of the 90s. With the changes in Eastern Europe and the subsequent opening up of new markets offering a more highly-skilled labor force, trade and investment are flowing from the North to the North. The voices of Latin American leaders in the 1970s-80s who once called for Latin American unity and warned of economic exploitation--such as Venezuelan President Carlos Andrés Pérez–have changed their message. In a financial world where Latin America seems to have been forgotten, governments are scrambling one over the other to open their economies as rapidly as possible and offer the most attractive conditions to foreign investors.

Nicaragua has not escaped this wave. While struggling to overcome the "stigma" of war and instability, the Chamorro government made significant changes in the economic structure to convince the international financial community that investment in Nicaragua is viable. A privatization program was begun to reduce and restructure the state sector. A new foreign investment law left the economy wide open, placing no restrictions on the percentage of stock that foreigners could own in national enterprises (foreign interests can own up to 99% of any national enterprise). At the same time, the government did not define any "strategic" areas of the economy (natural resources such as gold, forests, etc.) and indeed as Joaquín Gonzalez, the government Director of Foreign Investment declared: "all areas of the economy are open to investment."[29]

Before the government's imposition of an economic structural adjustment program in March 1991, production costs in Nicaragua were the highest in Central America given salaries and costs of inputs. The March measures devalued the national currency by 500% and brought salaries down by approximately 30%.[30] The most important single advantage that the Nicaraguan market now holds for foreign investors is cheap labor. In order to attract foreign investment the government must keep wages down, demonstrate that the unions are weak, and that there is a climate of political stability.

"The union movement is an obstacle to structural adjustment, because it makes it difficult to cheapen and exploit the labor force and tries to prevent the sacking of natural resources that comes with foreign investment," said José Angel Bermúdez, FNT leader.[31]

May Day for the Unions

The first of May, 1991, traditionally known as Labor Day throughout the world, was a sad day for Nicaraguan unions of both the left and right. The dusty streets of Managua were as deserted as on any hot Sunday afternoon. Approximately 2,000 Sandinista supporters gathered outside the CST headquarters to listen to the speeches, perhaps one third of the attendance in 1990. And many of those in the audience were either political analysts, journalists, or foreigners. The FNT estimated that nationwide attendance of Labor Day activities perhaps hit 10,000, the lowest showing in years.

The demonstrations of the right-wing unions were even sadder as to be expected given their lesser following. Approximately 500 participated in the CPT's march and perhaps 100 in the CTN's ceremony which was held separately because of its traditional political differences with the CPT.

The poor May day turnouts in 1991 were just one small example of the general weakness of the labor movement. On repeated occasions throughout the first two years of the Chamorro government, the unions had been unable to call a general strike and come close to the force they had demonstrated in 1990. The government was able to privatize state enterprises, firing thousands of workers, without any resistance from the unions in many companies. This weakness confirmed the success of the government's strategy to neutralize them, and particularly in undercutting the support of the FNT.

This government chose co-optation rather than confrontation, as its primary strategy for neutralizing the unions. The strategy is basically the same as the Mexican corporative model used by the PRI government to keep the unions at bay. Indeed, Presidential Minister Antonio Lacayo and other high government officials made several trips to the Aztec capital during 1990 and 1991 "to study" the Mexican concertation process.

There are three basic instruments which the government continues to use to neutralize the unions: the process of *concertatión* begun in October 1990; the "occupational reconversion" program introduced in 1991 to reduce the state sector, and the privatization process through which the government plans to promote "solidarismo" in Nicaragua.

Concertatión

The force demonstrated during the 1990 strikes by the unions brought the government to the bargaining table in the concertation process. However, the government also realized that it was not in its interest to meet the unions in the street while the unions were strong. Until the government achieved its goal of weakening the unions, it made sense to fight them in air-conditioned rooms with long discussions over inflation and cost-of-living increases.

As discussed previously, the government did not comply with most of the agreements signed, except regarding privatization, so the unions had very few concrete gains to take back to their base. In fact, the union leadership's signing of these accords affected its support among its base membership which questioned continuing participation. The only real salary increases that were gained were won outside the concertation process through strikes and work stoppages.

By the end of the first six months of the concertation process the FNT had begun to play the same double game as the government. This "double game" began with the base's natural reaction to defend itself-- such as during the health strike and others in early 1991– rather than as a conscious strategy of the leadership. The FNT did agree to a six-month "truce" on strikes during the six months of concertation. However, FNT leaders emphasized that the workers would have to "defend their rights in their workplace." In the end the only real rule of the concertation game was that the FNT would not launch another general strike like the July 1990 mobilization, that would threaten the stability of the government and damage its image with international creditors. In essence, what the FNT was agreeing to during the six months of concertation, was to fight with one hand tied behind its back.

Within two years, however, the government had succeeded in sufficiently weakening the unions, and by 1992 a general strike was no longer even possible. At this point, the government wasted no time in applying brutal repression against workers. In the final months of 1991 and throughout 1992, Nicaraguan newspapers would be filled with accounts of riot police severely beating and shooting at workers. By 1992, the FNT had filed 11 formal complaints for human rights abuses with international human rights and labor organizations against the Chamorro government.

Occupational Reconversion

This program was introduced in 1991 to reduce the state sector using funds provided by USAID. It was directed towards public servants and offered them four different monetary options for leaving their post and becoming "micro- empresarios." Given the complete saturation of the "micro-empresario" market, however, the plan was really just another slightly gilded road to long-term unemployment.

By July, 1991, nearly 10,000 workers had applied to the plan and left their jobs.[32] The plan had immediate detrimental effects in various government ministries given that some of the most qualified personnel applied, particularly in the health and education sectors. Health Minister Ernesto Salmerón protested vigorously and had the plan temporarily halted, but not before his ministry lost over 500 doctors who had been working in isolated areas.

The plan also had devastating effects for the unions. FNT leaders admitted that the plan hit the unions hard. José Angel Bermúdez estimated that at least 60% of the workers who had applied to the plan as of July 1991, were affiliated to the UNE. In the Finance Ministry, 150 of the 450 workers applied to the plan, all of them members of UNE, including the entire union leadership, according to Bermúdez[33]

"The salaries are so miserable that many prefer to take the plan. This was the direct effect of the March measures which brought salaries down. This plan is a trap because they're giving people money without any concrete project to invest it in or any training. In the end you are confronted with your family's immediate needs, and you eat the money. Many of those who joined the plan in March and April are desperately looking for work," Bermúdez explained in 1991.

The plan presented a major dilemma for FNT leaders over how to fight it and convince workers not to succumb to its temptation. Many Sandinista workers in the state sector feared they would lose their job sooner or later anyway (as many of them did), and decided to join the plan and at least have some financial security with which to face long-term unemployment.

The right wing and centrist unions in the CPT did not complain at all about the plan. As one CUS leader in the customs sector explained: "This plan is great. I know that many of the Sandinista union hotheads joined the plan, and our union has the majority for the first time."[34]

Privatization and *Solidarismo*

The third method for reducing the state sector which represented employment for 78,000 workers in 1990 and weakening the unions, is through the privatization process.[35] This process which should be completed by 1993, is a cornerstone element of the government's economic program and a requisite for receiving foreign aid from the Bush administration.

As with the occupational reconversion program, through privatization, thousands of workers were thrown out into the street. The government began returning confiscated enterprises to their original owners, many of whom who had returned from Miami following the change in government. The first thing many of these owners did was to fire Sandinista workers, and particularly union leadership.

The government agreed to "worker participation" in the privatized enterprises during the concertation negotiations. Through strikes and pressure the FNT did win shares in several enterprises, although as of 1992 it still was not clear exactly how those enterprises would be managed or how shares would be divided between workers. The concept of "worker's ownership" in Nicaragua is completely new, and there are no previous experiences. The union movement faces the same challenges as in other countries where labor movements grapple with the issue of becoming the "boss," and where the potential for division among workers can be exacerbated.

Another danger that existed was that the government would try to use the privatization process to introduce solidarism in Nicaragua. A government functionary stated in April 1991[36]

> We think that the shares workers receive should not be handled by the union. In Costa Rica, in the businesses where the workers own shares, they are managed by a labor development association, and this system has worked very well. It has never been tried in Nicaragua, but we think it can slowly be introduced. It's just a proposal, and we don't want the unions to get up in arms about it because they will see it as a threat and would surely oppose it. They think it will turn the workers into capitalists and they would lose their so-called class-consciousness,

Solidarism is neo-liberalism's arm against the labor movement–a subtle and effective method of debilitating unions that has worked in Costa Rica and Guatemala. The name might be misleading since solidarism has nothing to do with establishing solidarity between workers. It is designed in fact to do just the opposite–to divide workers, destroy unions, and have workers identify with the interests of the "patron" rather than their fellow workers. In Costa Rica "solidarist associations" have legal status with over 2,000 associations and approximately 200,000 members. There are 300 associations in Guatemala with over 80,000 members, and the phenomenon is expanding to El Salvador, Honduras, Panama, and now possibly, Nicaragua.[37]

Solidarism began to spread in Costa Rica in the 1970s when it was promoted by the business sector and backed by a conservative sector of the Catholic church. In Costa Rica, it has resulted in a weakening of the unions, particularly among the most radical banana workers' unions on the Atlantic Coast to which 60% of the banana workers were previously affiliated. By 1981, however, the percentage had dropped to 10%.[38] In each of the enterprises with a solidarist association, employees contribute between 5% and 8.3% of their salaries to a communal fund.

Employers match the fund which is used to provide credit for workers to build homes, for cafeterias, medical assistance, and other benefits. Funds can also be invested in enterprises or used to buy shares.

It may sound good on paper, but in reality solidarism is a death sentence for unions. In Guatemala, for example, it has had devastating effects. Solidarist associations in Guatemala have been used to break unions and drive them out, and function much in the same way as parallel unions. According to the Science and Technology Institute for Guatemala (CITGUA), solidarist associations have replaced unions in at least 17 enterprises and have provoked conflicts with the existing union in 18 others.[39] During the Sandinista revolution, solidarist associations did not attempt to penetrate Nicaragua because of the polarized political climate and highly unionized work force. Given the change in government and the weakening of the Sandinista unions, however, the conditions are ripe. Time has also proven to the United States and the AIFLD that the right-wing unions in Nicaragua which they have funded for years have not grown sufficiently to provide an alternative to the Sandinista unions. The privatization process provides a perfect vehicle for introducing solidarism and further weakening the labor movement.

There is also a general lack of awareness among union leaders in Nicaragua regarding solidarism and confusion over its possible consequences. In 1990, the Solidarist Association leadership in Costa Rica began inviting Nicaraguan union leaders and businessmen from the CUS and the FNT to seminars to convince them of the benefits of introducing solidarism. Most of the union leaders were not convinced and indeed were alerted to the possible arrival of solidarism.

The FNT which has gained shares in some state companies, is insisting on retaining a controlling percentage of the shares in any given enterprise, and insuring the unions continued belligerency in fighting for workers' rights. Only time will tell however, if these union leaders, soon to become shareholders, will continue to fulfill their role as the defender of workers' interests.

Conclusion

In short, the future looks bleak for one of the strongest labor movements in the region. However, there is hope in the new phenomenon of unity between unions on the right and left, and a growing autonomy of the union base from its leadership. Union leaders are being forced to follow along, or risk losing their base of support. This is the fruit of the Sandinista revolution, which regardless of the mistakes made in the 1980s, planted the seeds of consciousness in the minds of thousands of Nicaraguans.

FOOTNOTES:

[1] 1. The CST's General Report to the Second Congress, 1990-1992, April, 1992.

[2] Interview at the Caracol cocoa and coffee processing factory, Managua, October 15, 1990.

[3] George Black,*Triumph of the People* (London: Zed Press, 1981), pp. 70-72.

[4] The Regional Coordinator for Economic and Social Research (CRIES), Economics team, Managua, Nicaragua.

[5] From an interview in the German magazine "Nicaragua-Info," Number 38, October, 1990.

[6] CRIES.

[7] Interview with Commander Luís Carrion, Managua, November 8, 1990.

[8] CRIES.

[9] Interview with CST leader Damaso Vargas, Managua

[10] Off the record interview with a CST advisor, Managua, November 7, 1990.

[11] CRIES.

[12] Ibid.

[13] Marvin Ortega,*Elementos para una estrategia sobre la concertacion* (Managua: ITZTANI, May 1991). Unpublished manuscript.

[14] Ibid.

[15] Interview with FNT leader, Mario Quintana, Managua, June 25, 1991.

[16] Declarations made by a member of ANDEN, the Sandinista education union, during an FNT strategy meeting in Managua, March 2, 1991.

[17] Declarations in the Sandinista daily *Barricada* 3/23/92.

[18] Interview with Saul Cisnes, union leader at the Corinto port, Corinto, Nicaragua, August 17, 1990.

[19] Interview with CTN leader Sergio Roa, Managua, September 4, 1990.

[20] Interview with leader Marcial Cabrera, Secretary General of FETRAHORESTUC,Managua, April 10, 1991.

[21] Interview with union organizer, Dr. Efraín Fajardo, Managua, April 10, 1991.

[22] Interview with CTN leader Carlos Huembes on health strike, Managua, May 1, 1991.

[23] Interview with union leader Juan José Jarquín at the Intercontinental Hotel, Managua, April 10, 1991.

[24] Interview with Fernando Malespin, leader of the Frente Obrero union in Managua, April 5, 1991. The Frente Obrero is a small marxist union which does not belong to any confederation but is affiliated to the political party, the Marxist-Leninist Movement of Popular Action (MAP-ML). Malespin has been instrumental in the Nicaraguan labor movement in promoting unity at the base level.

[25] Interview with union leader Carlos Ortega at the Intercontinental Hotel, Managua, April 10, 1991.

[26] Interview with Juan Ramon Carvajal, CUS union leader at the Sandino customs office during the March, 1991 strike, Managua, April 12, 1991.

[27] Interview with Alberto Alvarez, head of the Sugar Federation of the CST ,Managua, April 28, 1992.

[28] Communiqué published in *Barricada,* March 25, 1992.

[29] Interview published in *Barricada,* July 1, 1991.

[30] Interview with Oscar Neira, CRIES economist, July, 1991.

[31] Interview with José Angel Bermúdez, UNE leader, Managua, July 3, 1991.

[32] CRIES Database of Nicaraguan press-labor, 1991.

[33] Interview with José Angel Bermúdez, July 3, 1991.

[34] Interview with Juan Ramon Carvajal, Managua, April 12, 1991.

[35] CRIES.

[36] Off the record interview with government functionary in CORNAP, the ministry in charge of the privatization process, Managua, April 30, 1991.

[37] *Envío* issue on Solidarism, May, 1991.

[38] Pensamiento Propio, May 1990, "Solidarism: a business association," by Edwin Saballos.

[39] *Envío*, May, 1991.

THE NICARAGUAN WOMEN'S MOVEMENT: FEMINIST REFLECTIONS FROM WITHIN

ANA CRIQUILLON

> *The perspective and analysis here is my own though the original source of these reflections comes from the ideas and experience of the Nicaraguan women's movement in all its breadth and diversity. Our movement represents a confluence of Nicaragua's history, the lessons of the revolutionary process, and the contributions of the women's movement in Latin America and other parts of the world. This means, of course, that not everyone in the Nicaraguan women's movement will agree with all or any part of this article. However, my intention in gathering and sharing these experiences is to try to represent as accurately as possible the dynamics of the movement as it was lived by some of us, perhaps many of us, in the women's movement over the last fifteen years.*

The Nicaraguan Women's Conference "Diverse but United," which took place in January 1992 with the participation of more than 800 women from all over the country, marked an unprecedented milestone in the history of the women's movement in Nicaragua. This conference was the first gathering of its kind not initiated or organized by the Nicaraguan Women's Association "Luisa Amanda Espinoza" (AMNLAE), the national organization of women associated with the Sandinista National Liberation Front (FSLN), which had been the heart and the leadership of the women's movement up until then. The idea for the conference had arisen in order to "reactivate" the women's movement after the defeat of the FSLN in the national elections.

However, when the leadership of AMNLAE decided not to participate in organizing the conference but chose instead to hold their own assembly on March 8, 1991, the result was the first formal rupture inside the movement since its birth in 1977 and the first public expression of what would come to be the current broad-based and autonomous women's movement (that is, autonomous of AMNLAE and, therefore, of the FSLN). In the context of Nicaraguan history, "broad-based" and "autonomy" are concepts that have taken on particular nuances over the past fifteen years.

In this article I will review the evolution of the Nicaraguan women's movement. This overview illustrates the diverse strategies which we have adopted in the course of the Sandinista People's Revolution to gain women's rights and to transform the relations between men and women in our country. For discussion purposes, I have divided the development of the women's movement into three principle stages. The first, which could be described as the period during which we developed a "gender-based revolutionary consciousness," lasted from the first large-scale entry of women onto the political scene in 1977 to our achievement of ideological autonomy as a movement in 1986. During this period, we went through a process of discovering--sometimes very much in spite of ourselves--that it was not sufficient "to struggle alongside men" for a more just and equitable society. In addition to our status as women workers, students or campesinas, victims of the dictatorship, and later victims of the war, we were an oppressed gender, and we aspired to our own liberation.

In this process we realized that we not only had to resolve the problems that are specific to ourselves as women (which derive from the reproductive role assigned to us) but that we also had to question the gender roles which throughout the world marginalize and oppress women. We began to demand--in addition to the rights to the same opportunities that men have for education, work and participation in the social and political life of the country--the right to control our own bodies, the right to freely choose whether to become mothers, and for an end to all domestic and sexual violence. We realized that there was not just one reality, but at least two: that of men and that of women. To transform both at the same time represented another whole revolution. However, even among ourselves, we found a great resistance to addressing our own needs: the Revolution should be our priority, we were told, and the rest would follow.

The second stage, in which we began to discover and accept the diversity of women's identities (particularly between urban and rural and among different social and economic classes) lasted from 1987 to

1990. These years saw the birth of the "sectoral" women's movements, showing us the importance of combining our specific interests as women with the social class or labor union or overall interests of the country with which we also identified. For us these years also saw the crumbling of a myth, the belief that there could exist the "revolutionary" who struggled in support of the interests of all of the oppressed. In reality, there are a multiplicity of revolutionary actors, each of whom demand their own space, pressuring for their own demands.

In the third stage, from 1991 to the present, we are facing and responding to the various political and practical aspects of organizational autonomy and independence from political parties. We are coming to terms with the tremendous diversity that exists among us, not only regarding our individual and collective identities, but also regarding our different political and party affiliations or even–among feminists–our differences in regard to strategies for building the movement.

Revolution and Raising Gender Consciousness (1977-1986)

In order to understand why the 1992 National Women's Conference represented such a landmark in the history of the movement, we return fifteen years back to 1977, when at the initiative and with the leadership of some women militants and cadres of the FSLN–which then operated in clandestinity–the Association of Women in the National Situation (AMPRONAC) was founded as the first mass women's organization in the history of Nicaragua. Led by AMPRONAC, many women–housewives, students, market women--participated in the revolutionary struggle, both in political activities such as protest marches and human rights advocacy, as well as in the guerrilla insurgency as combatants or as part of the logistical rearguard. The great majority became involved out of their ethical principles, that is, in order to oppose the terrorism of the state under Somoza, but also were motivated by their positions as wives, mothers, daughters or sisters of male combatants.

AMPRONAC included in its demands the recognition of our right to be treated with dignity as human beings: the elimination of prostitution and the use of images of women in advertising, the right to equal pay and other rights. In this sense it represented for us a first step toward addressing our specific problems as women. It legitimized our demands by defining them as social and political problems and related their solution to the establishment of "a government formed by the popular and progressive organizations which have struggled against the Somoza regime" (Program of AMPRONAC, 1980), thus giving a revolutionary perspective to the organized struggle of women.

With the victory of the Sandinista forces, the new governing junta responded to these demands by women with executive orders and overall social policies and laws which represented significant gains for women. One of the first decrees required employers to pay equal salaries for equal work, without discrimination based on age or sex; the decree prohibited all commercial use of women's bodies as sexual objects in advertising or in the media. Likewise, the following year, the Council of State (the legislature at that time) passed the agrarian reform law, the only such law in Latin America which explicitly recognized women as beneficiaries of an agrarian reform, regardless of their marital status.

Other laws of importance for women were approved during this period, namely the Family Relations Law and the Child Support Law. Both gave equal rights and responsibilities to men and women in regard to the care and raising of their children, regardless of whether or not the parents were married.

At the same time the government undertook a massive literacy campaign which succeeded in reducing illiteracy from 52% to 12%. This particularly benefitted rural women, who constituted the social sector with the highest level of illiteracy. The government also began a comprehensive program of maternal and infant health care which, among other achievements, succeeded in completely eradicating polio. It opened hundreds of pre-schools and schools both in the countryside and in the city and created dozens of childcare centers.

In this new stage, AMPRONAC became the Association of Nicaraguan Women "Luisa Amanda Espinoza" (AMNLAE), taking the name of the first Sandinista woman martyr. AMNLAE's principal objective was the integration of women into all the tasks, activities, organizations and goals of the revolutionary process, in the belief that this was the best strategy to achieve the emancipation of women. A slogan of that era (1980-81), "Building a New Country, We Make the New Woman," encapsulated the idea that as women became part of the revolution, we got out of the house, out of the traditional role assigned to us, and, therefore, liberated ourselves.

In the first two years of the revolution, AMNLAE sought to incorporate into the organization the largest possible number of women who were Sandinistas or at least identified with the revolution. By October 1981 AMNLAE had more than 25,000 members which gave it a solid base but also created an enormous workload for the leadership of the organization.

The organization's specific role at this point was not very well defined. It was not clear what distinguished AMNLAE from the other popular organizations which also tried to incorporate people into the social activities of the revolution. For example, all the organizations promoted the active participation of the people in civil defense through membership in the people's militias. AMNLAE as a women's organization also recruited women for the militias, but often found that women were already participating in the militias as members of the Sandinista Youth, labor unions or neighborhood committees. There was great confusion in regard to AMNLAE's role which led to tensions with the other popular organizations.

This led to a rethinking within AMNLAE, not of its objectives (which continued to be the integration of women into the revolution) but rather of its organizational structure and work methodology. Thus, at the end of 1981, AMNLAE moved to define itself as a political-ideological movement and began to work not as much as a separate organization but rather within the popular organizations and social sectors encouraging women to overcome the obstacles they encountered that limited or prevented more active participation at both the grassroots and leadership level.

However, AMNLAE's resistance to recognizing that power relationships of domination and subordination existed between men and women prevented the organization from developing a stronger concept of the women's movement. In spite of its reorganization of work methods and organizational structures, AMNLAE continued functioning like any other popular organization; its principal activities continued to be supporting the work of reconstruction and necessarily of women-specific issues.

Thus began this process of searching for the identity of the women's movement. There was still no discussion of the subordination of women as a gender, but there was awareness of the need to address "the specifics" of the situation of women and to confront directly "the obstacles" which limited the participation of women.

However, this embryonic development of our consciousness as women was truncated--as were many other projects whether political-ideological like ours or economic--by the U.S. aggression begun in 1982 under the Reagan administration. We went from being harassed by small counterrevolutionary groups to wholesale, total war. The whole country was mobilized for defense. The bill to enact a "Family Code" and other similar bills were relegated to the back burner, and in this new situation, the FSLN assigned to AMNLAE the role of supporting recruitment for the Patriotic Military Service (SMP), through working with the "Mothers of Combatants." AMNLAE's new principal responsibility was to borrow from the successful experience of AMPRONAC in the struggle against the dictatorship and apply all its energies to the struggle against the contras.

In practice, the work with the mothers consisted of facilitating communication between mothers and their sons who were serving in the military and responding to the economic and material problems of the soldiers' families. Many mothers were opposed to SMP for fear of losing their sons, so the political objective of this work was to convince mothers that military service was necessary for the survival of the revolution and all of its achievements. The FSLN did not want opposition toward SMP to lead to support of the counterrevolution at a time when the contras were creating an internal front.

In personal terms, AMNLAE enabled many mothers to move beyond the pain of the physical separation from their sons by creating a network of profound solidarity among women and developing a certain politicization of a space that until then had been private: motherhood.

However, because of AMNLAE's lack of reflection previous to the decision to prioritize this work and the lack of clarity in regard to the organization's strategic objectives as a women's movement, AMNLAE didn't know how to take advantage of the potential offered by such a large scale mobilizing project. AMNLAE was not able to lead women to question the monopoly of responsibility borne by mothers in regard to their children, or the irresponsibility of men as fathers, or even our identity which was determined exclusively by women's role as mothers.

At the same time, many of us who were feminists, and even AMNLAE activists felt that work with the mothers of combatants was a responsibility not solely for the women's movement but also for the state and the popular organizations. We feared that the work with mothers would totally absorb the movement, reinforcing the movement's tendency to be concentrated in urban areas, and distracting the movement from work that we believed was more important in the struggle for our liberation. In fact, one of the consequences of the focus on mothers was that AMNLAE gradually became more and more identified as an organization of mothers of combatants, heroes and martyrs. AMNLAE became more isolated from many younger mothers who did not have a son in the military.

Many of us continued to search for alternative solutions to the problems which we faced as women, problems which limited our participation both in production as well as in organizing and in domestic work.

There began to emerge in 1983 a large number of independent feminist initiatives in "coordination with AMNLAE." Officially and formally, AMNLAE continued to be the only revolutionary women's movement in the country, but in practice new initiatives had begun to emerge which would later become the diverse and autonomous women's movement that exists today. New efforts were clearly necessary. For example, two years had passed since the promulgation of the laws on family relations and child support. It was clear that there was a need to work more actively to ensure compliance with these laws.

This led to the founding on March 8, 1983 of the Women's Legal Office (OLM)–formally affiliated to AMNLAE–which was a legal aid office that also offered psychological services. Women in Managua sought help from OLM for all kinds of problems or legal claims related to the family: divorce, custody of children in cases of separation, domestic violence, rape, etc. This office was probably the first Nicaraguan feminist institution, and although it was ostensibly a project of AMNLAE, in fact, it functioned independently for many years.

The year 1983 also saw advances in the field of feminist social research. The Department for the Study of Rural Women, created as part of the Center for Research and Study of the Agrarian Reform (CIERA), was strengthened and two new research teams, one in the Center for Labor Studies (CETRA) and the other in the Association of Rural Workers (ATC), were created. The close coordination between the three research teams around a joint study of the situation of women agricultural workers resulted in the teams unifying their theoretical and methodological premises and in developing the foundation for subsequent analysis of the situation of subordination of Nicaraguan women in other sectors.

Other studies were later carried out and other teams created in institutions such as the government's Nicaraguan Institute of Economic and Social Investigations (INIES) and Nicaraguan Women's Institute (INIM). Projects were also developed in the area of health: a program for providing training to women who had been acting as midwives, some programs for family planning which were initiated by hospitals and health centers outside of Managua, and studies and promotion of the use of medicinal plants. Local projects also existed such as a jam and pottery factory in Estelí which was built by a group of 70 women who organized themselves as a cooperative to produce and administer the project.

The majority of these programs were financed by non-governmental organizations from Europe and Canada or by international solidarity committees with whom the Nicaraguan Women's Institute had developed relationships. This Institute, created in 1980 as the Government Office on Women and which became a government ministry, represented for many women--until the end of the decade of Sandinista government--an important feminist institutional reference point in the country. In effect, from 1983 on, while AMNLAE centered its efforts on supporting mothers of combatants, the Women's Institute worked to influence government policies related to the situation of women and attempted to define more clearly its role in relation to women's interests as a gender. The Women's Institute also sponsored a research department which carried out a number of high quality studies and maintained a center for documentation with a library of periodicals. The research department and the documentation center were the only ones in the country covering these topics.

Finally, there was a series of individual initiatives in the mid-1980s which played an important role in clarifying the ideology of the movement. Among these efforts was the work developed by a small team of women in the legal department of the National Assembly which in 1985-86 researched women's participation in the Open Meetings (consultative assemblies in which the Nicaraguan people could express their opinions in regard to the content of the country's new Constitution). The degree to which women's demands were incorporated in the final version of the Constitution, a document of transcendental significance, was due to the determined and effective work of this team.

Another initiative of a non-institutional nature was the publication in Nicaraguan periodicals and magazines of a number of articles written by a range of women--writers, lawyers, psychologists or feminist researchers. The articles covered diverse subjects such as: the double workload of women [having to do the housework, cooking and childcare as well as having a job outside the home], the need for greater responsibility for childcare on the part of society as a whole, machismo in the media, abuse and violence against women, and sexism in education. On two occasions there were even intense debates over abortion, its legalization or decriminalization. The social and educational impact of these debates was such that, together with other factors, they led to the defeat of an attempt by the conservative party to include in the Constitution a statement on "the right to life of all persons from their conception," which would have closed off all subsequent possibility of legal change in this area.

The discussion of these subjects in the media for the first time and the way in which they were treated in the context of Nicaraguan politics during a war was the determining factor in sensitizing public opinion and the views of the leadership in regard to the situation of women in the country.

By this point many of us who were involved in these diverse initiatives were identifying ourselves as feminists. However, at that time we felt that to call these initiatives "feminist" or to pressure AMNLAE to define itself as feminist would have bogged us down in internecine discussions when our main objective was to make sure that Sandinista policies towards women be as progressive as possible. Our tendency as feminists was more in the direction of looking for points of unity among ourselves and with AMNLAE instead of emphasizing our political differences with AMNLAE. Therefore, we talked about "coordinating" with AMNLAE. We considered ourselves feminists and asserted our demands as members of AMNLAE. That is to say that AMNLAE was all of this for us and potentially much more.

It was part of our strategy--although not explicitly--to unite women within the Sandinista popular organizations and within AMNLAE, offering feminist analysis and proposing alternative solutions to the problems of the women in these organizations. This is how, without actually forming a feminist movement as such, it was possible for a feminist analysis to gain much greater legitimacy in the country.

In addition to this, some of us had begun to work inside the popular organizations which enjoyed significant political power in Nicaragua in those years. We began our work in the Association of Rural Workers (ATC). This association united approximately 60,000 permanent agricultural workers, among them an increasing number of women. However, we documented the fact that women hardly spoke during union activities, and there was an almost total absence of women in the leadership.

This was the same conclusion reached by the national committee of the ATC--all men--who made the decision to begin doing work focussed specifically on women in the agricultural sector. The question was: what needed to be done to bring about real union democracy so that women would participate as they could and should participate? The male leadership accepted our proposal to begin a study within the union about the situation of women in the agricultural sector and the reasons for that situation.

This study, which was done with the participation of women and leaders at the grassroots level, caused considerable concern among and to some degree sensitized the leadership of the union. The leaders who were accustomed to see the workers' reality from their own perspective--obviously a male perspective--suddenly had to discover this reality as seen through the eyes of women. The study concluded that gender-based division of labor was a fundamental obstacle to the participation of women in production and in the union, and that this division of labor originated and was reproduced in the home; therefore, the union should take into account the totality of the conditions in which women lived their lives. In other words, it was not a question of women gaining a place within the union, nor of incorporating the demands of women into the list of things the union sought. Rather it was a question of transforming how the union operated, of developing a different concept of union work.

Where should this transformation begin? At the suggestion of the secretary general of the ATC, we chose as the focus of our work an aspect that didn't seem to be at all feminist, that is, the productivity of the workers. The union was deeply concerned about the low level of production in state enterprises. We analyzed productivity and its relationship with women workers, many of whom had continual pregnancies and double workshifts including childcare and domestic chores at home, as well as the kind of paid and unpaid jobs available to or assigned to women and their working conditions. This project offered a glimpse of the future strategy of the women's movement. Women's gender interests and issues had to be linked with their national, class and other interests.

Already by 1985, the relatively isolated nature of all these initiatives which existed parallel to AMNLAE's work demonstrated the inability of AMNLAE to control the movement. The situation was similar--but worse--on the Atlantic Coast where the process had already begun which years later would result in the official declaration of autonomy of the northern and southern Atlantic regions. Clearly the cultural differences between the two sides of the country and AMNLAE's unfamiliarity with the dynamics of the different ethnic groups on the Atlantic Coast did not facilitate the organizing efforts directed toward women, which, as a result, gradually died out, except in those places where local leadership had emerged.

AMNLAE's growing inability to lead the movement reached such a crisis level that the leadership of AMNLAE called for a national assembly in the first months of 1985. At this assembly Bayardo Arce, one of the nine members of the FSLN directorate, gave a speech in which he even questioned the need for a women's organization in a revolution like Nicaragua's. Of course, the reaction of all the women who attended the assembly was unanimous: there could be no question of the existence of AMNLAE as an organization which defended our specific interests as women, although we were also conscious that we could not go forward without first trying to re-orient AMNLAE to the new situation. In this assembly the women approved the idea of forming "interest groups" as a way of continuing work with mothers of combatants--at the explicit request of the national leadership of the FSLN--while at the same time leaving open the possibility of developing other areas of work that responded to the different interests of women.

Three months later all sectors of the population began preparing their input for the draft of the new Constitution. Since AMNLAE was supposed to speak for women and had to define its position on a wide range of topics, the organization deepened its reflections on the kind of society to which we aspired. In terms of defining its own vision and political goals, this was a qualitative leap for AMNLAE.

The second national assembly convened in 1985 to celebrate AMPRONAC/AMNLAE's seventh anniversary clearly showed the progress made. For the first time in the history of the women's movement in Nicaragua, we discussed our problems and obstacles in terms of gender. It was a beautiful moment. For AMNLAE this experience could have been decisive. At last the door was open to debate in terms of gender issues. This was an advance that could never be reversed. However, in spite of the strong political support expressed by the members during the assembly, during the course of 1986 AMNLAE still failed to develop a strategy that incorporated the most immediate and accessible issues which had been articulated at the assembly.

AMNLAE was aware of the ever more unavoidable need to take a clearer position in defense of the interests of women as a gender. However, there persisted in many of its leaders a certain feeling of guilt that attention was being "distracted" from the revolution. This was the result of seven years of the women's movement taking on the tremendous tasks of defending the revolution without ever having been able to integrate our own gender issues into the national agenda.

This left the AMNLAE leaders with the sense that they had to choose between the revolution and women. This feeling was reinforced by the lack of clarity on this issue by the FSLN leadership, in which, despite diverse ideas, there predominated a fear that people would get bogged down in a war between the sexes that would distract from defense and production, which were critical for the survival of the revolution during those years.

This internal contradiction paralyzed AMNLAE and further intensified its internal crisis. As a result, the organization began to lose influence with its own members. For its part the national leadership of the FSLN began to show concern about the situation and formed a high level internal commission, headed by Sergio Ramírez, then vice-president of the Republic, with the objective of analyzing the situation of women in the country and proposing political alternatives. The Sandinista leaders wanted to see what really worked in practice, what mobilized women and what responded to their gender-based demands, while at the same time fulfilling the demands of the revolution.

The first clues as to the direction taken by the FSLN appeared on November 8, 1986 at an event celebrating the 25th anniversary of the founding of the party. When Daniel Ortega began to read point 9 in the Sandinista proclamation a special intonation in his voice caused a hush to fall over the crowd of hundreds of thousands of people present: "The FSLN commits itself to guarantee the rights of women and to struggle with determination against the vestiges of machismo left us by the past." This was the first time that in an official public event there was an explicit reference to machismo.

From the Politics of Gender to the Politics of Identity (1987-1990)

Five months later the Sandinista Front made public its official proclamation on women during the third national assembly of AMNLAE on March 8, 1987. That day more than 3,000 women from all parts of the country heard *Comandante* Bayardo Arce state, "Nicaraguan women have historically suffered a social discrimination that has put them in a subordinate position in society." The proclamation went on to say that machismo, paternal irresponsibility, discriminatory laws and policies, and the subordination of women in families and society were real obstacles which impeded women from giving their energies to the construction of popular power in the new society.

That day we women felt legitimately proud that the revolutionary leadership had taken up our demands and made them policies that promoted equality between the sexes. Like the FSLN, we were convinced that it "is up to the whole society to solve the problems experienced by women and to struggle energetically against attitudes that impede new personal and social relations." (1987 FSLN proclamation.)

The organizing experiences of recent years involving thousands of women united around projects that integrated both class and gender consciousness led to the formation of a new AMNLAE leadership committee. Women from a number of social sectors and popular organizations were represented. The selection of new leadership for AMNLAE marked a new stage in the history of the movement, a stage characterized by a profound change in tactics and political organizing. In our struggle against subordination our focus shifted from the revolutionary government to the concrete context of the mass organizations and the labor unions, where we pressed the leadership--most of them men--to find concrete solutions to women's issues. This new national leadership committee's first objective was to better connect the movement's work with the overall political work of the revolution.

A section for women was established in the National Union of Farmers and Ranchers (UNAG), and a national women's commission was formed in the National Confederation of Professionals (CONAPRO). In the Association of Rural Workers (ATC), the department of women attained the status of a national secretariat, and the director of the secretariat became a member of the national executive committee of the ATC. In the other popular organizations, although special sections or commissions were not created, the women's movement's work became part of the work that was supposed to be promoted by the whole organization, and a woman was named to the national executive committee of each organization to ensure that the work was carried out.

Our demands, which up to now had been general, began to be more explicit and were increasingly articulated in conjunction with our class or organization-based demands. The ideological debate on the situation of women began to appear on the agenda of meetings and assemblies attended by both men and women. As a result, women became more deeply involved in organizations which up to that time had given little or no importance to women's issues. This generated new dynamics within these organizations.

Industrial and agricultural workers, *campesinas*, health workers, teachers and labor leaders (both men and women) began to take more seriously in an explicit and comprehensive manner what have historically been the most radical demands of women. The right to control over our own sexuality, reproductive rights, public denunciation of domestic violence, denunciation of the sexual abuse and harassment of women on the job and of all forms of sexual violence, as well as the decriminalization of abortion began to gain much greater political recognition.

The "specter of feminism" which was prevalent in Nicaragua began to be demystified. On the same day that Bayardo Arce spoke at the AMNLAE assembly, Ivonne Siu, who was then a member of the national executive committee of AMNLAE, stated

> The struggle for our demands and rights is revolutionary in itself. The struggle against a system of domination and the struggle of women are complementary struggles; they are part of the same struggle to transform social injustice and to achieve freedom and equality through transforming unjust relationships of production and reproduction in society.

We should also mention that the advocacy activities of a small nucleus of Sandinista feminists who had come together in late 1987 were also a factor in this process. The majority of the women who were involved in this group were among the high level leadership of government, party or popular organizations. Our coordination–and even "conspiracy"--enabled us to project a critical perspective which offered alternatives to AMNLAE's perspectives. We christened this new network with the name "P.I.E.: The Party of the Erotic Left," a name which both reflected a certain irreverence toward the formal structures of AMNLAE and of the Sandinista party and impeded any attempt on the part of those working for either body to control or formalize the network.

In spite of our gains at the theoretical level, it was clear from the Assembly of AMNLAE Leaders which took place in June 1988 that after the movement's high point–the FSLN Proclamation on Women--AMNLAE had again lost assertiveness.

In reality there persisted at a basic level within the leadership of the women's movement a certain lack of clarity and a lack of agreement in regard to what AMNLAE's strategy should be. There was a mechanistic acceptance of the idea of "working with the social sectors" without it being clear why and how. Theoretical reflection on the causes of the subordination of women in the country was not sufficiently formulated, hampering fundamental agreement on strategies for the struggle. What strategies in the short term would be viable and attractive for the different sectors of women? In what ways is the women's movement distinct from other struggles? How could we maintain the necessary autonomy from the political priorities of the mass organizations to which we belonged without losing our relationship with them, which is also necessary?

Clear ideological contradictions also continued to exist in the movement, even within the national leadership of AMNLAE. One example of this was when Eliette Elhers, then head of the media commission and a member of the executive committee of AMNLAE, was expelled for having publicly opposed on the radio the holding of a national beauty contest. Beauty pageants had not been held since the fall of Somoza. This event, promoted by the Sandinista Youth (the FSLN's youth movement), provoked intense debates, with well known feminists taking opposing positions. Ultimately, AMNLAE toed the Sandinista line and did not oppose the pageants. The Sandinista Youth pageant and others have been held every year since, marking the increase–in spite of the law prohibiting the exploitation of images of women in advertising–of ever more machismo in advertising.

At the same time AMNLAE was again experiencing a temporary paralysis resulting from a bureaucratic and top-heavy structure that included full-time employment of more than 130 professional activists, a structure that was no longer appropriate for the new political organization concept. The leadership's attention was taken up by matters related to maintaining this bureaucracy, including having to come up with specific workplans for each activist. Those of us who were working in the mass organizations continued to reject the strategy of "outside promoters" from AMNLAE working within our organizations. At best, we treated them with indifference. We were trying, each in our own sector, to define our own women's agenda, responding as we thought best to the FSLN's call.

This resulted in even more dispersion. Under these circumstances, it was not possible to give overall direction to so many initiatives, nor even to document all these experiences. As a result the leadership of AMNLAE tended to focus its attention inward on the organization, overemphasizing internal organizational matters and neglecting both women's own initiatives as well as mobilization and political education.

Under pressure from the women's secretariats of the mass organizations–who insisted that AMNLAE should be more democratic and that the women who emerged as leaders in these sectors should play a greater leadership role in the organization--AMNLAE made the decision to reduce drastically the number of professional activists in the organization and instead to make women who were leaders in other organizations the principal promoters of the movement. There was greater recognition of the heterogeneous nature of the women's movement including the differences in levels of organizational development among the different sectors. At the same time, there was a call for unified action around common issues.

On September 29, 1988 during the commemoration of its eleventh anniversary, AMNLAE made public its work plan for the new period and announced an opening of the political and electoral process within the movement. This would culminate with the convening of AMNLAE's national assembly and the election of a new leadership committee. For the first time both the representatives to the assembly and the national leadership would be elected democratically by the AMNLAE membership. During the following months there was extensive discussion and a gradual consolidation and profound democratization of the movement. Throughout the country hundreds of women in factories, on farms, in cooperatives, and in neighborhoods participated in the decision-making process of AMNLAE.

This led to deeper reflection on the significance of the subordination of and the discrimination against women in the context of each social sector. The differences between the situation of women workers, teachers, peasants, artisans, youth and homemakers in the poor districts of the city were examined. There was also a rediscovery of what women--regardless of their differences--have in common, and above all, of the solidarity among women from different social and economic backgrounds.

The most tangible manifestation of this was the first national gathering of women from mass organizations which was held on International Women's Day in 1989. More than 700 women from all of the country's labor organizations, including women from the Atlantic Coast women's movement (although insufficiently represented) and from the Sandinista Youth, forcefully told President Ortega of their desire to participate in the national economic and political *concertación* that the government was promoting. Adopting the slogan "Negotiate without Surrendering--in the Country and in the Home," women asserted the connection of their political demands in the house and in the national arena.

The 1989 gathering represented a show of strength which the FSLN and AMNLAE could not deny. It was a way of telling them: "Here are all of us women who are part of the 'fundamental forces of the revolution' speaking with one voice and represented by a leadership elected [from the bottom up]. Will you listen now?"

We were on the eve of the 1989 national assembly of AMNLAE and of the election of its new national leadership committee. The elections were considered almost superfluous; it was clear that the winners would be women who were feminists or sympathetic to feminism, mostly leaders in the women's secretariats of the labor unions and popular organizations.

But in May 1989, before the assembly and elections could happen, the FSLN carried out a *coup d'état* inside AMNLAE. Under the pretext that the priority of all Sandinistas was to prepare for the upcoming presidential and legislative elections and that now was not the time for internal debates, the FSLN froze the AMNLAE's internal election process and removed its national leadership. The FSLN replaced the former leaders with *Comandante* Doris Tijerino (who until this point had been the chief of the Sandinista Police), *Comandante* Mónica Baltodano and three trusted party activists. Their task was to "normalize" the functioning of AMNLAE and above all to win the women's votes for the FSLN. Given that the heads of the women's secretariats who belonged to AMNLAE also belonged to Sandinista organizations, this decision was received as a direct order from the National Directorate of the FSLN. In fact, for a year internal discussion was cut off. The AMNLAE assembly did not take place at the end of 1989 as planned. Likewise, the Second Latin American Feminist Workshop, which was to have been held in Nicaragua in the middle of the year, had to be moved to Ecuador. The workshop's agenda had included themes such as autonomy for the women's movement that were considered "too controversial" under the circumstances.

Women organized in the sectoral movements did not question the decision by the national leadership of the FSLN, nor did we confront the new leadership committee. In part this was out of respect for the political history or commitment of the new general secretary of the AMNLAE, Doris Tijerino, and in part because we were convinced of the importance of maintaining--in spite of everything--unity among Sandinistas during the pre-election period.

However, an attitude of passive resistance to these decisions prevailed, and each of the sectoral movements started to work more on its own. One of the most negative effects for the women's movement was the loss of coordination and horizontal communication among the organized sectors within the movement and the gradual atomization of the movement. It was difficult to maintain these relationships behind the back of AMNLAE's leadership, but at the same time, no one wanted to confer on AMNLAE the role of bringing the movement together.

While the distance between AMNLAE and the women workers who belonged to the mass organizations grew, AMNLAE devoted itself to strengthening its influence in the sector of homemakers and vendors in the cities. All of its regional and municipal offices were gradually converted into Women's Houses which began to provide the women of surrounding neighborhoods with legal, psychological and gynecological services in so far as they were able, as well as classes in sewing, typing, hairstyling, sex education and other areas.

The 1990 National Elections: the Gender Gap Strikes Again!

It is very common to hear that women by "nature" vote conservatively. In reality, at least in Nicaragua, it is not that simple.

In the 1990 elections the campaigns of the two presidential candidates represented two radically opposed agendas. For women, the UNO coalition was a return to the traditional, the known, the secure (although at the cost of our subordination and marginalization); the FSLN meant challenges, dignity, equality of rights and opportunities with men (in sight on the horizon), national sovereignty, the possibility of dreaming our own future and along with all this, an interminable war and insecurity.

In spite of such differences, each candidate played the traditional gender role: Doña Violeta de Chamorro, widow of a "hero and martyr" assassinated by Somoza, an elderly woman dressed in white, a pure and good mother who guaranteed the reconciliation of her children, the return to the "tranquility and peace at home;" and Daniel Ortega, the "strutting rooster," the young, strong man of the house, who worked hard to provide us with corn, rice and beans, and who was going to defend us against the attacks of neighbors and wrongdoers.

However, in a country where the absence of a man in the house is common, where paternal irresponsibility has become a national sport, and where the only absolute national value--extolled by the Sandinista Party itself--is motherhood, what woman was going to be convinced by Daniel? Only the activists and sympathizers of the FSLN and perhaps young girls seduced by the image of a political rock n' roll star which the election campaign sold us.

Doña Violeta seemed to be a woman who was not very political--as men understand and practice politics--and, as a result, many women identified with her. She was going to run the country more or less like a large household with many sons, daughters and grandchildren. She was going to clean everything up, get it in order, arrange everything in such a way that everyone had enough to eat, clothes to wear and was happy. In any case, it was widely assumed that the big bully of the north (the U.S.) would instantly turn into a sugar daddy, and all would be well. There is no doubt that these symbols made a deep impression on women. Nicaragua does not have a tradition of election campaigns based on the programs of political parties. Things function much more on the level of symbols and deep-rooted cultural meanings than on the level of the content of the parties' programs. In any case the Sandinista Party's program was not known in detail by the majority of the population, both in 1984 during the first elections and even less in the 1990 elections. Some points of the program relating to the immediate future were well-known, but these were not exactly the ideas that were going to inspire enthusiasm among women: the economic austerity plan and the military draft among others.

It was to be expected, therefore, although no one foresaw or imagined it, that the majority of women would vote for the National Opposition Union (UNO) and not for the Sandinistas. However, there were exceptions to the rule which are worthwhile to examine in order to understand this phenomenon better.

There were parts of Nicaragua where it was possible to identify voters by gender. Many state enterprises, particularly in the countryside, had their own ballot boxes and a number of these were enterprises where the workers were almost all women, such as the tobacco farms in the north and the banana plantations in the west. In these state enterprises, the Sandinista Front won by a large majority. Why did these women vote for the FSLN?

The reason may have to do with the specific attention and the political opportunities which the Association of Rural Workers (ATC) provided women in this sector. The ATC won the largest number of votes for the FSLN and a large part of its women members voted for the Sandinistas. The opening of more than a hundred rural children's centers, the establishment of clinics providing medical care to women, the offering of technical training courses to women, sex education and family planning workshops, and greater stability in employment for women, particularly during the first half of the decade, were some of the gains which women workers attributed to the ATC and the Sandinistas. During the election campaign, the ATC made a point in their election campaign of calling attention to these benefits as achievements of the revolution, something the other Sandinista organizations did not do, except for the Confederation of Professionals (CONAPRO) which was not large enough to be significant in the outcome of the election.

In the light of the election results, the Sandinista Front committed a very serious error in planning a national campaign designed uniformly for all sectors of the population, carried out by Sandinista activists without being adapted to the specific situation of the people in each locale.

This error was even more pronounced within the women's movement. The election campaign paralyzed us completely. Almost all of us active in the 1990s were Sandinistas or sympathized with the Sandinista Front. However, the tone of the election campaign was so macho that it brought us practically to the point of schizophrenia: either you were Sandinista and so went along with the election campaign or you responded to your feminist convictions or, at the least, the new image of women that you had acquired during these years and came into conflict with the election campaign. The result was a profound demobilization of many women leaders of the movement throughout the country who were literally silenced during these months. It is quite probable that this had a significant influence and impact on the vote for the Sandinistas.

In fact, throughout their ten years in power, the Sandinista Front had seldom departed from homogenous references to "the people" as though the people were not made up of different groups of real people with their own identities and interests. The Sandinista Front favored what its leadership considered the overall or general interests of the country. The specific demands of particular sectors or social groups, particularly women, ethnic minorities and the people of the Atlantic Coast, were for much of these ten years considered diversionary or--in the best of cases--secondary relative to the strategic interests of the Revolution.

However, it was precisely those of us belonging to these social groups who were the first to show that it was not necessarily the best strategy to subordinate specific interests to common interests, but rather to know how to integrate the two.

Political Autonomy: a Little More, a Little Less...

When the Sandinistas lost the election, we found ourselves with a dispersed movement, lacking internal communication at the base and with the national leadership committee of AMNLAE which itself was ever more isolated. Some members of the national committee had even deserted their posts and *Comandante* Tijerino was practically alone at the head of AMNLAE. After some months of "prolonged popular depression" on the part of women in the movement, some feminists and groups of women began again to try to develop horizontal relationships across social sectors, without waiting for a sign from AMNLAE, which in any case, like other formal Sandinista organizations, was only half alive.

In August 1990 AMNLAE began to recover and convened a meeting of women Sandinista activists as well as some independent feminists. The objective was the "reactivation of the movement." The idea was to develop a series of ongoing activities which would culminate in the internal elections frozen the year before by the FSLN. Although the objective of the reactivation was shared by all those at the meeting, our motivations were not the same, nor, as would be seen later, were the ways we envisioned achieving this objective.

AMNLAE had not undergone a process of self-criticism in regard to its role in the 1980s and thus understood the "reactivation" as a relatively quick way to prepare for holding elections for the national leadership of the movement, since it was clear that the legitimacy of Doris Tijerino's leadership was quite tenuous.

One of the first steps in the reactivation process was the formation of a "methodological commission" led by AMNLAE and composed of a number of independent feminists who had volunteered for the commission. Later the heads of the women's secretariats of the principal Sandinista labor organizations also became part of the commission. Unlike AMNLAE, a number of us in the commission considered it essential that the groups and organizations that made up the movement go through a process of reflection which would lead not only to the election of leaders, but above all to the development of a strategy for creating a broad women's movement which would be democratic, pluralist, autonomous and dedicated, of course, to the defense of women's interests.

The Commission proposed organizing a series of workshops throughout the country in order to consult with women on what kind of movement we wanted, what our platform should be, what sort of coordination we wanted to establish among ourselves and what relationship we wanted with the Sandinista Front, as well as the other political parties and the Chamorro administration. After the reflection process was completed, there would be a national women's conference where decisions would be made on these issues, including even the name of the movement since the current name was being seriously questioned.

Between August 1990 and February 1991 we were able to hold eight sectoral and regional workshops, organized principally by the women's secretariats. We also held one national workshop in spite of the differences between the Commission and AMNLAE regarding both the meaning and the methods of carrying out the reactivation. In effect AMNLAE resisted changes in regard to how it had traditionally functioned while the rest of the groups and organizations insisted--with more conviction every day–that for the building of a strong and assertive women's movement, internal democracy and autonomy vis-a-vis the FSLN were essential.

In January 1991 AMNLAE stated its intention to convene a national assembly in the near future in order to elect representatives of the movement, although all the other groups considered the process too hurried and the preparation insufficient. We believed that the intersectoral consultation process should continue and that the national assembly should be the culmination of this process.

By the end of February a schism within the movement was definite: AMNLAE withdrew from the reactivation process and confirmed its decision to hold its own national assembly on its own on March 8-9, turning a deaf ear to the concerns raised by the other groups represented in the methodological commission.

The rest of the groups, the women's secretariats, women's non-governmental organizations and centers decided not to attend the AMNLAE assembly as the only way of expressing our disagreement with the negative attitude of AMNLAE. In fact many of the organizations in the Commission were not even invited; in some cases because it had been clear for some time that they did not identify with AMNLAE's work methods; in other cases because AMNLAE did not consider them members of the movement since AMNLAE saw the women's movement in the context of mass organizations, that is, the women's secretariats of the Sandinista popular organizations.

Four of these secretariats (the ATC--the agricultural workers, the CST--urban workers, the UNE--state employees and the FETSALUD--health workers) stated in a public communiqué that they would not attend the AMNLAE assembly because they did not agree with the hegemonic way in which AMNLAE's leadership was acting vis-a-vis the rest of the movement. At the same time they contradicted AMNLAE's claim to represent all women and said that the assembly should be seen as the expression of one part of the women's movement which was called AMNLAE, but not as an expression of the whole women's movement.

Three Women's Houses in Managua, which disagreed with the decisions of AMNLAE, decided to participate in the assembly in order to demand positions that were more inclusive and democratic. The AMNLAE leadership did not allow them to participate and called them anti-Sandinistas and dissidents (as well as lesbians, diversionists, etc.).

The groups of women who did not attend the AMNLAE assembly celebrated March 8 with a three-day festival called the "Festival of the 52%," an allusion to the percentage of women in the population of Nicaragua. In other words the festival was for all women whatever their politics, ideology or religion. During this festival there were forums and debates on a range of themes including growing unemployment among women, a new interpretation of the Bible from a feminist perspective, solidarity with Palestinian women, and maternal mortality. There were also exhibitions on the work carried out by each group, videos, and artistic activities: women's poetry, music and theater. Without question one of the high points of the festival was the public appearance--for the first time in Nicaragua--of the Managua lesbian feminist collective, whose booth selling books and posters was one of the most well attended of the festival.

The festival and its success in terms of attendance--in spite of the explicit boycott by the Sandinista media--was an historic event in the development of the women's movement in Nicaragua. The "Festival of the 52%" marked the end of one stage of the women's movement characterized ultimately by considerable political dependence on the FSLN and the beginning of another characterized by a determination to develop internal democracy, to set its own objectives and methods of political work, and to build relationships with other social and political movements on the basis of autonomy.

After the events of March 8 and in spite of the break with AMNLAE, the forty women's groups and organizations needed to affirm their will to continue with the still uncompleted process of "reactivation" of the movement. However, for three months, these groups and organizations were practically out of touch with each other.

What was the reason for this? For women militants of the Sandinista Front, the festival represented a serious dilemma. The women's secretariats of the mass organizations were receiving strong pressure from the national leadership of their organizations and from the Sandinista party itself. How could Sandinista women be publicly confronting each other? Thus, between March and June 1991 the women's secretariats of UNE, CONAPRO, ATC, and CST pulled back, and the Sandinista Youth, the teachers and the health workers retreated even more. Meanwhile the majority of the other groups did not want to force a process that might result in a second break within the movement.

Because of the economic crisis, the unemployment which was pushing a growing number of salaried women towards the informal sector of the economy, and the economic problems of the labor organizations themselves, the women's secretariats found themselves losing strength within their own organizations and had ever greater difficulties responding to their members' anguished demands for support. There were clear limitations to the degree to which they--as members of the women's movement--could take positions radically autonomous of the FSLN, given the unfavorable array of forces within their own organizations.

At the same time the women's secretariats of the ATC and the CST, accustomed for years to being the "center of operations"--and of decisions--and at the heart of the movement, after March 8 made a dramatic cry to the rest of the movement to close ranks around their issues, without taking into account that because of mass unemployment, many women were no longer unionized workers and were identifying themselves now in terms of their neighborhood or community. The labor organizations continued to be an important force but no longer the only one, nor even the main one. They had to join forces with other women who were organizing themselves in other ways.

The resistance by the leaders of the women's secretariats of the ATC and CST to accept a more limited role as the movement consolidated led to accusations against them by other women's groups who worked at the neighborhood level--among them various centers, houses and feminist collectives--of again trying to assert hegemony over the movement.

At the same time, the intransigence of AMNLAE and the hostile attitude in certain Sandinista circles towards any proposal of political autonomy for the women's groups resulted in an intensified, almost visceral rejection of any kind of political tie with the FSLN on the part of the feminist groups and centers. This put the women who were active in the mass organizations between a rock and a hard place.

Obviously, on both sides the differences were not just about strategy but were also differences about what constituted the most important issues for the women's movement. For the labor and mass organizations, the focus was on the worsening economic crisis and issues of employment, working conditions, childcare centers, privatization of property and developing income-generating projects for women. For the groups which worked with women in poor neighborhoods, the emphasis was more on the issues related to the kinds of services these groups could provide such as responding to violence against women, skills training, sexuality and health. As a result of these different priorities, women from the mass organizations began to call their demands "the popular demands" of women and to call the demands of the other groups "feminist," thus regressing to the debate, which to a large degree had been overcome, over whether women's practical interests were feminist or not.

All of these resulted in a growing distance between the two sides and the distancing of the women's secretariats of the labor organizations from the rest of the movement. The unity among women labor unionists was even further strained when the women's secretariats of the ATC and the CST, as well as AMNLAE, opposed the candidacy of *Commandante* Dora María Téllez for membership in the national leadership of the FSLN during its first Congress in July 1991. In contrast, the women's secretariats of the UNE and the CONAPRO, together with the rest of the women's movement, actively campaigned to include at least one woman in the national leadership of the strongest opposition party in the country.

Thus by the middle of 1991 we found ourselves with the following currents of political positions: AMNLAE was on one hand and the ATC and the CST were on another; a series of groups and organizations including the women's secretariats of the UNE and the CONAPRO, centers and NGOs that work with women, and independent feminist collectives such as those of Matagalpa and Masaya and the women's

houses of Managua formed a third current; and finally a fourth current--
the majority--included many women's groups who did not identify
with any of the three other currents, nor involve themselves in
strategizing about the development of the women's movement. Groups
in this fourth current included women's agricultural collectives and
cooperatives and the majority of women organized around specific
themes: Christian women, disabled women, soy promoters, environ-
mentalists, etc.

The National Gathering

In August 1991, tired of waiting for AMNLAE, the ATC and the CST
to decide to participate in convening the reactivation conference, about
thirty groups, centers and organizations--the majority of them from
Managua--began to work in committees to prepare for the event. We
wanted to involve the participation of women from all the women's
groups and organizations in the country. Without imposing any kind of
limitations and respecting the identities, platforms, structures and
leadership of each of the participating groups, we hoped to agree on
some common actions.

Obviously there were different expectations within the organizing
committee for the national conference. Both the preparation process as
well as the results of the conference made clear what the disagreements
among the groups were. One of these revolved around different
strategies for building the movement. The organizers of the conference
were not totally conscious of these differences, nor were the differences
totally elucidated until after the gathering when they became for some
of us the cause of "un-gathering" among those who had been meeting,
with consequent repercussions for the movement in general.

On one hand there was an effort to build and consolidate a nucleus
of active, organized and self-proclaimed feminists, capable of bringing
together, coordinating and orienting the movement. This necessarily
involved defining a common political platform, creating a stable
coordinating structure, and designating those who would publicly
represent the movement. On the other hand there was an effort to
strengthen the broad-based women's movement and to overcome
polarization and dispersion; from our diversity find our common
interests or at least the majority's interests, without forcing the unity
process.

In this sense, the strategy was to construct unity and cohesion step
by step. By looking for concrete actions that would bring together the
diverse expressions of the movement, and allowing women's felt needs
to emerge little by little, the most appropriate and flexible forms of
coordination would facilitate and harmonize the process.

Many of us did not agree with the idea of creating, in the heat of the conference, a new movement. We knew that there was a lot of distrust among women's groups because of past attempts to impose hegemony and domination. It was not reasonable to expect that the women in AMNLAE and in the mass organizations would agree to belong to a new movement, regardless of what it was called. Therefore, an attempt to start such a movement would have excluded many of the women attending the gathering.

At last the long-awaited conference took place. The preparation itself marked another milestone in the history of the women's movement. First of all the conference was organized by individual women who voluntarily joined the organizing committee. It did not have the sponsorship of any political party or social organization. Second, the nature of the attendance at the conference was different from past conferences: instead of each group or entity sending a representative (as was the custom) any woman could attend as an individual.

As Sofía Montenegro wrote in *Barricada*,

> The system of individual registration avoided institutionalized representations and favored the freer expression of opinions, because everyone spoke as an individual. This had the advantage of promoting dialogue among equals, avoided lobbying and manipulation, and encouraged the participants to look for what they had in common and to reach consensus.

Third, the methodology was unique. As Sofía went on to write,

> There were no prefabricated documents or positions. There were only enough questions posed so that the participants could respond from their own knowledge and understanding, and on the basis of their responses, look for the common ground among them. This "style" of doing things encourages people to look for their own solutions to solve their most pressing problems and it enables them to take destiny into their own hands. In short, it strengthens the self-affirmation and autonomy of individuals and of civil society, breaking the cycle of people's paralysis and their sense of victimization and resignation.

Fourth, the participants were extraordinarily diverse. "Diverse but United" was the slogan of the meeting and made explicit the hopes of the conference's organizers to include women from different places, economic situations and organizational experiences. This objective was achieved, the only exception being that the great majority of the women participating identified themselves politically as "progressives" (although not necessarily as Sandinistas).

The event was praised for its resounding success, both by the women participating--800 women attended instead of the anticipated 250--as well as by the media (both left-wing and right-wing) which gave the conference unprecedented coverage. The results of the meeting were reached by consensus; first, to carry out three national women's actions; and, second, the formation of seven networks (Economy and Environment, Violence, Sexuality, Health, Education, Social Communicators and Political Participation) that would convoke and organize actions and follow up on the specific thematic proposals that emerged at the conference.

However, after the event, there was an assessment of the conference results that generally reflected the range of expectations that had preceded it. Some of the organizers felt frustrated that the conference had not produced a more organized feminist movement with its own voice capable of being effective in national politics and which could immediately overcome the dispersion of the movement.

This question of the efficacy of the networks was related to a debate which continues today, an internal debate over the different concepts and definitions of "feminism." Some Nicaraguan feminists think of themselves as an ideological current active within the women's movement while others would rather identify themselves as a political-organizing movement distinct from the broader women's movement and at the same time influencing it.

The first tendency maintains that the existence of a separate feminist organization with a clearly defined membership may in fact push women in the broad-based movement farther away from feminism instead of attracting them. This tendency sees feminism not as a preconceived given but rather as an individual and collective process. From the moment that there is a politically distinct group which defines itself as "The Feminists," it is clear that other women are not feminist. Crossing from one side of the boundary line to the other becomes much more difficult.

The second tendency does not consider the broad women's movement to be autonomous as long as each of the entities that are part of it are not autonomous. In this sense, when they speak of an autonomous women's movement they are referring to a movement made up exclusively of groups, centers and feminist collectives with organizational autonomy. This would not include the women's secretariats in unions, for example, or even AMNLAE. Obviously this concept makes imperative a much-needed discussion on the question of autonomy.

In all cases the demand for explicit "autonomy" on the part of this second tendency overlooked the fact that autonomy is not exclusively a question of will. Both at the personal level and at the collective or social level the ability to act independently and with self-determination depends to a large extent on the objective and subjective context. Economic and political dependency exist quite apart from the desire and interests of those who must suffer them. If there is a country which has experienced economic and political dependency firsthand it is Nicaragua. The problems that result from dependency may be confronted through alliances, but dependency does not magically disappear. It has cost us women a lot even to want, much less practice, autonomy. We still have to learn how to establish alliances and how to "change the world without losing ourselves."

What Has Happened Since the National Conference?

Some of the networks formed at the 1992 Nicaraguan gathering have flourished. For example, in May 1992 the women's groups who form the Women's Health Network carried out a successful national campaign against maternal mortality, organizing more than 200 activities in more than 20 municipalities throughout the country. One of the gains of their work has been that the National Commission Against Maternal Mortality, established by the Ministry of Health, has agreed to include organized women's groups in the commission instead of exclusively medical institutions.

The Network on Economy and the Environment has also been quite active. Among other activities it initiated the organizing of marches in three departments of the country for International Women's Day and, together with the Action Network of Women for the Environment of the Nicaraguan Environmental Movement, organized a "Green Festival."

The Sexuality Network, as part of the larger "National Commission for Sexuality Free of Prejudice" organized an intensive week of activities around the celebration of Gay and Lesbian Pride in June 1992. Currently, the network continues participating in a campaign to abolish a new article in the Penal Code, recently approved by the National Assembly, which condemns to one to three years in prison anyone "who promotes, propagandizes for, practices and induces anyone to practice in a scandalous way cohabitation between persons of the same sex."

Interestingly, Nicaragua is one of the few (if not the only) of the Latin American countries where lesbians and gay men form a unified movement and where since very early on there have been strong ties with feminist groups and even with the broader women's movement.

To end the year, the Women's Network Against Violence showed creativity and effectiveness in carrying out the strongest campaign ever in Nicaragua in commemoration of November 25, the Latin American Day Against Violence Towards Women. With more than 220 activities in a number of parts of the country, television and radio shows, distribution of flyers, educational displays, street theater and banners, the campaign involved many women from a range of sectors and also, for the first time, men, youth groups and children.

On the other hand, some of the networks which were formed at the conference have experienced setbacks or have completely ceased to function because of lack of interest or internal cohesion.

Parallel to the work carried out by the networks, which are comprised mainly of women's groups, collectives and independent centers, the women's organizations such as AMNLAE--which celebrated its 15th anniversary in September 1992--and the women's secretariats of the labor unions and mass organizations have succeeded, despite the economic crisis, in maintaining and even, in some cases, developing health and legal aid services and offering training to the women in their respective sectors.

Because of this new visibility and assertiveness of our movement, the tide turned in 1992 in regard to the representation of women in leadership positions in the country. The ATC and the CST went from having one to having three women in top leadership positions, and the CST also has two more women on their national council. When the UNAG and the UNE expanded their respective national executive committees, the UNAG increased the number of women members from one to two, and the UNE went from one to four, while the Sandinista Youth for the first time elected a woman as vice-coordinator at the national level.

Notwithstanding some disappointments, the actions carried out by the networks formed during the conference, the creativity and the initiative of the women's groups, collectives and organizations, and the active presence of a diversity of expressions of the women's movement in the media, clearly made 1992 overall a very positive year for women.

Even though the traditional organizing of large-scale or public political actions has diminished, in large part because of the absence of an external cohesive force, such as the FSLN or AMNLAE, the reality is that the women's movement has expanded throughout the country in a decentralized form.

According to a series of interviews of grassroots leaders from a variety of women's groups and organizations, carried out by *La Boletina*, a small feminist bi-monthly magazine published in Managua by the *Puntos de Encuentro* Foundation, the majority of women state that the movement has developed, diversified and gotten stronger and that it is now present among sectors of women who until recently had not been reached.

Women refer to the National Conference as the most important event of the year and agree on the importance of the realization that "all of us, from our different perspectives, have a place and a role in the women's movement." Some point out as an achievement the process of developing autonomy which liberates the women's movement from the control of the FSLN and the mass organizations and frees the movement from an exclusively class-based analysis and other forms of oppression experienced by women.

In regard to the main obstacles the women's movement experienced during the year, women identified "the lack of receptivity and concern that still characterizes government, popular and mass organizations in regard to women's issues." Within the movement, other factors were identified: "the economic crisis affecting the majority of the collectives, women's houses and women's groups"; "the lack of communication among women's organizations and groups"; and "the lack of assertiveness of women in leadership positions, women who could but, because of fear, fail to respond to women's issues."

The suggestions and proposals for the future of the movement are abundant. "We need a single front to confront this conservative government, and we need to demand fast and effective solutions to the socio-economic crisis we're suffering." "We need a project, in which representatives of all the groups participate, to draft laws that reflect the interests of women in all the areas that affect them." "We should continue the Campaign against Violence towards Women and Girls. The campaign should be permanent." "We should include disabled women in society so that they can study, work and enjoy themselves like all other women. People should look at the person, not at the wheelchair, crutches or cane." "We have to decide on a strategy that will give the movement attention in the media. We must continue making progress in training women, integrating theoretical and practical work, and offering follow up to forums on areas of interest to women." "We must work on our fears, even our most secret fears, so as to be able to be fully independent and to create new spaces and to strengthen existing spaces. We need to work with positive energy, with enthusiasm, and with honesty to overcome differences."

A number of the women interviewed even suggested forming a national women's coordinating group. The current women's movement in Nicaragua is clearly a broad social movement in which, despite geographic dispersion and a lack of infrastructure, the groups involved are interested in connecting in a context of independence, autonomy and equality.

Political action as an organized and cohesive force with new ways of working that are acceptable to all the groups–something which is an aspiration of many women and would be very helpful in developing the strength to confront the government's backwards policies on women's issues–is the challenge before us.

It will probably be a slow process, and it is a process which should be based on the mutual trust we are developing on the basis of collective actions, respect for diversity, and the certainty that the strength of each is the strength of all.

Farmers' Organizations and Agrarian Transformation in Nicaragua

Eduardo Baumeister

T his article is divided into four sections. The first section covers the period of the mobilization and organization of Nicaraguan campesinos before the July 1979 revolution. The second section will discuss the impact of the Sandinista agrarian reform on campesino mobilization. The third section will focus on organization among the campesinos and the medium-sized agricultural producers in the National Union of Farmers and Ranchers (*Union Nacional de Agricultores y Ganaderos-UNAG*) during the Sandinista period (1979-1990). The fourth section will treat the role of UNAG during the current period since the electoral defeat of the Sandinistas.

In the rural areas of Nicaragua certain tendencies have prevailed regardless of the party in power. Historically (before the Sandinista revolution) the mobilization and organization of Nicaraguan campesinos was relatively weak in terms of the number of campesinos involved and the organizational structures that developed. In comparison with similar countries such as Honduras and El Salvador and even Costa Rica which developed under structural and political conditions much less polarized than the rest of the region, peasant organizations in Nicaragua were much less developed.

However, the tendency of Nicaraguan campesinos to become involved in political and military struggles has been relatively high. In the 1959-1979 period there were networks in the countryside of campesinos that collaborated with the Sandinista guerrillas. The open support for the Sandinistas was even greater in the period immediately after the revolution when large numbers of campesinos swelled the ranks of both the Sandinistas and the contras.

In Nicaragua one finds a relatively low level of autonomous organization in terms of campesino mobilization and expression of demands, together with a high level of participation in political-military struggles. This has been characteristic of the rural sectors since the 19th century.

The other dynamic at play in Nicaraguan agriculture has been a nearly constant struggle between economically and politically important sectors. Earlier the liberals were pitted against conservatives, then the anti-Somocistas against the Somocistas, then the Sandinistas against the contras. Nearly always the "visible hand" of the United States has been at work.

Landowning classes or the political groups in power have almost always had difficulties in creating a viable agrarian model based on large landholdings. Large plantations, whether Nicaraguan-owned *fincas* or large plantations owned by international fruit companies like the ones established in Honduras and Costa Rica or state-owned farms which existed during the Sandinista government, have been difficult to sustain. Traditionally, the viability of large landholdings depends on a sustained capacity for capital accumulation and stable control over the work force whether this work force was *peones*, migrant workers, sharecroppers, daily laborers, or state workers. The plantation model's political viability also depends on its ability as an economic and sociopolitical instrument to influence other property-owning or politically influential sectors. Neither condition exists for long in Nicaragua.

During different periods the groups in power have used the State to build economic power that serves the interest of their group. After seizing power in 1937 the Somoza family not only enriched themselves but also created new business sectors among the groups politically close to them and tried to strengthen the economic sectors which supported them politically. At the end of the 1970s one of the aspects which most divided the Nicaraguan bourgeoisie was the attempt by Anastasio Somoza to strengthen one business group by parlaying benefits from the government to this group at the expense of the other bourgeois sectors.

During the Sandinista period the group-interest factor took other forms. The Sandinistas did not promote one sector of private enterprise as the Somozas did, but rather attempted to develop large, state-owned projects creating twenty such agro-industrial projects and nearly forty enterprises engaged in agriculture, cattle and capital-intensive agricultural services. These new enterprises, largely controlled by a group of educated Sandinistas who, for the most part, came from the country's traditionally wealthy families, were seen as the high-growth sector of Nicaraguan agriculture and were the first priority for the revolution. Growth in other agricultural production in the country was encouraged but could count on little access to state resources.

During the Sandinista period the picture was highly conflictive both because of the struggles within the dominant agricultural sectors and due to the attempts to create an agrarian sector based on large scale production units. Particularly the politicization of campesinos played a significant and contradictory role in three different ways. First, the campesinos readily responded to the calls to take sides in the internal political struggles or to opt either for or against foreign intervention. For the campesinos the struggle to either defend or to gain land determined whether they sympathized with the Sandinistas or with the contras. Second, the medium-sized and large landowners had great influence on the attitudes and positions of the campesinos and were able to coopt the campesinos into supporting political positions held by landowners. Third, for the campesinos basic ideological values such as nationalism and traditional religious piety had enormous significance, and these values were frequently appealed to in order to sway the campesinos to join one side or the other in the confrontation.

CAMPESINO MOBILIZATION BEFORE 1979

Analysis of Structural Factors

There are a number of structural factors that have affected mobilization of campesino groups. First of all, as Table 1 shows, rural Nicaragua has the lowest population density in all of Central America. Nicaragua is also one of the countries in Latin America where the medium-sized farms are most significant, both in terms of their percentage of total number of farms, as well as the percentage of land that they occupy.

The steady expansion of agriculture after World War II more than doubled the cultivated land area. This grew from 3.3 million *manzanas* in 1952 to a little over eight million *manzanas* by the end of the 1970s. This process had two important effects. One was the competition between the campesinos, who had cleared the land in order to raise basic grains, and the cattle ranchers who expanded their landholdings. The steady growth of cultivated land also increasingly brought campesinos under the subordination of patrons as the sphere of control of the landowners and the medium-sized producers (because of the resources that they could offer--tools, transportation, credit, animals, paid labor) grew. The demand for labor to clear brush, plant orchards,

TABLE I: LAND USE IN CENTRAL AMERICA

Land used for agriculture or cattle ranching per economically active population at the end of the 1980s in Central America (measured in manzanas/*person with 1* manzana *equaling 1.7 acres):*

El Salvador	3.3
Guatemala	4.0
Honduras	4.4
Costa Rica	9.3
Panama	10.7
Nicaragua	19.8

Source: Baumeister, 1990

and sow and fence pasture on the cattle ranches increased as the number and size of ranches grew.

The widespread effect of rural commercialization and wage labor reduced the community bonds and radically altered the traditional nature of the campesinos, particularly in comparison with other countries in the region which had a significant population of indigenous people. Increasingly, campesinos became wage laborers and not *minifundistas* (small landowning farmers); more often their labor and product was commercialized and not subsistence-oriented. Campesinos in Nicaragua did not feel as much pressure as campesinos elsewhere to defend their lands at any cost from the usurping large landowners or to invade privately held lands. With land available in Nicaragua, campesinos had escape valves; they could clear new land, take up occasional or low-wage employment, or look for work in the cities. Land invasions in Nicaragua did not reach the level reached in some neighboring countries, although there were periods of time and parts of the country when these were prevalent, particularly in the departments of Leon and Chinandega where cotton interests expanded creating disputes with communal and ejidal lands.

THE SANDINISTA AGRARIAN REFORM

Land Tenure Pre-1979

In order to understand the Sandinista agrarian reform, one must be aware of, first of all, the structure of land tenure at the time of the Revolution, and secondly, the political process (particularly the internal political alliances) which gave birth to the agrarian reform. In Nicaraguan agriculture there was neither sufficient pre-capitalist features which would have more easily triggered a land reform (in order to eradicate the semi-feudal structures which did exist); nor were the capitalist features sufficiently established (as had been the case in pre-revolutionary Cuba), which would have made possible a rapid and massive transition to state or collective forms of production.

The most striking feature of the land tenure system at the time of the revolution was the presence of an important sector of small and medium-sized producers, a rare phenomenon in the typical Latin American land patterns of large *haciendas* and landless peasants. There was a mixture of small farmers and a developed class of rural petty bourgeoisie. There did exist, however, a landowning sector which controlled an important part of the cultivable land, but their levels of production were correspondingly less. The large landowners cultivated extensive tracts of land, yet their yield per unit of land was the lowest in Central America. The agrarian reform, then, took place within a context of an extremely heterogeneous, yet changing configuration of producers. The base of very dynamic smaller and intermediate capitalist sectors which predominated in the three decades before the revolution had given way to new landowning classes--cotton growers in the Pacific region and a substantial number of the coffee growers in the Central region. The expansion of cotton fields and cattle ranches meant an increased demand for land and growth in the (low-wage) proletarianization of campesinos.

The Somoza family, high level officers of the National Guard, and politicians within the Nationalist Liberal Party had already usurped about 15% of the land, mainly sugar, rice, and export tobacco plantations as well as extensive tracts for grazing cattle. The overall picture in Nicaragua presented, from a structural point of view, a system of land tenure quite different from that in the other Latin American countries which have had major land reforms. Nicaragua was not a case of strong semi-feudal landowner/tenant relations resulting in confrontations between peasant masses and absentee landowners; nor of large plantations controlled by foreign capital, a situation favorable to the development of nationalism; nor did a peasant community with indigenous traditions capable of producing symbols of a return to a pre-Hispanic past which had communal characteristics. In other words, neither large coffee plantations as in El Salvador or Guatemala, nor plantations like those in Honduras, Costa Rica or Cuba, nor the peasant communities like those of the Guatemalan highlands prevailed.

Nicaragua had also not experienced agrarian stagnation, as had been common to the countries which later underwent agrarian reforms this century. Indeed the opposite is the case. The agricultural sector experienced rapid growth creating new sectors of agricultural technicians, small and medium producers in the central region, wage workers in the Pacific North and in some sectors of the modern bourgeoisie associated with cotton and sugar cane which ultimately fed into the revolutionary surge at the end of the 1970s. With the exception of the farmworkers in the expanding cotton production, farmworkers and producers largely had benefitted economically from the strong growth in the agricultural sector after World War II.

The weakness of the Somoza model for agricultural development was not strictly structural or economic; more accurately the problems were situated in the sociopolitical realm. Under Somoza rule, the agricultural system was unable to incorporate into the political system the social forces which emerged in the 1950s, 1960s and 1970s. This is true both of the modern sectors of the bourgeoisie, the small and medium producers of the central interior region, as well as wage laborers; *Somocismo* fundamentally was based on the principle of the three P's established by Somoza Garcia: *plata* (money) for friends, *palos* (blows) for the vacillating, and *plomo* (bullets) for enemies.

A large part of the modern and traditional medium-sized sectors which joined the Sandinista cause did not feel represented or included in the political system under Somoza. In effect, these new social forces had not been able to establish their own organizations or business associations, and when they did achieve this, it was only at the very end of the 1970s. The Association of Cotton Growers of León (ADAL), for example, which was founded in mid-1978,[1] was founded by young cotton growers who had ties to the FSLN and many of whom later played important roles in the revolutionary government.

The large sector of small and medium-sized producers--which includes both landowning small farmers as well as more commercial enterprises--did not have its own organization. There were attempts to form such an organization in the 1970s, but these attempts were weak and passing. Rather, groups of campesinos and medium producers who had collaborated with the Sandinistas would be among the founders of UNAG in April 1981. UNAG's first president, in fact, was Narciso González, who was a farmer from Estelí and an active clandestine collaborator with the FSLN. Something similar occurred in regard to the Association of Farm Workers (ATC) (*Asociación del Trabajadores del Campo*), which was founded in early 1978 at the initiative of one of the tendencies of the Sandinista Front and which was successful in incorporating salaried farmworkers sectors in the Pacific North and Central regions.

Political Factors in the Agrarian Reform

The program of the Sandinista-led Junta for National Reconstruction, which had the support of all sectors opposed to Somoza, proposed three broad areas of change in regard to agriculture: a) nationalization of the banks, b) nationalization of agricultural exports, and c) an agrarian reform based on the confiscation of those properties which were owned by Somoza's family, indebted to the national bank, or lay idle. The agrarian reform faced international problems, however. Though there was widespread support by the broad anti-Somocista coalition for expropriations of the property of the former regime and its conversion into agrarian reform lands, within that coalition there were splits between private banks, agricultural exporters, and large property owners who rented their lands to different strata of cotton growers.

Perhaps the "overpoliticization" during the time of the Sandinista insurrection impeded observers from recognizing these structural tensions within the more established sectors of Nicaraguan agriculture at the end of the 1970s. These tensions played out over the next ten years creating a succession of changing alliances within the social base of the ruling Sandinista coalition. UNAG was created in April 1981 by Sandinista supporters and gave campesinos, for the first time in the history of Nicaragua, an active role in the national political arena. As an organization founded at the initiative of the FSLN, however, UNAG suffered from a top-down approach and only in the past few years has gained organizational cohesion. Concurrently during these ten years, a large part of the rural bourgeoisie, which originally was part of the revolutionary coalition, moved away from Sandinismo.

The fundamental change, however, in the balance of power in Nicaragua dates to the rise of counterrevolutionary activity beginning in 1981. The first contra bands began to operate before the revolution was a year old, but they were decisively strengthened by the involvement of ex-National Guard officers and, obviously, the North American administration, "factotum" of this movement.

The contras were successful in influencing broad sectors of farmers in the regions which bordered Honduras and Costa Rica, and in the vast area which lay between the Central and Atlantic regions of Nicaragua (known as the agricultural frontier). The contras' first base of support in the rural areas were among medium-sized and large coffee producers as well as farmers adversely affected by the agrarian reform. The contras also gained the collaboration of wage laborers and campesinos who were economically dependent on the larger producers.

The contras were able to use the Sandinistas revolutionary discourse against the government. The contras claimed to defend the rights to private property and said how revolutionary policies were hurting farmers. FSLN policies of state control over land and the market made fertile ground for the contras as the gap between the government and the average rural farmworker and farmer grew.

Between 1980 and 1985 the State attempted to maintain a virtual monopoly over the marketing of basic grains, although according to the law, producers could sell freely; however, in practice there was pressure to sell to the state marketing board. In 1986 the FSLN instituted a new policy which ended state control over the marketing of grain within the country resulting in increased production of corn and also, though to a lesser degree, beans (the most productive areas for beans were in the most highly conflictive areas).

The contra war and the economic crisis led to a series of negotiated deals between the State and the farmers. It is interesting that in doing so the Sandinistas broke with the historical revolutionary pattern (which began with the French revolution) which some have called a "Jacobinization," or a radicalization of the revolution to defend itself from counterrevolutionaries. In Nicaragua this did not occur. Despite the intensity of the war and the level of human and material resources committed to the war (levels comparable only to those of European countries most involved in the Second World War), the FSLN did not harden its position in the countryside. To the contrary, beginning in 1986 the Sandinista initiated a series of policies towards the agriculture sector and the rural areas which party members summed up in the word "flexibilization." This meant, first, an increase in the pace of the land distribution to individual campesinos, based in large measure on the parcelization of lands that had belonged to state-run collective farms.[2]

Second, the government increased benefits to individuals as opposed to collectives or cooperatives (land allocated to individuals, individual access to credit and services through cooperatives, and semi-collective forms and services). Third, a process for giving titles to land squatters and those occupying state lands was developed. Fourth was the liberalization in regard to the sale of basic grains.

Although the land distribution process was modified and although the State ceased to control the sale of grain, the general nature of the ties between the State and the campesinos continued to have strongly statist and authoritarian characteristics.

As the February 1990 elections made clear, this process of "flexibilization" proved inadequate to overcome the accumulated mistakes which the FSLN had made in the treatment of the campesinos.

The wounds were still too fresh, and U.S. pressure convinced a large number of campesinos that the only way to end the war was to vote against the FSLN. The war and the economic crisis had changed the social landscape of Nicaraguan agriculture, but this by no means indicated the disappearance of the traditional private sector in agriculture which is represented by COSEP.[3] Post-election studies showed that approximately two-thirds of the voting campesinos cast their ballots for UNO.[4]

Impact of the Agrarian Reform

Over the ten years of Sandinista government, the agrarian reform profoundly changed the nature of the country's agricultural sector. By 1990 the agrarian reform sector represented approximately 28% of agricultural and ranch lands. Approximately 43% of all campesino families had received land; if we include those who received titles to national lands on which they lived in the central region of the country and the agricultural frontier, that figure rises to 60%. The small group of large landowners who before 1979 owned 36% of the land, by the end of 1989 owned only 13.5%.

Perhaps the greatest change in land tenure during the 1980s was the central role which small and medium-sized farmers and the cooperative sector began to assume. By the end of the Sandinista period, the amount of land which was controlled by large farmers (who number around 700 and who generally were organized in COSEP) and by the entire state sector had decreased to about 25% of the cultivable land, while at the beginning of the revolution almost 40% of agricultural land was in the form of large plantations.

TABLE 2: STRUCTURE OF LAND TENURE (1988)[5]
(according to size of property owned in manzanas)

Private Sector (Individually-owned)		1988	1978
+ 500 *manzanas*	1,087,149	13.5%	36.2%
200- 500 *manzanas*	1,033,586	12.8	16.2
50-200 *manzanas*	2,293,293	28.4	30.1
10-50 *manzanas*	1,218,261	15.1	15.4
0-10 *manzanas*	167,726	2.1	2.1

Reformed Sector (Cooperatively-owned) (*non-exstent in 1978*)		1988
State land	948,230	11.7
Producer Coops	921,491	11.4
Credit/Serv Coops	133,620	1.7
Work Collectives	23,509	.3
Other cooperatives	37,060	.5
Individual plots	209,974	2.6
TOTAL	8,073,899	100%

MOBILIZATION OF FARMERS (1979 TO 1990)

With the revolutionary victory of 1979 the situation of the largely unorganized campesinos changed markedly. For the next two years (until April 1981), the FSLN-aligned Association of Farm Workers (ATC) sought to bring together farm laborers and small and medium-sized farmers and represent their interests. With the support of the revolutionary government and the FSLN, the ATC's work expanded throughout the country, particularly in large expropriated farms which had become state-owned collective farms.

In spite of these efforts, small and medium-sized farmers largely did not become involved in the ATC choice to become more involved in credit, services and production cooperatives organized by promoters of the Agrarian Reform institute and the National Development Bank.

In April 1981 the National Union of Farmers and Ranchers (UNAG) was founded uniting activist members of the ATC with those small and medium-sized farmers who had collaborated with the Sandinista guerrillas before the revolution. UNAG's first president, Narciso González, as well as the third and current president, Daniel Nuñez, came from this background. The second president, Wilberto Lara, was among a group of activists from Chinandega who had worked with the Church in the mid-70s.

The birth of the UNAG reflected the growing realization among FSLN leaders that the agricultural sector was structurally complex and that some organizations such as ATC could not relate to all sectors. The government had needed to establish stronger ties with small, medium-sized and large farmers. Relations work was most necessary in the interior where the contras had already begun to win over landowners and were gaining popularity with the intermediate and poorer sectors. The FSLN also saw UNAG as a way to neutralize the influence of rural businessmen among small and medium-sized farmers, particularly in the coffee growing zones of Matagalpa and Jinotega. Not coincidentally, the first assemblies of what would soon be called UNAG took place in those departments.

For these reasons, from its beginning UNAG sought to appeal to a politically and socially broad constituency that included medium-sized and even large farmers. In this sense it never purported to be an organization of campesinos in the strict sense, but rather an organization of producers which would offset the influence of the large farmers organized in the traditional Chamber of Commerce of the UPANIC which was associated with the COSEP. Given the FSLN's ambiguity towards private enterprise, UNAG's identity tended to fluctuate; at times UNAG sought good relations with the private sector with the objective of increasing "national unity" while at other times distanced itself from large farmers and commercial interests and identified with the FSLN's revolutionary and radical goals.

Three tendencies within the organization surfaced as UNAG developed throughout this period, and in some ways these tendencies anticipated the changes which the organization experienced after the change of government in 1990. The first tendency followed the policies of the FSLN, particularly its positions as the ruling party which was in a war against the contra forces. The second tendency was made up of the small farmers and members of cooperatives, whose principal concerns were access to greater resources, including land, credit and technical assistance. The third tendency responded to the concerns of the influential medium-sized and even large farmers, particularly those located in the interior of the country, who sought to forestall the expansion of the revolutionary process and to diminish the role of the government in the economy.

The following table shows the representation of different social groups which made up the membership of UNAG and of its National Council. In the tables "Individual Members" refers to small, medium and large producers. "Members of Cooperatives" includes members both of production cooperatives (generally collectively owned property) as well as credit and service cooperatives.

TABLE 3: COMPOSITION OF MEMBERSHIP
OF UNAG AND NATIONAL COUNCIL OF UNAG[6]
in percentage

Types of producers	Membership in UNAG (1987)	Membership in National Council (1989)
Individual Members	22%	89%
Members of Cooperatives	78%	41%
	100%	100%

(total number of Members: 124,212)

A closer analysis of the membership of the National Council of UNAG more clearly demonstrates the influence of the medium producers in the organization. In 1989 individual farmers made up 59% of the representatives on the National Council of UNAG (out of fifty individual farmer representatives, 27 were medium-sized farmers, 22 were small farmers, and only one was a large farmer). Meanwhile representatives on the Council who were cooperativists only made up 41%.

This data reflect the growing influence of small and medium-sized individual producers within the National Council of UNAG. Their rise within the Council reveals certain perspectives of the FSLN as well as the nature of UNAG as farmers' organization, namely that UNAG was not a strictly mass organization and that its leadership was dominated by small and medium-sized landowners and not by campesinos.

To what degree, then, did UNAG become a sort of "Agrarian Front" for the FSLN or to what degree was it a more autonomous expression of the interests of agricultural producers? UNAG was a mixture of both. In part the rising prominence of the medium-sized farmers responded to the effort of the FSLN, particularly from 1984 on, to incorporate medium-sized and large farmers in the interior of the country into a Sandinista coalition and to impede the contras from gaining support from these groups. In part, too, their growing influence reflected the importance of these sectors in agriculture, particularly at this moment when medium-sized farmers were almost split in half, one part collaborating with the Sandinistas through UNAG and the other moving into positions of leadership and collaboration with the contras.[7]

While some medium-sized farmers were the object of competition, other groups in agriculture, namely poor campesinos who both farmed and worked in seasonal wage labor, found themselves with little support from agricultural organizations, either UNAG or ATC. ATC concentrated on the situation of year-round wage laborers in agriculture, particularly those laborers employed on state-run farms. On the other hand, UNAG's work was centered mainly on the sectors organized in cooperatives or commissions. In practice, these commissions usually succeeded in involving medium-sized and large farmers. As a result, significant numbers of largely landless campesinos did not find any organization that addressed their interests.

CONTRAS AND CAMPESINO MOBILIZATION

Throughout Nicaragua's political history popular sectors have been readily incorporated into political-military struggles either voluntarily or through coercion. The 1980s are yet another instance of this. A large number of young men of peasant origin joined the Sandinista Army voluntarily and many through forced military service. A large number of volunteers and conscripts also filled the ranks of the contras. The following breakdown shows the composition of demobilized contra groups:[8]

* number of demobilized troops was 22,000;

* 83% were from rural, agricultural backgrounds and were mainly landless peasants;

* 94% were from zones other than the Pacific region;

* 60% were less than 25 years old and the majority were illiterate.

Within the contra forces existed the same social stratification that existed in the rural interior of the country. For example, the Jorge Salazar Regional Commandos which operated in the zones of Matagalpa, Zelaya and Chontales, the positions of political leadership inside the country were held to a large extent by sons of large landowners; the intermediate positions were held by tenant farmers who rented from the landowners, and the ground troops were poor campesinos and wage laborers.[9] The majority of the leadership outside the country (in Honduras, Costa Rica or the United States) were men with political or military ties to the Somoza regime.

Significance of the Revolutionary Period for Farmers

Before the revolution the campesinos and medium-sized farmers were a more important social and economic sector in Nicaragua than similar groups were in other countries of Central and Latin America. Despite their high percentage of production of basic grains, beef and export of crops such as coffee, the access of Nicaraguan small farmers to bank credit, technical assistance, health care and education was very limited. There was also a large sector of seasonal wage laborers who also depended on subsistence farming although they had only precarious access to land. In the areas where new land was being opened up, many of the small and medium-sized farmers did not have titles to the land on which they were working. Marketing mechanisms, credit and agro-industrial processing of the most important products were to a large extent in the hands of big businessmen who did not have direct financial interests in agriculture and cattle ranching.

The decade of Sandinista rule left a mixed legacy for campesinos and medium-sized farmers. This period saw the entry of these groups as organized entities into civil society and politics. Today they have their own national organizations which unite different sizes of farmers (although the interests of the smallest-size farmers, basically poor campesinos, are under-represented). However, even this represents

The Sandinista agrarian reform gave access to land to tens of thousands of farming families.

considerable progress if one takes into consideration the situation prior to 1979 or compares the situation of Nicaraguan farmers to those in similar countries. UNAG, the largest organization of small and medium-sized farmers in Central America, has made considerable achievements in providing agricultural supplies to its base and, at the insistence of its members, is moving into marketing (both for domestic and for export). UNAG also has considerable interest in becoming a financial intermediary between farmers and credit institutions.

These achievements were no doubt furthered by the strong role that the revolutionary State and the Sandinista party played in the formation of the organization. This created for UNAG, however, a dependency on the government and a complex entanglement with the political party of the FSLN. However, given these limitations, UNAG's autonomy from the government and the FSLN was striking during the 1980s; since the electoral defeat of the Sandinistas in 1990, the trend towards greater autonomy has clearly sharpened.

There has been a strong effort on the part of UNAG to de-polarize confrontations with the counterrevolution (both during the war and subsequently), in part by UNAG's attempt to include the demands of the campesino supporters of the counterrevolutionaries in UNAG's platform. After the war ended, UNAG moved quickly to close the gaps between its base and elements of the National Resistance (the official name of the contras) and the two groups looked for common points of interest, a process which helped decompress the high level of tension in the rural areas.[10]

The agrarian reform increased campesinos and medium-sized farmers' control over the land as well as opened access to other resources; however, the country as a whole experienced a severe economic retraction, particularly in agriculture. Overall, this can be characterized as a process of redistribution of assets without economic growth. The alliance which overthrew Somoza and formed a support base for the Sandinistas could not--because of the war and its own errors--form an alliance for development. Policies which led to state capitalism in banking, agro-business and in domestic and export marketing were not effective at halting the slide in production, much less at increasing it.

One of the hopes that could arise out of the economic retraction would be the formation of a "development alliance" which would stimulate capitalist enterprises in the countryside and at the same time would maintain economic and institutional space for campesinos and medium-sized farming sectors. A "development alliance" would not be of wholesale benefit to campesinos and small farmers, and it is questionable whether their incorporation into such a market model of development would be positive on the whole. However, at the same time, Nicaragua offers some possibilities for development alternatives that would not necessarily be "zero-sum" (where one sector benefits only at the cost of the other); given the availability of farm lands and the vast areas still uncultivated, there are possibilities of increasing production using models that are labor-intensive and not capital-intensive.

On the other hand, the current policies of economic stabilization and structural adjustment create strong pressures of a "zero-sum" nature, particularly in regard to the competition for access to credit between campesinos/small farmers who produce for the domestic market and large farmers who produce for export. Another source of conflict is the allocation of profits between those who produce the goods (farmers) yet earn relatively little and the business interests (lenders, ag inputs vendors, middle-men, exporters, etc.) who earn relatively much more.[11]

A RETURN TO THE PAST?

In the 1990 elections, the vote against the Sandinistas was more pronounced in the rural areas and in the interior of the country than in urban areas. In the ten years since the Sandinista triumph, the dramatic turnaround indicates the degree of erosion of support for Sandinistas caused by the war and the economic crisis in the countryside. The blame cannot be fully laid with the contras, however, as the Sandinista agrarian policies that heavily prioritized state farms, state control of marketing and political authoritarianism antagonized many campesinos.

The Chamorro government has launched a number of initiatives in agriculture: a) partial reprivatization of lands affected by the agrarian reform; b) de-nationalization of export marketing and the banks; c) large-scale importation of food stuffs; d) elimination of guaranteed prices for the sale of basic grains; and e) drastic reduction in access to bank credit for small farmers and cooperatives.

It is difficult to predict how far this "return to the past" will go. Already part of the government-owned land has been returned to its former owners, and private business interests have gained control of the marketing of export crops. The private business interests have strengthened their financial position by gaining access to government credits for improving damaged coffee plantations and for rebuilding large herds of cattle.

Notwithstanding these reversals, however, the changes in the international economic context and profound political crisis that the country is experiencing make a complete return to the period before 1979 difficult. What is more imaginable is a long period of conflict and crisis in the countryside, where those who attempt to reproduce the agriculture of the past will not be fully successful and will be forced to coexist with small and medium-sized farmers and cooperatives who are defending their own space in production, marketing and financial management. This crisis of hegemony in the countryside is creating a situation of paralysis for government plans and programs. On the one hand, the government has not been able to placate former landowners, including many Somocista groups, who insist on the complete return of expropriated lands that currently belong to agrarian reform cooperatives. On the other hand the government has not met the demands of campesino and cooperative sectors for full legal entitlement of their lands and for access to credit and other government services. These disputes take place in the context of a delicate balance of concertation between the presidency and the FSLN in the hopes that an end to the polarization will help create conditions for the economic reactivation of the country.

The UNAG and the New Political Situation

With the electoral victory of the National Opposition Union (UNO) and the accession to the presidency of Violeta Chamorro the Nicaragua political picture changed radically. Contra military attacks ceased and conditions existed for a "normalization" of the country along the lines of what was happening in other Central American countries. The coalition of forces represented in UNO could not be considered a consolidated political power for various reasons. First, the Sandinista forces continue to control a very important amount of state power; they have 41% of the votes, which gives them a great deal of legislative power; and, above all, they have retained their capacity for social mobilization of urban labor unions, community associations, campesino organizations, social communications media and party activities.

Second, the UNO coalition is extremely disparate in terms of its political, class and ideological composition, and, since February 25, 1990, has experienced major internal conflicts. The coalition itself includes everything between the traditional conservative sectors to the Socialist and Communist parties, including liberals, Social Christians and Social Democrats. Executive power is controlled by non-party-affiliated technocrats and family members of President Chamorro. These reasons, in addition to the pressures imposed by the difficult economic situation in the country and international pressures, has resulted in a profound fragmentation of political power in Nicaragua after February 25.

Unquestionably the fragmentation of power in Nicaragua after the overthrow of Somoza in 1979 has its origins in the counterrevolutionary challenge which questioned the legitimacy of the Sandinistas. The contras succeeded in gaining support in remote areas near the Nicaraguan borders, although they were never able to permanently control any area of the country. The election results, rather than consolidating a new conservative hegemony, resulted in a greater fragmentation of power.

The influential group which surrounds President Chamorro is made up of young businessmen and technocrats from traditionally wealthy families who do not have formal ties with any of the coalition of parties in UNO. Typically they espouse the financial policies associated with the World Bank and believe that export of non-traditional products is Nicaragua's role in the world economy.

For these technocrats who are advising Chamorro, the ideal model of development is a neoliberal capitalist one. There is present, however, the influence of Social Christian thinking--or perhaps it is political calculation--as these technocrats are urging a socioeconomic develop-ment model that includes sectors of the small and medium-sized businesses which are organized in cooperatives, much like the model in Costa Rica. Part of the government plan includes "compensation" to the generally pro-Sandinista cooperatives for the privatization of their lands or businesses.[12] In many cases, the workers would be encouraged to purchase the enterprise from the government. Other enterprises to be privatized include the agro-industrial, marketing and financial interests which were initiated by UNAG. Under the Chamorro plan, the private sector would offer the financial backing to the workers who were purchasing formerly state-run enterprises. It is obvious that this plan does not rule out the probable failure of many, if not most, of these new worker-owned enterprises which arose out of the negotiations between the Sandinistas and the new government. Some observers feel that their failure is intended, in which case their assets would be ceded to groups of businessmen which the government considered more "authentic."

In a certain sense the chaotic situation arising out of the Sandinistas' electoral defeat and the formation of a new government is part of a continuum of early historic parallels. Particularly the crisis in the rural areas continues where neither the traditional sectors nor the modern-izing nor the cooperative sectors nor the contras have been able to establish pre-eminence. Within this political picture the role of the pro-Sandinista popular organizations changes considerably. When the FSLN lost the 1990 elections, they also lost much of the control they had exercised over the popular organizations. Since the elections, these groups have demonstrated a strength and militancy which were not seen earlier. The National Front of Workers (*Frente Nacional de Trabajadores*)) in particular has been a leading actor among the salaried labor unionists. It is important to point out that UNAG has been the mass organization that has been, relatively, the most autonomous and which has opposed many of the agrarian and economic policies of the revolution. In the period after April 25, 1990, UNAG no longer found enthusiastic support from the government which obviously ended the pseudo-statal role UNAG had played previously. In regards to relations with the FSLN, there is now a less dependent relationship although the majority of the leaders of UNAG are Sandinista activists. UNAG's autonomy strengthened both in relation to the FSLN and to government institutions.

The Rapprochement with the Contras

Immediately after the formation of the new government, UNAG took the risky step of approaching a sector of the contras, principally the forces lead by Commander "Franklin" (Ismael Galeano).[13] In May 1990 the President of UNAG Daniel Nuñez spoke with the contras in the hope of uniting the demands of campesinos belonging to the resistance, demobilized Sandinista Army soldiers and members of the Ministry of the Interior, as well as the members of the UNAG.

The first step proposed was a unified demand for lands, which could be resolved by distributing lands from state farms and in areas that had never been opened up for cultivation. In some areas, particularly in the department of Jinotega, demobilized contra forces had taken over private farms of UNO sympathizers who tried to have them forced off.

"Concertation" and Its Consequences for UNAG

Operating in a context of political instability, the Chamorro government in September 1990 initiated efforts at economic and social "concertation." The Nicaraguan concertation process resembles processes developed in other countries in Latin America: building a consensus on a number of sensitive topics between opposing social groups. In the case of Nicaragua the main issue has been property, although many other issues have been involved. The most significant aspects of the agenda in regard to property were: a) how much property should be returned to former owners; b) what rights do beneficiaries of the Sandinista agrarian reform have to keep their lands; and c) whether or not to let stand the redistribution of property that took place during the final period of the Sandinista government.

The business sector organized in COSEP has for the most part called into question the Sandinista agrarian reform and other land distribution with the exception of small individual plots of land for campesinos. On the other hand, the Chamorro government and the pro-Sandinista organizations have agreed in general to recognize the legitimacy of most of the property transferred during the revolution. The government and the organizations have also come to agreement on the privatization of state property in ways favorable to the interests of the workers. The agreement to transfer 25% of the state-owned assets to the workers also took place in the context of this understanding.

The UNAG has played a very active role in the concertation process. It has worked for privatization that benefits small and medium-sized agro-industrial producers--principally cotton processing plants, coffee refineries and cattle slaughterhouses. This is part of UNAG's strategy to strengthen the presence of such farmers in the processes of marketing, financing and agro-industrialization. Unlike the FNT, UNAG did not demand property claims although it has insisted on the right to direct negotiation with the State on issues of privatization. During the second stage of the economic and social concertation process (May through September 1991) UNAG negotiated certain benefits out of the inevitable privatization of the country's main slaughterhouse, el Carnic. The formerly state-run slaughterhouse was privatized becoming a cooperative in which the workers hold 25% of the capital and the producers hold the other 75%. The latter must purchase shares of stock (with each share worth U.S. $1,000), and no individual can acquire more than 14 shares. Payment is generally made in the form of livestock brought for slaughter.

UNAG and the Government: Towards a New Dependency?

The goal of government social and economic policies has been economic stabilization, and policies have followed the guidelines of international financial organizations. In terms of agriculture, this has important consequences. First, it has meant a major reduction in credit, principally in regard to basic grains raised by campesinos; this intensifies their traditional dependency on merchants and seasonal lenders (usually at exorbitant rates of interest). Second, the liberalization of the export trade as well as the increased international food assistance programs in Nicaragua make it extremely difficult for Nicaraguan campesinos to compete in the production of basic grains and raises serious questions about the economic viability of a significant sector of campesinos. Third, massive privatization of state property and the withdrawal by the state from providing support services to production, increases the vulnerability of small farmers, particularly in a market-driven economy which gives no allowances for drought, poor yields or other calamities.

As an organization, UNAG covers more of Nicaragua's territory than any other organization. Its leadership, in which medium-sized farmers predominate, has been very active in developing extensive relations with sectors of the government. Those relations have paid off in terms of government recognition of UNAG, for example, through the following means: a) UNAG representation on the directorate of the

National Development Bank; b) privatization on favorable terms to UNAG of the country's main slaughterhouse; c) government support in continuing to receive assistance from Sweden for an important marketing project; d) participation in the National Agrarian Commission which serves to arbitrate land conflicts and participation on similar commissions on the departmental level.

In April 1992 UNAG held its second National Congress in the Olof Palme Conference Center where Daniel Nuñez was ratified as the president of the organization and demonstrated an impressive ability in attacking the Ministers of his government in front of the campesino delegates to the Congress.

However, UNAG's legitimate role of intermediary between producers and the government on a spectrum of issues that range from integration of demobilized combatants to direct participation in negotiations with international financial organizations (such as the World Bank and International Monetary Fund) has left UNAG with a very compromising position in this new period in Nicaragua. The profound changes which brought about structural adjustment have dictated the terms of negotiations between popular organizations and the government in a totally different way from that which existed in the Sandinista period and in relation to other Latin American countries which also face an avalanche of stabilization and adjustment plans.

For small farmers the traditional agenda of negotiation with the government has been reduced significantly; basically, the government is no longer financing services to small farmers, and so little is left to negotiate. As Table 5 shows, the National Development Bank has cut support for campesinos under Chamorro.

TABLE 4: *CAMPESINO FAMILIES ASSISTED BY THE NATIONAL DEVELOPMENT BANK*

(from 1978 to 1991) [per thousands of families][4]

1978	16.0
1985	69.6
1986	80.6
1987	90.0
1988	102.2
1989	88.8
1990	74.1
1991	31.7

As in other countries in the region, the opposition (in Nicaragua's case, the Sandinistas), has not been able to offer viable economic alternatives to the policies of structural adjustment although it is clear from a number of perspectives that the neoliberal policies are deepening poverty and causing retraction in the national economy. This lack of alternatives is creating a crisis within organizations that represent popular interests; they do not know what to propose in terms of policies, plans or programs. The crisis makes essential a rethinking of the model of representation of small farmers and a rethinking of ways to confront the problems of the economic viability of these sectors.

While UNAG has been able to position itself vis a vis the government and its own base in the post February 1990 political scenario, it will take much longer for the organization to define its role within the new economic context as the central actor for small and medium-sized farmers.

Because of the factors elaborated earlier, production by the majority of the farmers organized in UNAG is suffering. As a result the organization is at a crossroads. One option is to try to integrate fully into the new economic model and to take an active role in export-oriented and domestic commerce, agro-industry and banking through cooperative-type enterprises. The other option is to concentrate on the defense of those sectors most vulnerable to the policies of structural adjustment; this would require a strong confrontational strategy in defense of land held by UNAG members and in defense of small and medium-sized producers.

Another important element in this analysis is the consequences of the new economic and political situation for the organizational structure of UNAG. During the revolutionary period, the UNAG had between 300 and 400 full-time promoters, as well as municipal and regional UNAG structures dedicated exclusively to the organization's work. UNAG's ties to governmental institutions were close, and UNAG received additional benefits through their government ties.

With the Sandinista loss in the elections and the installation of a new government the UNAG lost a considerable amount of material and institutional support, which resulted in a drastic reduction in the number of full time promoters. At present paid staff, including the national and departmental leadership, grassroots promoters and support staff, number less than 100 persons in the entire country. Grassroots work has suffered particularly among the poorest sectors of campesinos in the more remote zones of the interior and the agricultural frontier.

One cannot underestimate the extent to which the national leadership of UNAG has been based on the charisma of its president and principal leader since 1984, Daniel Nuñez. More than any other person, Nuñez was responsible for guiding UNAG towards positions of relative autonomy in relation to the Sandinistas during the revolutionary period, for initiating the rapprochement with the ex-contras, and for maintaining amiable relations with the Minister of the Presidency Antonio Lacayo. Nuñez, himself a well-known farmer and businessman, has been able to maintain a precarious equilibrium for UNAG between the positions of the influential medium-sized and large farmers who want to accept and fully integrate into the agro-industrial, commercial and financial system and the positions of the poorest sectors of the campesinos who want to struggle to have their most basic demands met.

Conclusion

Our interest in this article has focused on what kind of agriculturally-based organization emerges from a process of profound political changes, such as those that occurred during the Sandinista revolution. What kind of organization is UNAG? Within UNAG one can see the presence of a number of profiles. They could be characterized as:

a) UNAG as an "agrarian front" used to mobilize a popular base of a political party which, in this case, also controlled the government. In this way UNAG shared characteristics in common with the Mexican *Central Nacional Campesina* and the corporativist model promoted by the Mexican government under the rule of the PRI since the presidency of Lazaro Cardenas. The role of an "agrarian front" also resembles the National Association of Small Farmers (ANAP) in Cuba.

b) UNAG as an organization which in the past decade almost tried to be an interlocutor of the revolutionary government in the rural areas promoting policies of "national unity" and which tried to incorporate the more conservative agriculture-based business interests.[15]

c) UNAG as an organization of small and medium-sized farmers broken into different factions of working-class in the style of organizations of farmers in Southern Cone countries, or more recently, UPANACIONAL in Costa Rica or AHPROCAFE in Honduras.

d) UNAG as a more classic campesino organization which tries to represent and incorporate the campesinos, especially the poorest sectors, who are semi-proletarianized. In this model, the struggle for land plays a central role.

e) UNAG as an agricultural services organization playing a role in agricultural supplies, market and potentially financial activities. This role was reinforced after the electoral defeat of the Sandinistas.

All five dimensions are present almost from UNAG's birth as an organization emerging out of a broad political mobilization (in the late 1970s) and later supported and oriented by the revolutionary State. One has the impression that this process, to a large degree, is similar to the processes of agrarian reform in Latin America, though it is perhaps intensified in the case of Nicaragua by the absence of organizations prior to the revolution. The fundamental questions in regard to UNAG have to do with 1) the possibility of fully incorporating the poorest campesino sectors, including demobilized contra sectors, into the organization and into the national economy, and 2) the challenge of proposing and advocating for types of economic institutions that serve small and medium-sized farmers in the difficult postwar period. The fragmentation of political and state power could "feudalize" rural Nicaragua and lead to scenes of violence similar to what has occurred in Columbia. The instability is heightened by the policies of structural adjustment, which make the situation even more precarious for campesinos.

FOOTNOTES:

[1] Although there had been organizational precedents in earlier years.

[2] The state gave up a substantial amount of its lands. In 1980 the state owned approximately 1.3 million *manzanas* and by 1983 that had increased to 1.5 million *manzanas*. At that point the state was giving up more land than it was acquiring and by the end of Sandinista rule, the state had reduced its ownership to 948,000 *manzanas*.

[3] Perhaps their economic strength was overestimated at the beginning of the revolution, because their political power was so significant. However, at the beginning of the 1980s, the traditional private sector could claim only about 25% of agricultural and cattle production; by the end of the decade it was responsible for less than one fifth. The agrarian reform policies, migration out of the country, economic apathy or boycott by the wealthy, and the serious limitations experienced by the country in general contributed to this reduction.

[4] See *Envío* (July, 1992) which is published by the Jesuit Central American University in Managua, Nicaragua.

[5] These figures are taken from the CIERA publication, *The Land Reform in Nicaragua 1979-1989 Vol. IX* which are based on estimates made by the General Directorate of Agrarian Reform of the Ministry of Agriculture and Agrarian Reform. On the basis of these figures we have made our own estimates.

[6] Sources: Membership statistics for UNAG from the Project UNAG-Ecodepa Project, 1987; and our own calculations based on data of 85 representatives (out of 150 representatives) of the National Council of UNAG at the beginning of 1989.

[7] Ciera, 1989, vol. vi, Estudio sobre Matiguas

[8] Source: Civil Association of the National Resistance: Overview of the Process of Reinsertion [for ex-combatants] and Development Pole Projects. (document circulated in November 1990.)

[9] Ciera, 1989, vol. VI

[10] See the September 1990 issue of *Envío* for reporting on Daniel Nuñez.

[11] See Baumeister, 1992.

[12] These generally fell under the category of Workers' Property Areas *(Area Propriedad de los Trabajadores)* organized by the ATC and the labor union federation of the FNT.

[13] Galeano was the head of the general staff of the Northern Front of the FDN, which operated in the fifth region (the area of Nueva Guinea and El Almendro in the department of Zelaya). In 1992 he died in a car accident.

[14] The beneficiaries in 1991 break down into 23,800 families who belong to cooperatives or are individual small farmers, 6,700 families who were part of the process of demobilization of the contras, and 1200 more families (primarily repatriated refugees and demobilized contra families) who were assisted by the U.N. program PRODERE. Source: Department of Statistics of the National Development Bank, 1991 Yearly Statistics.

[15] This line was inconsistently applied because the leadership of MIDINRA [Ministry of Agriculture/Agrarian Reform] generally did not pass along these policy decisions to the leadership and promoters of UNAG.

The euphoric hopes of the early days of the Sandinista revolution were ground down by the contra war and a combination of internal factors. Neo-liberal policies have turned Nicaragua into the second poorest country in the hemisphere.

Unbinding the Ties That Bind: The FSLN and the Popular Organizations

Midge Quandt

As the July 1992 Sao Paulo Forum in Managua clearly revealed, the move away from vanguard politics is a distinguishing feature of the Latin American left today. The more than 60 movements and parties gathered there came out in support of "a national, democratic, and popular project" that included the strengthening of the social movements of civil society. "The left should stimulate the organization and participation of women, indigenous peoples, Blacks, youth, workers, campesinos, and the informal sector," declared the Forum working paper. "We have asked the people to understand the liberating imprimatur of our battles, but we do not sufficiently understand the same revolutionary character of the particular histories of persons, ethnicities, sexes etc. in their struggle."[1] This emphasis on grassroots organizing is part of a pervasive critique of traditional left politics. The reliance on cadre parties and top-down leadership styles; the subordination of social movements to political parties; the fetishizing of state power--all these have come under attack.

In Central America, the struggle of civil society is moving to center stage as the left, faced with the negotiating posture of modernizing, neoliberal regimes, tries to redefine itself. In the process of reformulating a democratic project, it is giving greater weight to the social movements and the popular organizations that embody them. And it is in Nicaragua and El Salvador that these movements have the greatest strength and vitality.

Since the electoral defeat of the Sandinista National Liberation Front (FSLN) in 1990, the popular organizations have insisted on greater independence from the Party. The party leadership, in turn, has agreed to bury the verticalist model, though what will replace it is unclear. There are still problems securing the autonomy of the social movements, but much has already been achieved. In addition, there is widespread acceptance of the values historically associated with social movements, especially those outside the scope of classical political parties and labor movements. These values include popular participation, group empowerment, the primacy of each sector's specific interests, and a less bureaucratic, more egalitarian ethos. Unlike many social movement activists in Latin America and the United States, however, those in Nicaragua do not make a fetish of autonomy and diversity.[2] For the most part, they do not believe that an alliance with a party like the FSLN automatically co-opts them, limits their independence, or diverts them from their goals.[3] Moreover, grassroots activists are in principle willing to go beyond the particular needs of their own organizations, though in practice the acute economic crisis makes this difficult to do.

The challenges facing the popular organizations and the Sandinista Front go beyond the issue of autonomy, however. What the left needs is not only grassroots empowerment but also a cohesive strategy to counter the logic of neo-liberalism. If autonomy is not to end in fragmentation, Sandinismo must find a way to articulate a popular project that links the different movements without compromising their independence. Though there is still no consensus on how this would work, the dual emphasis on organizational autonomy and coordinated struggle is part of the discourse of the left.[4] Consequently, Sandinista activists are typically hospitable to the notion of a vanguard party capable of coordinating a popular project as long as it sheds its elitism, authoritarianism, and intolerance of minority views.

Lack of Autonomy in the 1980s

After the victory of the United Nicaraguan Opposition (UNO), the FSLN had to face a surge of criticism from within the Party and the popular organizations. At the base and at the leadership level, Sandinistas voiced their discontent with the party structure. In addition, grassroots activists complained that their goals had too systematically and for too long been subordinated to those of the Sandinista Front. Misgivings about the authoritarianism of the Party were not new, but the elections served as a catalyst for a drastic reevaluation of its internal workings and external relations. Clearly the time had come for the Sandinistas to rethink their methods of organizing.

Running through the chorus of criticism was a unifying note–the rejection of verticalism and the top-down chain of command. Sociologist Virginia Villalobos made this not uncommon observation:

> Because the FSLN went from being a guerilla army into a situation in which the masses and the FSLN constituted "a single army" as the slogan goes, there wasn't time to develop and perfect more democratic styles of leadership. War leaves little room for democracy and considering this, the FSLN was extremely democratic. Nevertheless, the priorities of defense of the country constantly interposed itself between the base and the intermediate and higher levels of FSLN leadership in discussions regarding other problems that weren't considered as much of a priority as the war. Discussions around different topics were constantly postponed because "it wasn't the right moment" or "there weren't conditions to deal with them."[5]

War and economic crisis were not the only factors operating here, however. The hierarchical character of the FSLN was rooted in the vanguardism of a (partly) Leninist-style party. The Sandinista Front consisted of a self-selected, ideologically motivated, and disciplined revolutionary elite whose historical mission was to lead the people's struggle. A tension runs through the notion of a vanguard party. Its task is to guide, instruct, and transform the politically immature masses; at the same time it must listen to the people and empower them. This means taking account of the grassroots organizations that serve as channels for the expression of popular interests. In practice, however, the needs of the FSLN and the party-controlled state generally came first. Speaking about the Sandinista Front and the unions, María Teresa Blandon of the Farmworkers Association (ATC) noted that "being in power and at war made the Sandinistas subordinate the interests of the trade unions to the national interest as they defined it."[6]

Some of the organizations, due to their histories, leadership capabilities, and the strength of the sectors they represented, were more prepared than others to defend sectoral demands. The unions, as well as the other popular organizations, generally went along with party priorities. Choosing a low profile, the Sandinista Workers Confederation (CST), a union of mainly industrial workers, quietly acquiesced to government directives on production and belt-tightening. The ATC, operating in a strategic sector of the economy, agro-exports, was more militant in defense of its members' interests. The Civil Defense Committees (CDSs) received considerable resources from the state but were saddled with carrying out some of the more unpopular government policies, such as food rationing and military recruitment. Probably the least independent was the Sandinista women's association, "Luisa

Amanda Espinoza" (AMNLAE), since gender issues were largely postponed due to defense and production needs. The most autonomous and assertive of all the popular organizations, the Farmers and Ranchers Association (UNAG), played a key role in determining the Government's agricultural policy, but it too had to tailor its work to the demands of the State.[7] Thus after a decade of restraint and deferred hopes, the simmering dissatisfaction of grassroots activists was released by the FSLN's fall from power.

The Growth of Autonomy Since 1990

Although the electoral defeat opened the door to critical voices within the Sandinista Front and its allied organizations, other sources were at work to foster grassroots independence.[8] The conditions which had bred a verticalist style of leadership–the clandestine struggle against Somoza, the capture of state power, and the prosecution of the contra war–gave way to conditions which favored the growth of civil society.

The loss of the state made a critical difference. "For the Frente, the loss of power had nuances more dramatic than those faced by a party that only considers itself in government temporarily, renting the buildings as it were," said Commandante Dora María Téllez one and a half years after the defeat. "We weren't renters. We were part and parcel of the state apparatus."[9]

Without this meshing of party and government and without the concomitant material resources, the FSLN can no longer control the popular movements. "The popular organizations operate independently now," explained Managua party chief Victor Tinoco. "They organize themselves and get their own money. Even if we wanted to, we couldn't interfere, and even if we did, they wouldn't take any notice of us."[10] Though interference occurs more often than Tinoco suggests, it is neither as pervasive nor as heavy handed as it was during the 80s. As CST head Lucio Jimenez noted in June of 1992: "No longer does the Frente consult with the popular organizations on every major decision. And we in the CST no longer run to the Party about everything. Before there was subordination, now there's coordination."[11]

The loss of the State has led the social movements to a different conception of power. There has been an uncoupling of the classical triumvirate of party-state-mass organizations that for so long characterized the left in Nicaragua as elsewhere. Ronaldo Membreno, the CST's Organizational Secretary, sees the difference this way:

> We used to believe that change came from the top down, that the State was the mechanism. Now we don't have the State or the Party that can be an instrument of social transformation. Now change must come from the group most affected by the current

> economic crisis. The popular movements, not the Party, are the
> vanguard.[12]

The FSLN leadership, in turn, has a different attitude toward power. In the opinion of the Atlantic Coast's Francisco Campbell, who directs the Africa Program at the Center for International Studies, "The leadership has backed off, at least in part out of self-interest. Whoever wants to lead the popular movement must listen to the different sectors, not dictate to them, since it is civil society that is now the arena of struggle."[13]

Another factor that has encouraged autonomous organizing on the left is the Chamorro Government's draconian economic measures and its hostility to the popular sectors and their struggles. "There is no question that grassroots movements define themselves most clearly when in opposition to the status quo,"[14] writes Central American Historical Institute Director Lisa Haugaard in her article, "In and Out of Power: The Dilemmas of Grassroots Organizing in Nicaragua." And she adds:

> The fact that the conservative Chamorro administration has spawned a revival of grassroots organizing points to the central irony of the grassroots-government relation. Sandinista organizing has revived because the revolutionary grassroots movements find themselves in the more comfortable role of opposition -- free to mobilize for their sectoral interests. The pro-business Chamorro administration offers them a far clearer target against which to organize.[15]

The Government's economic war on women provides such a target for AMNLAE. The 1991 campaign of AMNLAE against violence against women was directed not only at domestic violence but also at violence inflicted by the state. In AMNLAE's view, the increase in prostitution and sexual abuse can be attributed directly to state-sponsored unemployment.

In the areas of health, education, and jobs, government policy led to feminist mobilization and protest. In May, 1992, AMNLAE organized a National Day Against Maternal Mortality, which pointed the finger at the Government's derelict health and family planning services. Together with the women's sections of the trade unions, it is also working to provide non-traditional job training for women.

The Chamorro Government's role in privatizing enterprises in the state sector of the Nicaraguan economy has led to a new belligerence on the part of the ATC. When the Government floated the idea of privatization in 1990, both rural and urban unions vehemently opposed it. But when it became clear that the Chamorro administration was going to go ahead regardless, the unions demanded that a share of the property be sold to the workers. (It was workers who in the 80s improved state farms after the original owners decapitalized their holdings and moved to Miami or other more congenial places.)

Even before *concertación* II, the negotiated social pact between government, business, and labor that established the principle of a 25 percent share to the workers, ATC members were occupying state cattle ranches. And takeovers of former state farms continue, though the situation is quieter than it was in 1990 and 1991. The union backs the land seizures when returning owners have tried to evict those guaranteed a job, a house, and a plot of land.[16] And according to Alba Palacios, ATC Secretary of International Relations, the union leadership was implicated in the takeovers early on. During *concertación* II, she said, ATC leaders "were talking to workers 'on the quiet'" about land occupations as a means to ensure that privatization proceeded in their interests.[17]

To a greater or lesser extent, all the social movements have been invigorated by the changes of the last three years. The fallout from the Sandinista's electoral defeat, the end of the FSLN's grip on government, and the Chamorro administration's harsh neo-liberalism have ushered in a time of vitality and independence for the popular organizations.

Obstacles to Autonomy

Although changing political circumstances have improved the climate for the social movements, old styles of leadership do not disappear overnight. As former Minister of Education Fernando Cardenal notes, "autonomy is not a still photo, it's a film, a process."[18] As inherited ways linger on, they present problems for grassroots organizing. "Since the elections, the popular organizations have won formal autonomy, but not one is really independent of the FSLN," maintains William Grigsby, Director of the pro-Sandinista radio station, *La Primerisima*. "For one, there's a shared mindset. But more important is the matter of work style. We all went to the same Stalinist school, the same verticalist school, and that legacy is still with us."[19]

The habits of top-down leadership exist at all levels of Sandinista organizing. There are those in the leadership of the FSLN who are cautious about giving away power and influence, still viewing the social movements through the lens of the 80s.[20] The Sandinista Assembly of Managua is a case in point. For journalist Sofia Montenegro, the fact that the FSLN coordinator for the Department of Managua, Victor Tinoco, invited the popular organizations to participate in its deliberations is an example of how verticalism lives on. "The Sandinista Assembly is not the Council of State," notes Montenegro, referring to the legislative body that from 1980 to 1984 represented Nicaragua's popular organizations and political parties. "The Party should let the popular organizations alone," she added. "It should stop being the father, let the children wander, leave home and grow up. Then later they may reunite on different terms."[21]

The top-down legacy of the 1980s affects the grassroots organizations in different ways. The heir to the CDSs, the Communal Movement, experiences it in the barrios of Managua where some of the Party's district secretaries try to by-pass local leaders in an effort to coordinate the Movement's work.[22] In the case of AMNLAE, the FSLN's way of subordinating patriarchal oppression to class oppression, influencing as it does the long-time party militants who run the organization, is an ideological inheritance of the Sandinista period. And for the trade unions, there's a point beyond which militant and disruptive tactics bring Party reprimands. Finally, almost all of the popular organizations are subject to FSLN Secretary General Daniel Ortega's habit of by-passing them on issues that involve them directly. In October, 1992, for example, the unions' umbrella organization, the National Workers Federation (FNT), which is reportedly a vehicle for Ortega's efforts to dominate the politics of the left, issued a 17-point agenda for the popular movement. Although it covered the needs of all sectors, only the CST people, according to William Grigsby, got to talk with Ortega about the statement. "That's not vanguardism," he added, "that's plain authoritarianism."[23]

The top-down nature of party leadership has left its mark on the popular organizations, affecting both the leadership and the base. At both levels there are people who still look to the FSLN for guidance. "It's not surprising," says Francisco Campbell, "that there's a reluctance on the part of grassroots activists to take full responsibility. Consciously or unconsciously they still think hierarchically and therefore revert to old ways."[24] The trade unions sometimes ask the FSLN to help them in areas where they could be influencing the Party. Leaders of the Communal Movement sometimes act as if they were still the transmission belts of the Party. And AMNLAE let Ortega monopolize an entire day of its 1992 Congress. In addition, some in the popular organizations have been known to turn to the FSLN when they are involved in power struggles within their own organizations. The conservative faction of the ATC, for instance, has tried unsuccessfully to get the Party's official seal of approval. (Ortega was careful not to attend the 1992 Congress, said Luis Carrión, lest he appear to tap one group as the Sandinista group.)[25]

Inherited methods of organizing and top-down leadership are not the only roadblocks to grassroots autonomy. There is also the matter of Daniel Ortega's partial, qualified alliance with Minister of the Presidency Antonio Lacayo. It involves Ortega in an intricate and difficult balancing act between the demands of the popular sectors and those of the Chamorro Government. On the one hand, he defends strikes and property seizures in order to wring concessions from the Government on a range of issues. (The 1992 sugar ·strike broke the logjam on privatization.) On the other hand, he can back popular militancy only up to a point. Since Ortega wants to maintain a working relationship with Lacayo, he must blow the whistle on actions that threaten unacceptable levels of chaos. In addition, he must support the privatization pushed by the international lending agencies which, as they coordinated structural adjustment in 1991, made sure that *concertación* II institutionalized it.[26] Since Lacayo is beholden to these agencies, the party leadership cannot officially back the property takeovers that violate the agreement.

Both Ortega and Lacayo benefit from what journalist David Dye calls "a marriage of convenience for both sides." A discerning and long-time analyst of Nicaraguan politics, Dye believes a tacit agreement exists between the two which has advantages for each.[27] For Lacayo, cooperation with an FSLN that can neutralize the unions and other rebellious popular movements brings a measure of stability to the country. The international lending agencies that confer legitimacy on Lacayo--isolated as he is from the political parties that make up the UNO coalition--require a certain level of social peace as a condition for aid. These agencies also insist on structural adjustment policies that make few concessions to Sandinismo. To keep Lacayo from falling into the arms of the far Right, Ortega has not pushed for macroeconomic changes.

The FSLN also gains a considerable amount from the deal (though many Sandinistas question its utility). In return for clamping down on serious disruption, whether by urban strikers or rural mobs, the Party is shielded from the ultra Right and from Washington; it is allowed to keep control of the police and the army; and it has been able to build on at least one of the gains of the revolution--the Area of People's Property (APP)--through the process of privatization to the workers. When asked what the Sandinista Front got out of helping the Government keep the lid on the powder keg that is Nicaragua, National Directorate member Luis Carrión replied:

> I'll be candid. The agreement between us enables both sides to save a democratic start in Nicaragua, and it enables the FSLN to defend the popular project. After all, the ultra Right wants to exterminate us and has the backing of the U.S. Right and recently, Bush. It's also in our immediate self-interest to have an alliance with Lacayo. It ensures that privatization moves forward, it prevents repression of popular forces by the police, and it gives us political space.[28]

The costs to the FSLN of an entente with Lacayo and cooperation with the Government are considerable, however. For they place the Party in the unenviable position of attempting to diffuse the impetus for change coming from its traditional base of support. And for the FSLN there is no denying the frustration and desperation of the popular sectors. "The people at the base are really confronting hunger, their backs are to the wall," acknowledges former General Secretary of the Foreign Ministry, Alejandro Bendana, who is close to Ortega. "Sandinistas who favor law and order don't like roads being blocked and lands seized, but there's a genuine struggle at the bottom that goes beyond legal means."[29] Having said this, Bendana went on to defend the Party's pragmatic middle course:

> Both the FSLN and the unions have to do this balancing act between the needs of the base and what you can reasonably expect from the Government. It has to keep the base from being too disruptive. That's what leadership is all about. It doesn't simply respond, it conducts, and in this type of situation it has to conduct responsibly. It can't just incite people to riot.[30]

Not only does the FSLN not incite people to riot or encourage property takeovers, it also exerts a restraining influence on those worrisome grassroots organizations that contribute to instability. Though the Party backed union militancy in the months following the elections, by the summer of 1990 it had decided to adopt a posture of moderation and negotiation. When the general strike of July, 1990, coordinated by the newly formed FNT, produced street barricades and armed vigilantes, Daniel Ortega stepped in to mediate between the unions and the Government. Though some say both sides asked him to intervene, many in the unions believe that Ortega sided with Lacayo, isolating the far Right but leaving the FNT, in the words of political scientist Richard Stahler-Sholk, "to fend for itself."[31] As Victor Tinoco put it with reference to the CST's 1992 sugar strike, "When strikes involve deeper matters, when they involve national issues, the Party must intervene."[32]

Although it is clear to everyone that the FSLN involves itself in the affairs of the popular organizations from time to time, opinions differ on what that signifies. Someone like Fernando Cardenal believes that what looks like externally imposed curbs on autonomy are actually the expression of a shared vision. Along these lines, David Dye argues that despite the threat of mass protest at the time of the sugar strike, CST head Lucio Jimenez agrees with Ortega on the dangers of massive violence to the revolutionary project.[33] Both leaders, Dye maintains, favor a policy of pressure, negotiation, and compromise. As Cardenal notes, "What we've got is mature thinking on the part of the popular organizations' leaders. They know they can't just go their own way, that the struggle for a national project can't be carried out by each independently of all the rest."[34]

Others, often of a more radical bent, interpret the maneuvers of the Party and the popular organizations in a different light, attributing more control to the FSLN. Economist Trevor Evans contends that the Sandinista Front dampens the unions' militancy by its commitment to stability and by the calls for social peace that it puts out regularly. And in the judgment of sociologist Oscar Rene Vargas, "verticalism is alive and well. The few people who see themselves as demi-gods who make decisions need little Stalins, yes-men, below them running the popular organizations."[35]

While the marriage of convenience between Ortega and Lacayo has put limits on Sandinista militancy and grassroots mobilization, there are signs that it may be crumbling. Since September, it seems that the party leadership has found the alliance more restrictive than enabling. Victor Tinoco, who according to Dye is usually allied with Daniel Ortega on party strategy, expressed these doubts: "The convenient agreement of the last two years is being increasingly questioned and is fast becoming obsolete."[36] This change in attitude is due in part to the Government's failure to honor commitments to the FSLN. Under pressure from the Bush administration, which has held up aid since the late spring of 1992, Chamorro fired long-time Sandinista Chief of Police, Renee Vivas in what was clearly a breach of the Transition Accords. ("Baker sent Lacayo a message,"[37] said Vivas later.) It also introduced a plan to review and return a large number of properties to claimants whose holdings had been expropriated and to indemnify others.

Simultaneously the Government began to renege on a new round of privatization to workers that involved the CST, announcing it would sell 25 factories to Miami-based Nicaraguans without negotiating the 25 percent to the workers that *concertación* II had mandated. In October, unionists occupied the factories, demanding worker ownership and protesting the return of any properties to Somocistas. A week after the takeovers, they mounted a street demonstration in Managua. The FSLN backed them up in what was a clear shift in attitude toward property seizures. Tinoco, who in June had spoken of the need to rein in an obstreperous and destabilizing CST, referred to the burning of tires and blocking of traffic on the Caretera Norte as "legitimate actions to defend the right to privatization, to defend the gains of the revolution."[38] (The privatization to the workers of all or part of 34 former state companies in January, 1993, represented an important political victory for the CST.)

Not only is the entente between the FSLN and the Government fraying at the seams because of the actions of the Bush and Chamorro administrations. It is also eroding because of attacks on it from an increasingly critical rank-and-file. Since February, 1992, when the first of a series of open forums was held to discuss Sandinista goals and strategy, many at the base, including most intellectuals, have complained loudly about the FSLN's cooperation with the Government. What had heretofore been talked about privately was now being said publicly in what Oscar Rene Vargas calls "collective therapy."

The open debate that began with the forums of February 12 and March 15 has taken on increased importance, according to forum organizer Aldo Díaz Lacayo, because it continues in the "organic structures" of the Party–the Sandinista Assembly and the district committees.[39] In August, the Assembly called into question the Party's conciliatory posture and came out in favor of a popular project.[40]

Sandinista militants criticize the alliance on several counts: it promotes a phony stability, and one that does not benefit most Nicaraguans; it does little to counter the economic stagnation caused by neo-liberal policies; it prevents the popular movements from using more militant tactics to effect change; and it limits the ability of the FSLN to lead the popular struggles and to communicate with the popular sectors.

These criticisms are central to a redefinition of the Party's relation to the grassroots. In the eyes of many Sandinistas at the base, the only counterforce to structural adjustment policies is a strong, organized mass movement in which the popular organizations are able to mount high-profile protests and engage in militant actions. Such a strategy could be coordinated by an FSLN less committed to cooperating with the Government.[41] By February of 1993, this attitude had spread to the Party's regional leadership in the North. The political secretaries of the Departments of Matagalpa and Jinotega were publicly asking the national leadership to co-govern less and to champion the diverse popular struggles more.[42]

The concern with the Party's inability or unwillingness to communicate with the base and with the popular sectors is integral to the question of strategy and is symptomatic of confusion over the FSLN's role. For Sandinista militants, the Party's failure to articulate a popular project makes it incapable of a dialogue with the grassroots. This sentiment is shared by some of the Party leadership. As the National Directorate's Luis Carrión sees it, "The Frente may have discarded the idea of vanguard leadership, but it hasn't developed a new way to relate to the people in the popular organizations and--just as important--the growing numbers of the unorganized."[43] Commandante Dora María Téllez makes a similar point. She maintains that communication is especially bad with the unorganized sectors--the unemployed, the informal sector, youth, women.

Like the rest of the left in Central America, the FSLN neglected their interests during the 80s while it focused on organized workers, a practice which continues. As an instance of this, Téllez mentioned in October, 1992, that the Party leadership had as yet said nothing about the Managua Mayor's property tax from which the poor had heretofore been exempted. "The leaders aren't tuned in to people's everyday needs," says Téllez. "If they go to a barrio they talk at people, they give a speech, rather than asking 'what are your problems and how could we go about solving them.'"[44] Even National Directorate member Victor Tirado, an unabashed advocate of the alliance with the Government, admits the FSLN may have a problem. "Maybe we should be in the streets, making our physical presence felt at strikes and takeovers. Maybe we should have maintained a permanent dialogue with the popular organizations and the people as a whole,"[45] he admits.

While internal criticism of the Sandinista Front died down during the U.S. aid crisis in the summer of 1992, by mid-October it had revived. And Daniel Ortega was taking notice: "In recent weeks there's been pressure on the National Directorate from the [party] base and the popular organizations to be more militant," he said in early November. "Currently things are too dispersed, too fragmented. A new phase of struggle is about to begin."[46] That phase may, in fact, have begun in November and December as popular protests, strikes and work stoppages grew in number and intensity.[47]

According to Ortega, as well as some of his critics, the FSLN could coordinate a popular project without compromising the independence of the social movements. Father Xavier Gorostiaga, the Rector of the Central American University in Managua, conceives the project this way: "There's a need for a microprocess whereby the popular sectors define their own interests. No global macroproject will work. It didn't work in the 80s, and it won't work now. The popular project and the Party must consider civil society."[48]

Another factor that may contribute to a new political alignment is the election of Bill Clinton. Three days after the U.S. presidential elections, Ortega was mulling over the meaning of the Clinton victory for Nicaragua, remarking that it reduced the power of the ultra Right while it opened up space for the struggles of the left.[49] (On a visit to the U.S. in December, National Directorate member Jaime Wheelock also spoke optimistically about Clinton.[50])

Although the marriage of convenience between the FSLN and the Chamorro Government may weaken further, until now it has clearly hampered the ability of the popular organizations to push more energetically and forcefully for change.

THE ATC: WALKING A TIGHTROPE

The 1980s

During the 1980s, the Rural Workers Association (ATC) was somewhat more independent of the Party and the State than was the

CST. It had strong organizational roots in the pre-insurrectionary period, emerging out of the Rural Workers Committees formed to protest National Guard repression and peasant working conditions. Founded in 1977, the ATC developed a more democratic mode of organizing than the CST. It also displayed a religious and political radicalism that emphasized collective as well as individual responsibility for social betterment. (Edgardo Garcia, one of its founders and currently its head, was a lay preacher for the Delegates of the Word, a progressive Catholic movement.[1])

But like other popular organizations in the period preceding the Sandinista triumph, the peasant and rural workers' movement was limited by historical circumstances. For one, there was considerable repression in the countryside. And unlike the popular movements in El Salvador, which, as Lisa Haugaard notes, were able to organize in liberated territory and in refugee camps in Honduras over a 10 year period, their counterparts in Nicaragua had a shorter time to build strength. "For most Nicaraguans, the insurrectionary experience was at most a one-or-two year affair," she reminds us. "A small amount of time was available to build organizations and learn through collective action."[2]

During the 1980s, the state's emphasis on production and defense put constraints on the ATC, but it was able to press for the needs of its constituency more militantly and more effectively than the CST, beginning with an ATC-organized demonstration in 1980 that brought some 30,000 rural workers and peasants to Managua.[3] Its central role in the agro-export sector of the economy gave it greater leverage with the Government. Moreover, the ATC leadership was more skilled at pressing workers' demands.

The ATC successfully pushed for a number of changes in government policy that substantially benefitted workers employed on state farms. Such things as job security, higher wages, and education and health benefits came about because of work stoppages, demonstrations, and on occasion, the takeover of management offices, despite public scolding by party leaders. And Edgardo Garcia was always willing to criticize the FSLN when its policies hurt the rural sector.[4]

Next to UNAG, the ATC was the most independent of the popular organizations, but it too had to tow the line and bow to the requirements of a war economy, especially after the introduction of austerity measures in 1985 and again in 1988. The Government's unwillingness to meet salary demands and the increase in the cost of basic consumer goods were things that the ATC had to acquiesce to.

The ATC Faces the Chamorro Government

The economic policies of the Chamorro Government that adversely affected rural workers prompted the ATC to mobilize in protest. What strengthened the hand of the union in the ensuing struggle was the fact that there were few pro-UNO unions in the agricultural sector to divide the workforce. Rural workers, moreover, earn dollars via export, and this strengthened the bargaining power of the ATC.

Soon after taking office, Chamorro announced two executive decrees that were a direct assault on Sandinista agrarian reform. Decrees 11-90 and 10-90 enabled the Government to rent, then sell, to pre-revolutionary owners land that had been confiscated by the previous regime. As the original owners began returning from Miami to stake their claims, workers began seizing state farms.

During the same period, the Government announced plans to privatize state enterprises throughout the Nicaraguan economy, the agricultural sector included. The nationalized portion of the economy, the Area of People's Property (APP), consisted of some 400 companies, with agricultural land and agro-industry comprising 60 percent of the value of all state property. Although the unions protested this plan, the Chamorro administration would not be deterred. Once it was clear that privatization would proceed (a World Bank loan was conditioned on compliance with its privatization scheme), the ATC began to mobilize. In the spring and summer of 1990, workers took over a number of enterprises. The privatization to the workers of 30 percent of state cattle ranches was negotiated because of worker occupations. Privatization in coffee, cotton, and bananas soon followed.[5]

From the start, there were people in the ATC who disliked the notion of privatization. Some objected to the division of workers into owners and non-owners, arguing that it would weaken the union movement. Others wanted to behave like classical unionists and fight for higher wages rather than shares in an enterprise, suspecting that the experience of the 80s, when worker interests were subordinated to other goals, would be repeated.[6] Critics in the union's three dissident federations--rice, cotton, and 1/2 of coffee--who have strong differences with Garcia and the leadership of the majority faction, claim that it was the FSLN that pressured the unions to accept privatization in the first place. (Garcia insists that the idea was first broached by the ATC[7]) Having lost the State, claim the critics, the Party leaned on the unions in order to salvage something of the nationalized sector. [8]

The Dilemma of the ATC

The process of privatization begun in February, 1991, and continued in the *concertación* II negotiations of May-August, have delivered to the

ATC a large number of viable enterprises in cattle, coffee, bananas, and rice (cotton is a disaster). The rural portion of the Area of Workers Property now consists of 240,000 acres of agricultural land, more than 14 agroindustrial units, and five service units. Its success marks a contrast with the CST, where the existence of bankrupt industries and deteriorating physical plants has, until recently, weakened the hand of the union.

The ATC's accomplishments were offset, however, by the problems they created inside the union. One thorny issue was the size of the share that members thought the leadership should demand. After the Government proposed a 15 percent share and the ATC insisted on more, a compromise of 25 percent was worked out in the *concertación*. Many in the union were unhappy with this figure. Though the FSLN leadership claims it was arrived at through negotiations between labor, business and government,--"The Party didn't say 'settle for 25 percent,' that resulted from reality,"[9] says Victor Tinoco--dissidents charge that the FSLN pressured the unions to accept this "straitjacket" because of its new conciliatory posture toward the Government.[10] According to María Teresa Blandon, who works with the rice federation, "the figure of 25 percent was a party proposal that the union agreed to, thereby exhibiting its persistent and enormous dependence on the Party."[11]

After the *concertación* II accords were signed, the union began a new round of negotiations with the Government over particular properties. This has involved the ATC in an unpleasant game of winners and losers that has pitted some members against the leadership. "With privatization," admits executive council member Martha Juárez, "a lot of people were going to lose out, and that's hard, but the pie was too small."[12] Though workers get 25 percent, a much larger share goes to the original owners and others in the private sector. "That leaves a lot of workers out in the cold," notes economist Trevor Evans. "Garcia dumped his own men; that's pretty bad for a union leader."[13] The union bureaucracy's desire for property, according to economist Oscar Neira, meant that "it had to step on somebody's toes."[14]

Among those whose toes were stepped on were coffee workers in Matalgapa and cotton workers in Chinandega. Angry over the 25 percent deal to begin with, they took over farms that had been negotiated back to the original owners. In June of 1992, the army began evicting some 6,000 families from the land. Then the new owners came in, burned their huts to the ground and had anyone who resisted arrested. Though some of the union leadership sympathizes with the marginalized and victimized, not all are charitable. "They're a renegade group on the loose," women's section director Dora Ivonne Herrera told Donna Vukelich, who was researching an article on the rural crisis. "They're flouting the leadership and that makes the ATC look bad."[15]

(The union has reportedly undertaken a publicity campaign to refurbish its image.) As for Garcia, he accepts the constraints of *concertación* II and the need to deliver 75 percent of the land to the private sector. "The 25 percent plan is practical," he insists. "It's more than *solidarismo* [a conservative scheme], and it helps us pay our debts by selling some enterprises to the Mexicans. We have to live with capital!"[16]

The problems of the ATC go beyond the issue of worker shares. Also involved is the way decisions about privatization and property are made. Martha Juárez acknowledges that the national leadership does not discuss or consult with the base in preparation for negotiations with the Government. That top-down manner extends to the regional leadership. Workers on a cotton farm near Leon were visited by union officials who surprised them with the news that 100 percent of the land was going back to the original owners. There was no discussion or advance warning. When the workers challenged the leadership, they were told that the decision was outside their purview. This process is not uncommon.[17]

A further dilemma for the ATC leadership is worker takeovers of land. Sometimes, as in the coffee region of Matagalpa, farm workers seized land that was returned en masse to the original owners. In other cases, workers would hear that the Government wanted to cut them out and would simply occupy the farms. Takeovers are a useful bargaining chip for the union when it is negotiating with the Government, and they have enabled it on some occasions to get as much as 35 percent of the land. In addition, the leadership recognizes that people at the base need takeovers as a weapon to defend what they see as their legitimate interests.[18] So once land seizures occur, the union backs them. It also typically pushes for legalization of worker claims if the original owners have violated the agreement to let them keep their jobs, houses, and a subsistence plot. [19]

Land takeovers, however, make it difficult for the ATC to deliver the agreed upon 75 percent to the private sector. "We're under pressure from the Government to comply with the *concertación* agreements,"[20] said Martha Juárez, explaining why the union cannot fully support the workers. (It plans to give up some occupied land and negotiate others.) Garcia straddles the fence this way: "Certainly no farms should be returned to ex-[National] Guard members, but the private sector has rights to property too."[21]

Not only is the union feeling the heat from the Government. It has also been under pressure from other quarters. As Juárez explained, "Just because the original owners were Somocistas, we couldn't go for 100 percent to the workers. We had to listen to the international lending agencies. We're an occupied country in economic terms because they tell us what we can do."[22] In addition, Nicaraguan banks are reportedly threatening to withhold loans from APT enterprises as long as takeovers continue.[23] Thus with pressure from all sides, the ATC finds itself in a tight spot. "It's an unmanageable situation,"[24] admits Juárez.

The Dilemma of the Leadership and the Issue of Autonomy

The conflicting demands on the ATC and the contradictions inherent in the process of privatization put the union leadership in a difficult position. Because it is pulled in various directions, sometimes taking a confrontational position toward the Government, sometimes a conciliatory one, it is sometimes difficult to ascertain what is really going on.[25] It is also hard to tell to what extent the leadership sets the course for the ATC, and to what extent it falls in behind the FSLN.

Much about union autonomy revolves around the issue of land takeovers. The Party does not have an official line, and there are different opinions within the National Directorate. According to Luis Carrión, "The position of the party leadership is ambiguous because takeovers are politically destabilizing; on the other hand, people's lives are being destabilized."[26] As already noted, the deal that Ortega has with Lacayo puts a premium on stability and makes support for disruptive and illegal tactics problematical. As Ortega put it last June:

> Stability is the point of departure. Without it the economic situation would worsen. We can't bet on the deterioration of the Government just to win votes. The FSLN disagrees with dislodging those who take over land, but what's negotiated has to be fulfilled.[27]

When it comes to the ATC, the common perception is that the leadership is fully behind the land seizures. That impression stems from the fact that not only does it refrain from publicly criticizing the tactic or the people involved, but it also backs workers' demands.[28] Whereas Ortega is openly apprehensive about takeovers, the union leadership is clearly not. For economist Trevor Evans, this is an indication that it determines policy independently of the FSLN. Edgardo Garcia may agree with Ortega on the need to coexist with capitalists, says Evans, but on issues of property and class struggle, the union is to the left of the Party. "Garcia may be influenced by Ortega, but he thinks like a worker," Evans maintains. "Anyway the union isn't a footsoldier of the FSLN anymore. It can't be switched on and off at will."[29]

But some think that the ATC leadership, though unable to publicly condemn takeovers, has serious reservations about them. Alejandro Bendana maintains that the union leader dislikes takeovers. "Garcia is of the opinion that no, we can't countenance that [takeovers] because it would put in danger rural property owners who are Sandinistas and who might be alienated by the seizures, the instability."[30] Oscar Neira believes that land occupations threaten the entrepreneurial ambitions of the union bureaucracy: "As future landowners, it's not in the ATC's interest to encourage takeovers. After all, its property may someday be in jeopardy."[31] And Luis Carrión thinks that Garcia, like Ortega, waffles on land seizures because of their destabilizing effect. Moreover, if the ATC cannot keep its part of the bargain, the Government may torpedo the process of privatization to the workers altogether.[32] The President of the ATC's rice federation, Domingo Goméz, confirms Carrión's observations. Goméz states unequivocally that on the issue of takeovers the union leadership has the same views as the party leadership--they threaten stability. "As a leader, he's one of those closest to the leadership of the FSLN," says Goméz. "Some people say he's more a militant of the Sandinista Front than of the ATC."[33]

Insiders like Domingo Gomez and observers like William Grigsby go beyond saying that Garcia and Ortega are on the same wave-length. To them what is involved is verticalism. The picture is muddied, according to Goméz, because the Party does not send down "orientations" as it did in the 1980s. But it does not need to. "He's been trained to think in terms of how the National Directorate thinks and what it wants," explains Goméz. "Garcia is in the verticalist tradition, he depends heavily on the views of the FSLN leadership. Therefore he works in the interests of its national project, not in the interests of the workers. The ATC has been castrated by the Party."[34] Grigsby agrees: "The union responds to the Party's need for stability, not to the workers' need for land and jobs."[35]

Garcia depends on the FSLN and the National Directorate in other ways. According to dissident unionist María Teresa Blandon and economist Oscar Neira, the heavy hand of the Party, in the person of Jaime Wheelock, is evident in the ATC's position on corporate structure and professional management. The former Minister of Agriculture takes as the model for the rural portion of the Area of Workers Property the big state farms heralded by Marxism-Leninism as the most efficient way to organize agricultural production.[36] This was the model for much of Sandinista agriculture in the previous decade, and the ATC leadership is perpetuating it in the present one. The corporation model of the state sector, tailored to the needs of the 90s, but with the 80s bureaucratic structure and top-down management, is the plan for the APT. Both Blandon and Neira contend that it is Wheelock's ideas and administrative style--in the Sandinista years his sector was the most paternalistic and bureaucratic--as well as Wheelock himself, that exert such a powerful influence on the union.[37]

The Area of Workers Property, acquired through pressure tactics and negotiation and structured along corporate and hierarchical lines, represents a significant achievement for the union. The cautious posture of the leadership stems in part from its stake in the APT. What this stake entails can be seen in the proposal that the national executive council has put out to the coffee federation about corporate structure. According to this proposal, a large number of shares in each enterprise would go to the ATC itself, another large number would go to the professional managers of those enterprises, and a smaller number would go to the workers. María Teresa Blandon believes that, should it carry the day, it would significantly strengthen the union bureaucracy.[38]

With regard to the APT, the union and the Party have a shared interest that leads them to see eye to eye on a number of issues. In both cases, the leadership believes that such an economic base will give the ATC a political voice and enable it to push for economic and social change.[39] In addition, the union and the Party share what Oscar Neira calls "a corporate interest:"[40] they want to create an entrepreneurial group that can succeed in a free market environment. To their mind, that requires the kind of corporate structure–Edgardo Garcia refers to it as a limited liability corporation–that Jaime Wheelock advocates. It also requires the use of professional managers. This from Wheelock: "The workers can't run the enterprises, they don't have the professional training. The production process is complex, and you need to know the macro and microeconomic picture to run them properly."[41]

It seems that the entrepreneurial ambitions of the ATC and the FSLN, together with what they perceive to be the constraints of a market economy, push the leadership in a conservative direction, one in which the workplace democracy so strongly advocated in the 1980s makes way for other priorities. The democratic potential of the APT would appear to no longer interest either party.

Contested Terrain: Workplace and Union Democracy

The issues of democracy in the workplace and in the union currently divide the ATC. The conservative majority faction represented by the national leadership is pitted against 2 1/2 dissident federations–rice, cotton and 1/2 of coffee. Although Garcia maintains that the conflict is about personal power--the geographic organization of the federations would weaken the power of the product federations--it is clear that democracy is the real issue. Even Wheelock, who in December of 1992 said Goméz just wanted Garcia out, went on to say that "democratization is the true problem."[42] The dissidents charge the leadership with riding roughshod over demands for worker control of enterprises, worker participation in privatization, and democratization of the union. According to Olga María Espinoza, the leadership is almost as verticalist as it was in the 1980s, when it sent down orientations and expected the mid-level leadership and the base to comply.[43]

The question of worker management has its roots in the previous decade. Worker participation in running state farms and factories was a persistent demand of the Sandinista unions in the 80s, and many collective bargaining agreements contained provisions for a worker say in administrative decisions. It was seen as an important aspect of revolutionary democracy, one that challenged bourgeois principles of authority. Both the FSLN and the unions took on the task of promoting worker participation and of training the rank-and-file so they could participate more effectively. But there was a fairly low level of involvement due to lack of education and motivation. What also discouraged participation was the verticalist mindset of government ministries and state-appointed managers. The Ministry of Agriculture and Agrarian Reform (MINSA) under Wheelock's tutelage was especially guilty in this regard. Paternalistic practices pervaded MINSA, whose functionaries thought that only they had the requisite technical knowledge to make decisions.[44]

The tension between workplace democracy and top-down management is being played out again in the 90s, with one addition to the cast of characters–the World Bank. The World Bank pushed privatization in 1991 and is known to favor professional managers. As such it was one part of the equation for the ATC leadership. Secretary for International Relations Alba Palacios, speaking about the union's preference for professionally trained people, spoke of the pressures it felt: "We need people with specialized knowledge to run the APT. We have to be efficient and competitive within the international marketplace, within the policies of the Government, and within the area of international lending agencies like the World Bank."[45] The World Bank is known to frown on worker management and worker involvement in decision-making. In its view, the APT should look like a hierarchically organized private corporation where control is vested in a board of directors and decisions are made by its appointees.[46] And the union's executive council proposal to the coffee federation resembles this model. According to María Teresa Blandon, the World Bank was instrumental in the ATC's decision to opt for professional managers.[47]

Then there is the persistent influence of Jaime Wheelock. "The ATC leadership is dependent on Wheelock," maintains Oscar Neira, "but it also shares his views on corporate structure and management." According to Neira, most of the people appointed to run the rural segment of the APT are "Wheelock's bureaucrats" from MINSA.[48] In the 90s, the union leadership continues in the corporate mold set in the Sandinista years. As Garcia is quick to point out, "Qualified professionals have always run Sandinista enterprises."[49]

The dissidents have put forward an alternative proposal, one that is more democratic and participatory. In their plan, workers would have a majority of the shares and would determine how the enterprises are managed. "Workers should participate in running the APT enterprises through worker assemblies,"[50] insists Domingo Goméz. (Currently the Camillo Ortega farm in Masaya is run by the workers, who are addressing the problem of unemployment in the region and are working with the community to set up social services.[51]) The need for technical expertise is not ruled out, however. Goméz noted that professional administrators have a role to play, albeit a circumscribed one.

Currently, managers are chosen by the board of directors of each enterprise. Garcia defends the process as a democratic one: "Professional administrators may make decisions about investment and production, but workers elect the board in every corporation of the ATC."[52] But dissidents say that appearances are deceptive. "The structure and the decision-making process have been imposed from above," Goméz maintains. "Sure, there were elections, but everything was controlled at the top."[53] El Divisadero, a rice farm near Leon, is a case in point. According to Donna Vukelich, who wrote about privatization and its problems in the countryside for *Pensamiento Propio*, the union leadership installed a friend and political ally to run it. He proceeded to bar workers' participation, suggesting that they were "not competitive." As one unionist put it, "The leadership thinks we're the same dumb workers we used to be."[54]

The dissidents also criticize the national leadership for dealing with privatization in an undemocratic way. Martha Juárez acknowledged that "some workers weren't heeding the decisions of the leadership because they weren't brought into the decision-making process,"[55] adding that pressures on the union made this necessary. Workers at El Divisadero had wanted an open, participatory process, but the leadership ignored them. "We're just peons when we thought we would be partners," said one worker. "All that happened was that we changed bosses."[56]

According to the dissidents, the 1992 Congress of the ATC was also handled in a verticalist way. In the planning stage, the national council "just papered over differences and imposed its views,"[57] says Goméz; the dissident federations proceeded to boycott the Congress. Garcia and the rest of the leadership were reelected to their posts, but Trevor Evans, who attended the Congress, thinks the elections might have been stacked. Though there was no fixed slate, dissident candidates were systematically vilified from the floor.[58]

Despite its top-down leadership style, the ATC has become more democratic in the 1990s. The behavior of the dissidents testifies to that. In the Sandinista era, there would not have been the vigorous debate or sharp conflict that now exists. Nor would there have been such a marked lack of deference to the leadership.

The decentralization of the union is also part of the democratization process. In the crop sectors of coffee and cotton, there has been a significant dispersion of decision-making. The small enterprises in these sectors have been partially delinked from the executive councils of their federations.[59] Commenting on this development, Jaime Wheelock said at the end of 1992 that he had rejected the corporate model and was now in favor of small enterprises. "I tell Garcia and the rest of the leadership that success requires that they respond to the will of the workers and not try to impose a fixed model on them."[60] (It is possible that Wheelock was wearing his second hat when he said this. Like the rest of the Party leadership, he often talks like a conservative bureaucrat but has a radical line when there is pressure from the grassroots.[61])

Crisis, Democracy, and Civil Society

The ATC's verticalist mode of organizing and its preference for stability and bureaucratic corporatism have led to serious division within the organization and have created a crisis of leadership. According to Domingo Gómez, there has been a deterioration of the leadership because it has been unwilling to think creatively about new strategies; nor has it been willing to face the challenge inherent in the demand for democratization. In addition, because of the union's bureaucratic character, the leadership is distant from the base, and many workers have stopped listening to it.[62] Luis Carrión points to the ATC as an example of a disquieting tendency on the left–the disintegration of organized leadership:

> First, the popular organizations go their own way from the party leadership. Then local groups within these organizations start to break away from the national leadership, as in the case of the ATC. The union leadership is losing the control it once had over the base. There's a lot of confusion.[63]

While the leadership seems mired in old ways, the dissidents have an alternative vision for the union and for the other popular organizations. This vision speaks to the need for grassroots participatory democracy. It also envisages a way of bringing about social change that does not rely on a vanguard. "The old school of leadership must compete with alternative forces," maintains Gómez. "In the 80s the leadership was everything, but not anymore. There's been a growth of civil society at the grassroots."[64]

Both factions converge in their thinking about state power, however. This reflects changes in the way the social movements think about the apparatus of the state and its relation to party structures. The popular organizations tend to regard revolutionary governments and parties as severely constrained by global neoliberalism and a world economy in crisis. Although they believe that a Sandinista electoral victory would help the popular sectors, unionists on both sides concede that the U.S., the lending institutions, and a neoliberal environment limit what any regime can do. As a result, the popular organizations have to depend on themselves.[65] Martha Juárez puts it this way:

> It's critical that popular movements have a higher profile and presence than the FSLN. If we're clear about our own agenda and have an economic base, that gives us the chance to have a significant political voice. The popular organizations could be the motor of social change.[66]

Not unexpectedly, María Teresa Blandon goes further. "It's wrong to think a big party, a big leader can solve everyone's problems." she says. "That's a messianic conception, an old illusion."[67]

With its internal divisions and divergent politics, the ACT currently faces in two directions: toward the verticalist and corporatist past and toward the participatory civil democracy that distinguishes the post-vanguardist left. What will be the outcome of the struggle within the union is still unclear. [The conflict has since been resolved. The majority faction won out.]

Sandinismo: Between Vanguardism and Fragmentation

If verticalism is the legacy of the 1980s, fragmentation may be the danger of the 1990s. Of course many in the social movements and the Sandinista Front do not believe that this is a hazard; they think that the FSLN still plays too vanguardist a role with regard to civil society. And they object to the notion of the Party as the coordinator of a newly defined Sandinista project. Commandante Dora María Téllez, for example, believes that even facilitating a "horizontal dialogue" among the different popular sectors would be "too bureaucratic and vanguardist."[1] But many Sandinistas agree with Victor Tinoco's sentiments: "The new reality is characterized by autonomy and a need for coherence. Often autonomy has been more important, causing dispersion. The FSLN should act as a link between different groups."[2] Luis Carrión agrees. He contends that the Party should encourage discussion among the different movements so that they can create popular alliances. "It could be a broker, helping the groups find common ground."[3] This would be a new and less hierarchical role for a vanguard party. "And vanguardism isn't bad," says journalist William Grigsby, "if it promotes dialogue and the search for common solutions."[4]

But there are obstacles to the creation of a political agenda that preserves the autonomy of these groups yet links them to the FSLN and to each other in a more cohesive way. At present, the economic crisis leads the popular organizations to put their own interests first. And political constraints have inhibited both the articulation of an alternative vision for Sandinismo and the creation of a post-vanguardist role for the Party. The FSLN has yet to create a flexible leadership style, one more attuned to the needs of the popular sectors and more in touch with the grassroots. Nor has it been able to respond to the increasingly desperate situation of Nicaragua's poor. Given this situation, a set of forces is converging which may lead Daniel Ortega to a new initiative. The economic crisis, which shows no signs of disappearing; the diminishing returns that accrue to the Party from accommodation to the Government; and his own political vulnerability – all these have led to an effort to reach down to the grassroots. Just after Clinton's election, Ortega worried aloud about the party leadership's weak links with the base.

> The problem certainly exists. We've just begun to work on it. The FSLN needs to develop new structures of communication, organization, and mobilization. We need to invert the pyramid, so that the ideas of the leadership reflect proposals from the base. Until now, however, the formal links have been missing.[5]

One important factor inhibiting the development of a post-vanguardist vision has been the Sandinista Front's alliance with the Chamorro government. Now that this marriage of convenience seems to be faltering, perhaps a breakthrough is in the offing. In November, Ortega was talking about new directions. As noted earlier, he spoke of "recent pressure from the [party] base and the popular organizations to be more militant. Currently things are too dispersed, too fragmented," he said. "A new phase of struggle is about to begin."[6] Meanwhile, the popular movements, backed by a firmer National Directorate, upped the ante in November and December of 1992 by engaging in work stoppages, strikes, and demonstrations.[7]

The election of Bill Clinton is also part of the new political equation, allowing the FSLN and the grassroots movements to be more militant in their pursuit of a popular project. Three days after the U.S. elections, Ortega claimed that they had "reduced the threat of the [Nicaraguan] far Right, which sees the Clinton victory as a victory for the Sandinistas, and had given us more space for struggle."[8] But if Ortega is to succeed in positioning himself and the FSLN as the leaders of increasingly militant popular struggles, he will have to find a way to reinvent the relationship between the Party nd the movements. If the Sandinista Front can meet this challenge, then, in the words of Orlando Nuñez, "to the Party and the organizations alike would belong the task of persuading and incorporating the majority of the Nicaraguan people in the revolutionary project."[9]

FOOTNOTES:

1*Crossroads* (Oct., 1992), 13.

2For a discussion of social movements in historical and comparative perspective, see Samir Amin et.al., *Transforming the Revolution: Social Movements and the World System* (New York, 1990) and Arturo Escobar and Sonia E. Alvarez, eds., *The Making of Social Movements in Latin America: Identity, Strategy, and Democracy* (Boulder, CO, 1992).

3Judith Helman argues that the anti-state and anti-party bias of social movements and their theorists reflects the disillusionment with socialism on the left and the indifference to class analysis on the part of post-modern critics. See "The Study of New Social Movements in Latin America and the Question of Autonomy," in Escobar & Alvarez.

4For a recent contribution to this discourse and its double emphasis, see Orlando Nuñez, *En Busca de la Revolution Perdida (In Search of the Lost Revolution)* (Managua, 1992).

5Interview, *Monitor,* Nicaragua Network Education Fund, July, 1990.

6*The Guardian* (Sept. 19, 1990), 15.

7For an excellent analysis of the changing fortunes of the popular organizations in the 80s and 90s, as well as a consideration of the autonomy question, see Lisa Haugaard, "In and Out of Power: Dilemmas of Grassroots Organizing in Nicaragua," *Socialism and Democracy,* 7.3 (1991) 157-184. She provided the ranking of the organizations that appears here. Interview with Lisa Haugaard, 11/30/92.

8For a discussion of the conditions that encourage and discourage autonomy, see Haugaard and Andre Gunder Frank and Marta Fuentes, "Civil Democracy: Social Movements in Recent World History," in Amin, 139-180. For an analysis of Nicaraguan politics in the post-election period, see George R. Vickers and Jack Spence, "Nicaragua: Two Years After the Fall," *World Policy Journal,* IX. 3 (1992), 533-559.

9*Envio* (Sept. 1991), 31.

10Interview with Victor Tinoco, 6/19/92

11Interview with Lucio Jimenez, 6/22/92

12Interview with Ronaldo Membreno, 10/23/92

13Interview with Francisco Campbell, 6/22/92

14Haugaard, 157.

15Haugaard, 158.

16Interview with Edgardo Garcia, 10/16/92

17Interview with Alba Palacios, 10/27/92

18Interview with Fernando Cardenal, 7/22/92

19Interview with William Grigsby, 6/29/92

20Interview with Luis Carrión, 9/15/92

21Interview with Sofia Montenegro, 6/17/92

22Interview with Carolina Espinoza, 7/17/92

23Interview with William Grigsby, 11/5/92

24Interview with Francisco Campbell, 6/22/92

25Interview with Luis Carrión, 9/15/92

26Richard Stahler-Sholk, "Labor/Party/State Dynamics in Nicaragua: Union Responses to Austerity Under the Sandinista and UNO Governments." Paper presented to the Latin American Studies Congress (LASA) (July, 1992), 27-29.

27David Dye 7/11/92 This section is based on Dye's analysis.

28Interview with Luis Carrión, 9/15/92

29Interview with Alejandro Bendana, 7/30/92

[30]Interview with Alejandro Bendana, 7/30/92
[31]Stahler-Sholk, 20.
[32]Interview with Victor Tinoco, 6/19/92
[33]Interview with David Dye, 7/11/92
[34]Interview with Fernando Cardenal, 7/23/92
[35]Interviews with Trevor Evans, 7/6/92; Oscar Renee Vargas, 7/15/92
[36]Interview with Victor Tinoco, 10/15/92
[37]Central American Historical Institute, Nicaragua News Service, #260.
[38]Interview with Victor Tinoco, 9/15/92
[39]Interview with Aldo Díaz Lacayo, 9/22/92
[40]Interview with David Dye, 10/7/92
[41]Interviews with Trevor Evans, 7/22/92; William Grigsby, 6/29/92
[42]Interview with Donna Vukelich, 2/8/93.
[43]Interview with Luis Carrión, 9/5/92
[44]Interview with Dora María Téllez, 9/18/92
[45]Interview with Victor Tirado, 10/29/92
[46]Interview with Daniel Ortega, 10/6/92
[47]*Envio* (Jan.-Mar., 1993), 5-7.
[48]Interview with Father Xavier Gorostiaga, 6/15/92
[49]Interview with Daniel Ortega, 11/6/92
[50]Interview with Jaime Wheelock, 12/7/92

The ATC: Walking a Tightrope

[1]Jeffrey Gould, *To Lead As Equals: Rural Protest and Political Consciousness in Chinandega, Nicaragua, 1912-1979.* (Chapel Hill, 1990), 272-5.
[2]Haugaard, 162
[3]Gilbert, 89.
[4]Interview with Lisa Haugaard, 8/19/92
[5]*Envio* (May, 1991), 16-19.
[6]Interview with Trevor Evans, 7/6/92
[7]Interview with Edgardo Garcia, 6/19/92
[8]Interview with María Teresa Blandon, 6/16/92
[9]Interview with Victor Tinoco, 6/19/92
[10]Stahler-Sholk, 30.
[11]Interview with María Teresa Blandon, 6/16/92
[12]Interview with Martha Juárez, 11/3/92
[13]Interview with Trevor Evans, 7/16/92
[14]Interview with Oscar Neira, 10/15/92
[15]Interview with Donna Vukelich, 11/11/92 For more on the conflict between the leadership and the base in the region of Leon, see Donna Vukelich, "Reforma Agraria: La tierra prometida," *Pensamiento Propio* (October, 1992), 10-13.
[16]Interview with Edgardo Garcia, 6/19/92
[17]Interview with Donna Vukelich, 11/11/92
[18]Interview with Luis Carrión, 9/15/92
[19]Interview with Trevor Evans, 7/22/92
[20]Interview with Martha Juárez, 11/3/92
[21]Interview with Edgardo Garcia, 6/19/92
[22]Interview with Martha Juárez, 11/3/92
[23]Interview with Paola Perez Aleman, 8/9/92
[24]Interview with Martha Juárez, 11/3/92
[25]Interview with Oscar Neira, 10/16/92
[26]Interview with Luis Carrión, 9/15/92
[27]Stahler-Sholk, 21.
[28]Interview with Richard Stahler-Sholk, 7/15/92
[29]Interview with Trevor Evans, 7/22/92
[30]Interview with Alejandro Bendana, 6/30/92
[31]Interview with Oscar Neira, 10/15/92

[32]Interview with Luis Carrión, 9/15/92.
[33]Interview with Domingo Goméz, 10/21/92.
[34]Interview with Domingo Goméz, 10/21/92.
[35]Interview with William Grigsby, 6/29/92.
[36]Gilbert, 86-88.
[37]Interviews with María Teresa Blandon, 10/19/92; Oscar Neira, 10/15/92; Donna Vukelich, 2/8/93.
[38]Interview with Richard Stahler-Sholk, 8/14/92.
[39]Interviews with Martha Juárez, 11/13/92; María Teresa Blandon, 10/19/92.
[40]Interview with Oscar Neira, 10/15/92.
[41]Interview with Jaime Wheelock, 12/7/92.
[42]Interview with Jamie Wheelock, 12/7/92.
[43]Interview with Donna Vukelich, 11/11/92.
[44]Carlos Vilas, "The Workers' Movement in the Sandinista Revolution," in Harris and Vilas, 133-142.
[45]Interview with Alba Palacios, 10/27/92.
[46]Interview with Paola Perez Aleman, 8/9/92.
[47]Interview with María Teresa Blandon, 6/16/92.
[48]Interview with Oscar Neira, 10/15/92.
[49]Interview with Edgardo Garcia, 10/16/92.
[50]Interview with Domingo Goméz, 10/21/92.
[51]Interview with Oscar Neira, 10/15/92.
[52]Interview with Edgardo Garcia, 10/16/92.
[53]Interview with Domingo Goméz, 10/21/92.
[54]Vukelich, 11-13 and Interview 11/11/92.
[55]Interview with Martha Juárez, 11/3/92.
[56]Interview with Donna Vukelich, 11/11/92.
[57]Interview with Domingo Goméz, 10/21/92.
[58]Interview with Trevor Evans, 7/6/92.
[59]Interviews with Jaime Wheelock, 12/7/92; Domingo Goméz, 10/21/92.
[60]Interview with Jamie Wheelock, 12/7/92.
[61]Interview with Oscar Neira, 10/15/92.
[62]Interview with Domingo Goméz, 10/21/92.
[63]Interview with Luis Carrión, 9/15/92.
[64]Interview with Domingo Gómez 10/21/92.
[65]Interviews with Dora Ivonne Herrera, 7/7/92; Martha Juárez, 11/3/92.
[66]Interview with Martha Juárez, 11/3/92.
[67]Interview with María Teresa Blandon, 10/19/92.

Sandinismo: Between Vanguardism and Fragmentation

[1]Interview with Dora María Téllez, 10/19/92.
[2]Barricada Internacional (Aug., 1992), 21.
[3]Interview with Luis Carrión, 9/15/92.
[4]Interview with William Grigsby, 11/5/92.
[5]Interview with Daniel Ortega, 11/6/92.
[6]Interview with Daniel Ortega, 11/6/92.
[7]Envio (Jan. - Mar. 1993), 7.
[8]Interview with Daniel Ortega, 11/6/92.
[9]Nuñez, 141.

Notes on the Contributors

Guatemala:

Rolando Alecio is a Guatemalan anthropologist currently doing research on environmental issues in connection with the Guatemalan refugee return in the Petén. For three years he was an investigator with AVANCSO (Association for the Advancement of Social Sciences in Guatemala), a Guatemalan research institute, during which time he completed a field study of the Rabinal area. That serves as the documentation for this article.

Rigoberta Menchú is a Guatemalan indigenous leader and for many years served as a leading spokesperson for the Committee of Campesino Unity (CUC) despite her forced exile from Guatemala. Her autobiography *I, Rigoberta Menchú* (Verso) has been translated into nine languages. In 1992, Menchú won the Nobel Peace Prize in recognition of her struggle in behalf of indigenous peoples. Other members of CUC, working principally in Mexico City, co-authored this article.

Minor Sinclair is the coordinator of the Ecumenical Program on Central America and the Caribbean (EPICA) and has worked on Central American issues for twelve years. He wrote *Out of the Shadows: The Communities of Population in Resistance*, an EPICA report, and other articles have appeared in *The Christian Century, The Witness* and *Social Justice: A Journal of Crime, Conflict and World Order.*

EL SALVADOR:

MARTHA THOMPSON is a specialist on Central American refugee issues for an international development agency. For eight years she worked with Salvadoran refugees in the Honduras refugee camps and upon their return to El Salvador. In 1978-1979 Thompson worked as a journalist in Argentina.

MARIO LUNGO UCLÉS is a Salvadoran social scientist currently associated with the Central American University in San Salvador. He is the author of several books and articles, including *El Salvador en los 1980s: insurgencia y contrainsurgencia* which won the prestigious *Premio de las Americas* from Havana, Cuba.

NICARAGUA:

TRISH O'KANE is a free-lance journalist currently based in Guatemala. From 1989-1992 O'Kane worked in Nicaragua for CRIES (Region Coordination for Economic and Social Investigations) and wrote regularly for *Pensamiento Propio.* Her articles have appeared in *The San Francisco Chronicle, Houston Post* and other newspapers.

ANA CRIQUILLON has been active in the Nicaraguan women's movement since 1977. She co-founded the Secretary of Women of the ATC (Farmworkers' Association) and also helped establish Gender Studies Area in the Sociology Department of the Central American University in Managua. In 1990, together with other women, she founded *Puntos de Encuentro,* a training and educational center that works with the women's movement.

EDUARDO BAUMEISTER is a Nicaraguan sociologist who has written frequently about the agrarian situation in Nicaragua and Guatemala. Baumeister has worked as a consultant with UNAG (the National Union of Farmers and Ranchers) in Nicaragua.

MIDGE QUANDT holds a PhD. in History and is an independent researcher. She has written widely about Nicaragua and Central America. Her articles have been published by NACLA's *Report on the Americas, Z Magazine* and others.

INDEX

A

ACG 101-2
ADAL 244
AEU–Asociación Estudantil
    Universitaria 71
AFL–CIO 160, 195
agrarian reform
  in El Salvador 158, 176
  in Nicaragua 243, 245, 247, 253
Agrarian Reform Ministry 185
Agua Fria , Guatemala 32
AHPROCAFE 261
AIFLD 158. See also AFL–CIO
Alecio, Rolando 17
Alliance for Progress 7
alternative development 14, 20
American Institute for Free Labor
    Development. See AIFLD
AMNLAE 209, 212, 213, 214–
    16, 218, 220, 221, 222, 224, 227,
    234, 236, 268, 269, 271
Amoco 85
AMPRONAC 211, 212, 213, 218
ANAP 261
APP 272, 278
APT 280, 282, 283, 284
Arbenz, Jacobo 6, 78
Arce, Bayardo 218, 220
ARENA government 165. See also
    political parties: in El Salvador:
    ARENA
Arévalo, Juan Jose 6, 78
Arias, Arturo 38
Army
  Guatemalan 26, 39, 43, 52, 55, 57, 77,
    85, 90
    civil defense patrol 26, 28, 30, 31,
      32, 33, 41, 67, 70, 71, 75, 93, 99
    military commissioners 28, 33, 42
    recruitment 28, 37, 39
  Nicaraguan
    recruitment 251
  Salvadoran 109, 112, 115, 123, 125,
    128, 139, 140, 157, 161
    ORDEN 112, 117
Association of Cotton Growers of
    León. See ADAL
Association of Farm Workers. See ACT
Association of Nicaraguan Women "Luisa
    Amanda Esp. See AMNLAE
Association of Women in the National
    Situation. See AMPRONAC

ATC 215, 217, 220, 226, 230, 231,
    236, 244, 248, 250, 267, 269, 271,
    276, 277, 278, 279, 281, 282, 283,
    284, 285, 286.
    See also Campesino Organizations: in
      Nicaragua: ATC
austerity program
  in Nicaragua 185
Autonomous Workers' Federation of
    Nicaragua. See CTNa

B

Baumeister, Eduardo 19
Belli, Humberto 198
Bendana, Alejandro 273, 281
Bermúdez, Fernando 77
Bermúdez, José Angel 201, 203
Blandon, María Teresa 267, 279, 282,
    283, 284, 287
Bloque Popular Revolucionario. See BPR
BPR 155
Bush administration 194, 272, 274

C

Cabrera, Alfonso 68
Cabrera, Monsignor Julio 101
Campaign for Peace and Life 99, 102
Campbell, Francisco 269, 271
Campesino Committee of the Highlands.
    See CCDA
Campesino Organizations 4
  in El Salvador
    FECCAS 154
    UTC 154
  in Guatemala
    CCDA 90
    CUC 16, 29, 31, 47, 50, 51, 53, 86,
      87, 89, 102
    publications 61, 62, 67
    repression 61, 62, 63, 65, 68, 70, 87, 90
    UNAGRO 68, 70
  in Nicaragua
    ATC 11, 20, 215, 217, 220, 226, 231,
      236, 244, 248, 250, 267, 269, 271, 276,
      277, 278, 279, 281, 282, 283, 284, 285,
      286, 287
    UNAG 11, 19, 220, 236, 239, 244, 245,
      248, 249, 250, 252, 255, 257, 258,
      260, 261, 268, 277
Canchún, Guatemala 30

Cardenal, Fernando 270, 273
Cardenas, Lazaro 261
Carrión, Luis 185, 271, 272, 275, 281, 282, 286, 287
Catholic Church 17, 28, 41, 50, 51, 56, 76, 78, 87, 99, 100, 204
  Catholic Action 17, 77, 79, 80, 81, 82, 85, 86, 87, 89, 92, 95, 102
  in El Salvador 123, 124, 126, 168
  in Guatemala
    CEG 99
    CONFREGUA 101
  repression 78, 79, 85, 87, 89, 91, 98
CAUS 184, 193
CCDA 90
CCR 138, 139, 143, 146
CCTEM 160
CDSs 267, 271
CEG 99
Center for Labor Studies. See CETRA
Central American Economic Integration Bank 29
Central Nacional Campesina 261
Cerezo, Vinicio 64
CERJ 69, 71, 99
CETRA 215
CGT–i 184, 193
Chajul, Guatemala 57
Chamorro government 18, 183, 186, 189, 190, 194, 199, 200, 254, 257, 269, 271, 274, 277, 278, 288
Chamorro, Violetta de 183, 187, 188, 189, 191, 193, 225, 255, 274, 278
Chichupac, Guatemala 25
Chixoy River Dam 26, 29, 30
Christian Committee of Displaced Persons in El Sal. See CRIPDES
CIA 184, 194
CIA–led coup in Guatemala 7, 78
CIEDEG 99, 103
CIERA 215
CIPHES 168
CITGUA 205
Civil Defense Committees
  in Nicaragua 267
civil defense patrol 26. See also mentality of the Army
CLAT 156
Clinton administration 276, 288
CNR 126, 144, 159
CODYDES 159
CoMadres (Committee of the Mothers of the Disappeared) 10
Comité de Campesinos del Altiplano. See CCDA
Committee of Campesino Unity 50. See also CUC

Committee of Unemployed and Fired Workers. See CODYDES
Committees of National Salvation 195
Communal Movement 271
Communist Union 199
Communities of Population in Resistance (CPRs) in 12, 17, 40, 75. See also CPRs
Community organizations 27, 29, 35
CONAMUS 21. See also CONAMUS
CONAPRO 220, 226, 230, 231
CONAVIGUA 69, 71
concertación 189, 257
concertación
  II 270, 272, 274, 278, 279, 280
CONDEG 43
Confederation of Workers. See CPT
Conference of Evangelical Churches of Guatemala. See CIEDEG
Conference of Guatemala Bishops. See CEG
CONFREGUA 101
conscientization 2, 26, 82, 84, 91, 154
contra war 8, 194, 246, 268
contras 189, 245, 251, 255
  Jorge Salazar Regional Commandos 251
Coordinating Council of State and Municipal Worker. See CCTEM
COPAZ 174
Corinto, Nicaragua 194
COSEP 248, 257
Council of Trade Union Unification. See CUS
CPDN 163, 168, 173
CPRs 75, 76, 77, 78, 93, 94, 95, 98, 101, 102
CPT 193, 195, 198, 199, 201, 203
CRCC 138, 139, 146
CRIPDES 124, 125, 126, 159
Criquillon, Ana 19
Cristiani, Alfredo 160
CST 159, 184, 185, 186, 192, 194, 195, 201, 228, 229, 230, 236, 267, 268, 273, 274, 277, 279
CTN 184, 193, 195, 197, 201
CTNa 193
CTO 160
CUC 9, 16, 29, 31, 47, 50, 51, 53, 86, 87, 89, 102; CONACO 65
CUS 184, 193, 194, 198, 199, 205

D

de León Carpio, Ramiro 70
decade of development 7
Declaration of Iximché 58
Declaration of Metepec 71

depopulation
  in El Salvador   114, 125
Development Bank   50
displaced persons
  in El Salvador   122, 125
  in Guatemala   33, 36, 41
    CONDEG   16, 43
  in Honduras   122
Duarte government   158, 160
Duarte, Napoleon   114, 157
Dye, David   272, 273, 274

E

education campaigns
  in El Salvador   128, 133, 136
  in Nicaragua   212, 233, 277
EGP. See guerrilla organizations
El Barillo, El Salvador   127
El Divisadero   285
Encuentros Cristianos   103
Espinoza, Olga María   283
Esquipulas II   10
Evans, Trevor   274, 279, 281
exhumations of clandestine graves   25

F

Fajardo, Efraín   196, 197, 198
Falla, Ricardo   93, 96
FAPU   155
Farabundo Martí National Liberation
  Front. See FMLN: guerrilla organiza-
  tions
Farmworkers Association. See ATC
FDR   155, 171
FECCAS   154, 169
Federation of Christian Campesinos in El
  Salvador   9
Federation of Health Workers. See FITS
Federation of Trade Union Action and
  Unity. See CAUS
feminism. See women
FENASTRAS bombing,   161
Festival of the 52%   229. See also
  women: in Nicaragua
FETRAHORESTUC   196
FETSALUD   196, 229
Figueres, José "Pepe"   6
FITS   196, 197
FMLN   11, 20, 109, 112, 114, 123,
  125, 127, 131, 132, 140, 146, 149,
  154, 157, 159, 160, 161, 164, 167,
  168, 169, 171, 174. See also guerrilla
  organizations
FNT   187, 188, 189, 190, 191, 192,

195, 196, 199, 202, 203, 204, 205,
  257, 271, 273
Frente de Accion Popular Unificado. See
  FAPU
Frente Democrático Revolucionario. See
  FDR
Frente Obrero   198
FSLN   19, 183, 186, 187, 188, 189,
  190, 191, 192, 193, 194, 209, 211,
  213, 219, 224, 225, 230, 236, 244,
  245, 248, 249, 250, 253, 256, 259,
  260, 266, 268, 270, 271, 272, 273,
  274, 275, 276, 277, 279, 281, 282,
  287. See also guerrilla organizations;
  political parties
FUNDASAL   126

G

GAM   64, 69, 71
Garcia, Edgardo   281, 282, 283, 284,
  285
gender roles. See women: in Nicaragua
General Confederation of Labor–
  Independent. See CGT–i
Gerardi, Juan   101
Getty Oil   85
Godoy, Virgilio   188, 189, 190, 193,
  195
Goméz, Domingo   282, 283, 284, 285,
  286
Gonzalez, Joaquín   200
González, Narciso   244, 248
Gorostiaga, Xavier   276
Government Office on Women. See INIM
Grigsby, William   270, 271, 282, 287
Grupo de Apoyo Mutuo. See GAM
Guatemalan Christian Action   101. See
  also ACG
Guatemalan Church in Exile   94
guerrilla organizations   87
  EGP   30, 33
  FMLN   11, 18, 112, 114, 123, 125, 127,
    131, 132, 140, 146, 149, 154, 157, 159,
    160, 161, 164, 167, 168, 169, 171, 172,
    173, 174, 176
  FSLN   55
  URNG   11, 20, 71
Gurriarán, Fr. Luís   83

H

Haugaard, Lisa   269, 277
health care campaigns
  in El Salvador   120, 121, 133, 136
  in Nicaragua   212, 215, 233, 235, 269, 277

Hernández, Fidel   88
Herrera, Dora Ivonne   279
Huembes, Carlos   193, 195, 197
human rights   6, 99
   CoMADRES   10
   Guatemala
      Mutual Support Group (GAM)   10, 43,
      64, 69, 71

I

INDE–National Electrification Institute
   29, 31
indigenous people
   in Guatemala   16
      Achis   16, 27, 41
INIES   215
INIM   215
INTA   85
Inter–American Development Bank   29
International Monetary Fund (IMF)   14,
   16, 259
ITZTANI   190
Ixcán jungle   17, 85, 93, 95
Ixil, Guatemala   94

J

Jarquin, Juan José   198
Jimenez, Lucio   187, 192, 268, 273
Juárez, Martha   279, 280, 285, 287

K

Kennedy, John F.   7

L

La Estancia, Guatemala   86, 91
labor unions
   in El Salvador   156, 158
      CCTEM   160
      CODYDES   159
      CST   159
      CTO   160
      FECCAS   154, 169
      MUSYGES   158, 159
      UNOC   160
      UNTS   160, 163, 172
      UTC   154, 169
   in Guatemala   52
      UASP   65, 70
      UNAGRO   68, 70
   in Nicaragua   18, 183, 184, 217, 230, 284
      ADAL   244
      ATC   215, 217, 220, 244, 248, 250,
      267, 269, 271, 276, 277, 278, 279,
      281, 282, 283, 284, 285, 286, 287

CAUS   184, 193
CGT-i   184, 193
CNT   184
CPT   193, 195, 198, 199, 201, 203
CST   184, 185, 186, 192, 194, 195,
   201, 267, 268, 273, 274, 277, 279
CTN   193, 195, 197, 201
CTNa   193
CUS   184, 193, 194, 198, 199, 205
FETRAHORESTUC   196
FETSALUD   196
FITS   196, 197
FNT   187, 188, 189, 190, 191, 192,
   195, 196, 202, 203, 204, 257, 271
UNE   187, 203
Lacayo, Aldo Díaz   275
Lacayo, Antonio   187, 188, 189, 190,
   201, 260, 271, 273, 274, 281
land reform
   in El Salvador   158, 176
   in Nicaragua   8, 212, 242, 245, 247, 253,
   278, 280
land takeovers
   in El Salvador   155, 159
   in Nicaragua   279, 280
land tenure
   in Guatemala   47, 54, 56
   in Nicaragua   243, 247
Lara, Wilberto   248
Las Palmas group   190
Ligas Campesinas
   in Guatemala   52
Ligas Populares 28 de Febrero. See LP–28
lliteracy campaigns
   in El Salvador   120, 121, 136
   in Guatemala   56
   in Nicaragua   212, 233
Local Popular Powers in El Salvador   12
Los Encuentros, Guatemala   30
low intensity conflict   123, 125
LP–28   155
Lungo Uclés, Mario   18

M

Malespin, Fernando   198
Martínez, Maxmilian Hernandez   6
massacre   27, 32, 38, 42, 54, 55,
   57, 90
   in El Salvador   127
   in Guatemala
      exhumation in Chichupac   25, 42
      exhumation in Plan de Sanchez   43
      exhumation in Rio Negro   25
      in the Spanish Embassy   17, 58, 89
Matus, Juan Ramón Carvajal   199
Membreno, Ronaldo   268
Menchú, Rigoberta   17, 47
mentality of the Army   10, 17, 31, 32,

33, 38, 47, 52, 55, 57, 64, 77, 90, 128
Mesa Grande, El Salvador   129
migrant labor
   in Guatemala   48, 56, 64, 68
Ministry of Agriculture and Agrarian
   Reform. *See* MINSA
MINSA   284
Montenegro, Sofia   233, 270
Morazán, El Salvador   112, 127
Mozote massacre. *See* massacre: in El
   Salvador
MUSYGES   158, 159
Mutual Support Group (GAM)   10, 43,
   64, 69, 71

N

Nahuaterique, El Salvador   128
National Agrarian Commission. *See*
   agrarian reform: in Nicaragua
National Association of Small Farmers. *See*
   ANAP
National Confederation of
   Professionals. *See* CONAPRO
National Council for Displaced Persons
   (CONDEG)   16
National Day Against Maternal Mortal-
   ity   269
National Development Bank
   in Nicaragua   258, 259
National Directorate. *See* DN
National Electrification Institute. *See* INDE
National Front of Workers   256
National Opposition Union. *See* UNO
National Resistance. *See* Contras
National Union of Earthquake Victims. *See*
   UNADES
National Union of Farmers and
   Ranchers. *See* UNAG
National Union of Salvadoran Workers. *See*
   UNTS
National Women's Conference   232,
   235. *See also* Nicaraguan Women's
   Conference
National Worker and Peasant Union. *See*
   UNOC
National Workers Federation. *See* FNT
National Workers Front. *See* FNT
Neira, Oscar   279, 281, 282, 283, 284
new social movements   4
Nicaraguan Institute of Economic and
   Social Invest. *See* INIES
Nicaraguan Research Center. *See* ITZTANI
Nicaraguan Women's Association "Luisa
   Amanda Esp. *See* AMLNAE

Nicaraguan Women's Conference   209
Nicaraguan Women's Institute. *See* INIM
Nuñez, Daniel   248, 257, 258, 260
Nuñez, Orlando   288

O

Obando y Bravo, Cardinal   195
O'Kane, Trish   18
OLM   215
Operation Phoenix   126
ORIT   156
Ortega, Daniel   185, 192, 219, 225,
   271, 273, 274, 276, 281, 282, 288
Ortega, Carlos   199
Ortega, Humberto   188, 190, 193

P

PADECOMSM   137, 141, 146
Palacios, Alba   270
Panzós, Guatemala   55
Patriotic Military Service. *See* SMP
Peace Accords
   in El Salvador   146, 148, 167, 174
Peralta, Rodil   65
Perez, Fabián   87
Permanent Commissions of Guatemalan
   Refugees   71
Permanent Committee of the National
   Debate. *See* CPDN
Plan de Sánchez, Guatemala   32
political parties
   in El Salvador
      ARENA   160, 161, 165, 174
      Christian Democratic Party   114, 157,
         158, 160, 161, 174
      FMLN   20, 109, 112, 114, 123, 127,
         131, 132, 140, 146, 149, 154, 157, 159,
         160, 161, 164, 167, 168, 169, 171,
         172, 173, 174
   in Guatemala
      Christian Democrats   64, 86, 87
      National Liberation Party   86
   in Mexico
      PRI   261
   in Nicaragua
      FSLN   19, 183, 186, 187, 188, 189, 190,
         191, 192, 193, 194, 209, 211, 213,
         219, 224, 225, 230, 236, 244, 245,
         248, 249, 250, 253, 256, 259, 260,
         266, 268, 270, 271, 272, 273, 274,
         275, 276, 277, 279, 281, 282, 283,
         287, 288
      UNO   187, 188, 193, 194, 199, 225,
         226, 255, 257, 266, 272, 278
Pope John Paul II   100
Pope Pius XII   79

popular organizations
  in El Salvador   159, 167, 168, 172
    BPR   155
    CPDN   163, 173
    FAPU   155
    FDR   155
    LP-28   155
    UNADES   159
PRI   261
protests
  in El Salvador   141, 160
  in Guatemala   57, 58, 59, 63, 67, 90
  in refugee camps   122

Q

Quandt, Midge   19
Quezada Toruño, Monsignor   101

R

Rabinal, Guatemala   16, 27, 28, 30, 31,
    34, 36, 37, 38, 39, 41
Ramazzini, Monsignor Alvaro   101
Ramírez, Sergio   219
Reagan administration   213
refugee camps   117
  in El Salvador   115, 116, 117, 121
    CRIPDES   124, 125, 159
  in Honduras   116, 120, 121
refugee returns
  in El Salvador   18, 109, 110, 126, 127
    CCR   138, 139, 143, 146
    CNR   144, 159
    CRCC   138, 139, 146
    economic organization   133, 142, 147, 149
    Mesa Grande   129, 130
    organization   131, 142, 146
    PADECOMSM   137, 139, 140, 141, 146
    political organization   132
    social services   135, 143
religious organizations
  in Guatemala
    ACG   101, 102
    Campaign for Peace and Life   99, 102
    CIEDEG   99, 103
    Encuentros Cristianos   103
    SINE   101, 102
repopulation
  in El Salvador. See refugee returns: in El
    Salvador
Research and Study of the Agrarian
    Reform. See CIERA
Revolutionary Coordination of the Masses
  in El Salvador   9
Río Negro, Guatemala   25, 29, 32, 41
Ríos Montt, Efraín   90
Roa, Sergio   195
Rossell Arellano, Monsignor Mariano

  78, 79, 99

S

Salmerón, Ernesto   203
Salvadoran United Labor and Association
    Movement. See MUSYGES
San Idelfonso Ixtahuacán mine strike   52
San José de Las Flores, El Salva-
    dor   109, 127
Sandinismo   266, 287
Sandinista Assembly   192, 275
Sandinista Assembly of Managua   270
Sandinista government   18, 184, 185,
    193, 194, 247, 251, 252, 255
Sandinista National Liberation Front. See
    FSLN
Sandinista unions. See labor unions: in
    Nicaragua
Sandinista Workers Confederation. See
    CST
Sandinista Youth   213, 223
Sandoval, Marcial Cabrera   196
Sao Paulo Forum   265
Science and Technology Institute for
    Guatemala. See CITGUA
"scorched earth" campaigns   9, 63, 91,
    112, 128, 148
sectores surgidos
  in Guatemala   16
Shenadoah Oil   85
Simolox, Vitalino   99
SINE   101, 102
Siu, Ivonne   221
Social and Popular Unity of Action. See
    UASP
Solidarism   203, 204
  in Guatemala   204
  in Nicaragua   203, 204
Somoza, Anastasio   7, 240
Somoza regime   184, 188, 194, 211,
    240, 243, 268
Stahler-Sholk, Richard   273
strikes
  in El Salvador   156, 160
  in Guatemala   52, 55, 59, 61, 62,
    68, 69, 86
  in Nicaragua   187, 188, 190, 196

T

Tehuantepec plantation, Guatemala   59
Tellez, Dora María   268, 275, 287
Texaco   85
Thompson, Martha   17
Tijerino, Doris   224

Tijerino,Doris 227, 228
Tinoco, Victor 268, 270, 273, 274, 279, 287
Tirado, Victor 276
Torres,Luciano 185
Trujillo, Saul Cisnes 194

U

U.S. AID 174
U.S. backed contra war. *See* U.S. policy: to Nicaragua
U.S. economic blockade. *See* U.S. policy: to Nicaragua
U.S. policy 14
  Alliance for Progress 7
  to El Salvador 9, 114, 115, 128, 157, 158, 176
  to Guatemala
    1954 CIA coup 7
  to Nicaragua 12, 195, 202, 205, 272, 276, 288
UASP 65, 70
UITA 196
UNADES 159
UNAG 220, 236, 239, 244, 245, 248, 249, 252, 255, 257, 258, 260, 261, 268, 277
UNAGRO 68, 70
UNE 187, 203, 229, 230, 231, 236
UNHCR 116, 121, 122, 129, 141
Union of Public Employees. *See* UNE
United Nicaraguan Opposition. *See* UNO
Universal Declaration of Human Rights 6
UNO 187, 188, 193, 194, 199, 225, 226, 255, 257, 266, 272, 278. *See also* political parties: in Nicaragua: UNO
UNOC 160. *See also* labor unions: in El Salvador
UNTS 160, 163, 172. *See also* labor unions: in El Salvador
UPANACIONAL
  in Costa Rica 261
UPANIC 248
URNG 11, 20, 71. *See also* guerrilla organizations: URNG
UTC 154, 169. *See also* Campesino Organizations: in El Salvador: UTC

V

vanguardism 265, 267, 269, 271, 287
Vargas, Damaso 186
Vargas, Oscar Rene 274
Vatican II 81

Vegas de Santo Domingo, Guatemala 39, 41
Villalobos, Virginia 267
Vivas, Renee 188, 274
Vukelich, Donna 279, 285

W

Wheelock, Jaime 282, 283, 284, 286
widows
  in Guatemala
    CONAVIGUA 16, 36, 42, 43
winning the hearts and minds 38, 123. *See also* mentality of the Army
women
  in El Salvador 117, 144
  in Honduras
    in refugee camps 120
  in Nicaragua 19
    National Day Against Maternal Mortality 269
    national gathering 232, 235, 236
    Network on Economy and Environment 235
    Sexuality Network 235
    Women's Health Network 235
    Women's Network Against Violence 235
Women's Legal Office. *See* OLM
women's organizations
  CONAMUS 1
  in Guatemala
    CONAMUS 21
  in Nicaragua
    AMNLAE 209, 212, 213, 214, 216, 217, 218, 220, 221, 222, 224, 227, 234, 236, 268, 269, 271
    AMPRONAC 211, 212, 213, 218
    OLM 215
women's studies
  in Nicaragua
    ATC 215, 217
    CETRA 215
    CIERA 215
    INIES 215
    INIM 215
Woods, Father Bill 85
Workers' Federation of Nicaragua. *See* CTN
Worker's Solidarity Coordination. *See* CST
World Bank 14, 16, 29, 255, 259, 284

X

Xococ, Guatemala 27, 30, 31, 32, 39, 41, 43

Z

Zapón, Petrona 82